The Book of the Kings of Egypt

Sir E. A. Wallis Budge (1857-1934) was Keeper of the British Museum's department of oriental antiquities from 1894 until his retirement in 1924. Carrying out many missions to Egypt in search of ancient objects, Budge was hugely successful in collecting papyri, statues and other artefacts for the trustees of the British Museum: numbering into the thousands and of great cultural and historical significance. Budge published well over 100 monographs, which shaped the development of future scholarship and are still of great academic value today, dealing with subjects such as Egyptian religion, history and literature.

First published in 1908, this is the first of two volumes dealing with the kings of Egypt. Using a variety of material from the British Library's extensive collections, Budge meticulously collated the names of the Pharaohs and royal personages from the 1st to the 19th Dynasties of Egypt. With a detailed discussion concerning Egyptian chronology, this classic work will be of great interest and value to scholars and students of Ancient Egyptian history and archaeology.

The Book of the Kings of Egypt

Vol. I: Dynasties I - XIX

E. A. Wallis Budge

Routledge
Taylor & Francis Group
ROUTLEDGE REVIVALS

First published in 1908
by Kegan Paul, Trench, Trübner & Co. Ltd

This edition first published in 2013 by Routledge
2 Park Square, Milton Park, Abingdon, Oxon, OX14 4RN

Simultaneously published in the USA and Canada
by Routledge
711 Third Avenue, New York, NY 10017

Routledge is an imprint of the Taylor & Francis Group, an informa business

Publisher's Note
The publisher has gone to great lengths to ensure the quality of this reprint but points out that some imperfections in the original copies may be apparent.

Disclaimer
The publisher has made every effort to trace copyright holders and welcomes correspondence from those they have been unable to contact.

A Library of Congress record exists under LC control no: 09001578

ISBN 13: 978-0-415-81079-1 (hbk)
ISBN 13: 978-0-203-06714-7 (ebk)
ISBN 13: 978-0-415-81448-5 (pbk)

Books on Egypt and Chaldaea

THE BOOK
OF
THE KINGS OF EGYPT

OR THE KA, NEBTI, HORUS, SUTEN BÁT, AND RĀ NAMES OF THE PHARAOHS WITH TRANSLITERATIONS, FROM MENES, THE FIRST DYNASTIC KING OF EGYPT, TO THE EMPEROR DECIUS, WITH CHAPTERS ON THE ROYAL NAMES, CHRONOLOGY, ETC.

BY

E. A. WALLIS BUDGE, M.A., LITT. D., D. LITT., D. LIT.
KEEPER OF THE EGYPTIAN AND ASSYRIAN ANTIQUITIES
IN THE BRITISH MUSEUM

VOL. I.

DYNASTIES I—XIX

LONDON
KEGAN PAUL, TRENCH, TRÜBNER & CO., LTD
DRYDEN HOUSE, 43, GERRARD STREET, W.
1908

PRINTED BY
ADOLF HOLZHAUSEN,
19-21 KANDLGASSE, VIENNA.

PREFACE.

The present work represents an attempt made to gather together the Ka, Nebti, Horus, Suten Bȧt, and Rā names of the Pharaohs and royal personages of Egypt found on the monuments, and though the lists printed in it make no pretension to be complete, they are, I believe, the fullest hitherto published. I have drawn but sparingly for variants upon the unrivalled collection of scarabs in the British Museum, some 11,500 in number, because an exhaustive Catalogue of these is in course of preparation by Mr. H. R. Hall. Little apology is needed for the appearance of this work, for both the "Königsbuch" of Lepsius, and "Le Livre des Rois" of Brugsch and Bouriant have been out of print for some years. Moreover, since these works were issued the excavations carried out in Egypt by Amélineau, J. de Morgan, Naville, Petrie, Garstang, Quibell, Legrain, Daressy, and others have produced monuments inscribed with scores of royal names which were unknown to Lepsius, Brugsch, and Bouriant.

The grouping of the names into Dynasties is substantially that of Manetho, and transcripts of his King List, the Book of the Sothis, the Old Chronicle, the Table of Eratosthenes, etc., have been added for convenient reference. In the Chapter on Egyptian Chronology in the Introduction the reader will find the difficulties of the subject indicated, and the comparative table of the chronological systems which have been proposed from the days of Champollion Figeac to the present time will illustrate the divergence of opinion about a most troublesome branch of Egyptology. A list of recent papers bearing on the Chronology of Egypt has also been added.

I am indebted to Herr Adolf Holzhausen for the care which he has devoted to the printing of this book.

E. A. WALLIS BUDGE.

BRITISH MUSEUM,
April 11*th*, 1908.

CONTENTS.

	PAGE
PREFACE	XI
CHAPTER I. EGYPTIAN ROYAL NAMES	XIII
„ II. EGYPTIAN CHRONOLOGY	XXVIII
THE GREEK LISTS:	
MYTHICAL PERIOD: MANETHO AND PANODORUS ...	LX
„ „ MANETHO (BOECKH) ...	LXI
THE KING LIST OF MANETHO	LXII
THE TABLE OF ERATOSTHENES	LXXIII
THE OLD CHRONICLE	LXXV
THE BOOK OF THE SOTHIS	LXXV
JOSEPHUS. XVTH, XVIIITH AND XIXTH DYNASTIES ...	LXXIX
LIST OF PAPERS BEARING ON EGYPTIAN CHRONOLOGY ...	LXXX
THE KINGS OF EGYPT:	
PREDYNASTIC KINGS OF THE NORTH	1
DYNASTY I	3
„ II	9
„ III	14
„ IV	17
„ V	24
„ VI	31
„ VII AND VIII	38
„ IX AND X	42
„ XI	44
„ XII	51
„ XIII–XVII	65
„ XV AND XVI	93
„ XVIII	106
„ XIX	156

INTRODUCTION.

CHAPTER I.

EGYPTIAN ROYAL NAMES.

The year 1849 is a memorable one in the annals of Egyptology, for it saw the appearance of the "Chronologie der Ägypter" by Richard Lepsius, to whom we owe so much work that is solid and enduring. Nine years later he published the supplementary volume entitled "Königsbuch der alten Ägypter", in which, for the first time, was published a series of synoptical tables of the Egyptian Dynasties, together with seventy-three tables containing nearly one thousand names of the kings of Egypt. This work was, and still is, of the first importance for the study of Egyptian chronology, for it represents the first serious attempt made by a competent scholar to reduce to order the confused chronological and historical statements made in Egyptian texts, and to compare the systems of Egyptian chronology formulated by writers in Greek, almost all of which are based upon the famous List of Egyptian Dynasties compiled by Manetho for Ptolemy Philadelphus. This investigation in the domain of Egyptian Chronology threw much light on the subject, and at the same time incited other scholars to turn their attention to the correct arrangement of the historical facts which the results of the newly discovered decipherment of Egyptian hieroglyphics had placed in their hands. Lepsius's conclusions were undoubtedly the best which could be drawn from the facts available at that time, and they were adopted by Egyptologists generally throughout Europe, but his materials were insufficient for the scope of his work, and some of his chronological theories, in the face of the facts which have been steadily accumulating during the last fifty-one years, must now be rejected. That this is so is not to be wondered at, indeed the marvel is that so many of his theories have been proved correct by recent discoveries, and that so many of his guesses are supported by facts. To attempt to enumerate the important results which he formulated in the books mentioned above would be out of place here, but attention may be drawn to the fact that he was the first to show by the royal protocols which he published, that the greater number of the Pharaohs, and the Ptolemies and Roman Emperors after them, possessed five names, the import of which may be thus described:

The FIRST was the "Horus Name", or that which was borne by the king as the representative of Horus, the great god of heaven, whose symbol was a hawk. Originally this Horus was "Ḥeru-ur", *i. e.*, "Horus the Great", the Arouëris of the later Greek writers, but in later periods his attributes included those of Horus of Beḥuṭet, the great War-god of Edfû and the district round about that city, and those of several other forms of Horus, among them being Horus "the son of Isis, the son of Osiris". The object of calling the king "the Horus" was, as M. Moret has aptly remarked, to indicate that he was the "son of the gods", and "son of Rā" in particular.[1] The Horus name of a king is that which was given to his KA, or "Double", and it is written inside a representation of an object called the "Serekh", in the manner shewn here. The example given is the Horus name of Seneferu, the last king of the IIIrd, or first king of the IVth dynasty, and it reads *Neb Maāt*, "Lord of Maāt", *i. e.*, "Lord of Right", or Truth, or Law; above the "Serekh" is the hawk of Horus wearing the Crowns of the North and the South. The KA, as is well known, is a shadowy or ghostly form of the man, or a "shadowy second self", like the *Kra* of the Tshi-speaking peoples of the Gold Coast,[2] and the *Doshi* of the Ba-Huana.[3] About the "Serekh"  there has been some difference of opinion among Egyptologists. By some it has been regarded as a representation of a fringed banner, and by others as the plan of a building, more especially of a tomb.[4]

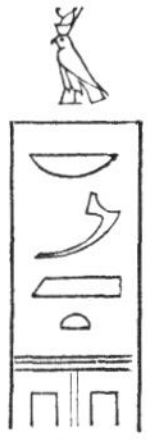

1. *Du Caractère Religieux de la Royauté Pharaonique,* Paris, 1902, p. 19.

2. A. B. Ellis, *The Tshi-speaking Peoples,* London, 1887, p. 149.

3. E. Torday and T. A. Joyce, *Notes on the Ethnography of the Ba-Huana.*

4. Maspero, *Revue Critique,* 1888, p. 118.

The most recent writer on the subject, M. A. Moret, regards it as the plan of either a temple or a tomb, wherein the Double of the king received both during his life-time and after his death the divine cult and the funerary cult.[1] And he shews that in placing the hawk of Horus on the "Serekh" the Egyptians intended to indicate that the king had taken his seat upon his throne as king, *i. e.*, had been officially enthroned. The custom of giving a Horus name to the king dates from the Ist dynasty, and proofs of this fact will be found *infra*, p. 8. Here we have the Horus names Tcha and Khent, and if Āḥa really be the Horus name of Menes, it follows that we have the Horus name of the first king of the Dynastic Period. The Nubian kings followed the Egyptians in adopting Horus names; thus Shabaka employed as his Ka name "Seqer-taui", Tirhâḳâh, "Qa-khāu", and Tanuath-Ȧmen, "Uaḥ-mert". The Ka name of Cambyses the Persian was "Sma-taui"; of Alexander the Great, the Macedonian, "Ḥeq-qennu"; of Ptolemy IV, the Greek, "Ḥunnu-qenu", or "Ḥunnu-qenu-skhā-en-su-tef-f"; and of Domitian, the Roman, Ḥunnu-qen. Some kings used their Ka name for their second and third names also. Thus "Neb-Maāt" was the first and second names of Seneferu (vol. I, p. 17); "Ṭeṭ-Khāu" was the first and second names of Ȧssȧ (vol. I, p. 29); and "Ānkh-mestu" was the first, second, and third names of Usertsen I (vol. I, p. 53). Now Horus was in all periods associated with Set, in fact was the counterpart of this god, and we find

1. *Op. cit.*, p. 20.

from the monuments that one king at least possessed a name as the representative of Set, as well as that of Horus. Thus the Horus name of one of the kings of the IInd dynasty was "Sekhem-åb", and his Set name was "Per-åb-sen"; in the former case the hawk of Horus, stands above the "Serekh", and in the latter, the symbol of Set (vol. I, p. 13). In another case the hawk and the Set-animal are written above the "Serekh" which contains the Horus-Set name "Khā sekhemui" (vol. I, p. 9).

The SECOND name of the king is preceded by the group of signs, the true reading of which, thanks to M. Daressy,[1] is shown to be "Nebti". In it the vulture is the symbol of Nekhebit, the goddess of the city of Nekhebet, and the goddess of the South *par excellence*. Among the earliest representations of this goddess is that on the granite vase found by Mr. Quibell at Hierakonpolis.[2] In this we see the vulture of Nekhebit standing, with her right talon placed on the symbol of the "seal", which contains the name of king BESH, and her left on the symbol of the union of the North and South *i. e.*, of Upper and Lower Egypt. Whether she appears as a vulture, or an uraeus, or a woman, she always bears or wears the symbols of the South, viz., the White Crown of the South, or or the

1. *Recueil de Travaux*, tom. XVII. p. 113.
2. *Hierakonpolis*, Plate 37.

White Crown with feathers, or the papyrus plant, or the papyrus sceptre. The uraeus in the group represents Uatchit, the goddess of the city of Pe-Ṭep, or Buto, the goddess of the North *par excellence*. Whether she appears as a serpent, or a woman, she always bears or wears the symbols of the North, viz., the Red Crown of the North, or, or the lotus plant, or the lotus sceptre. In a drawing by Lanzone,[1] she is represented in the form of an uraeus wearing, and she has before her the sceptre and the seal. Thus the Nebti group means that the king represents the goddesses Nekhebit and Uatchit, and that he is the lord of the Two Egypts, or the Two Lands, *i. e.*, of the North and the South. The oldest form of the Nebti group is given by an ivory plaque in the Museum at Cairo, where it appears as; in this the hawk symbolizes the South, and the serpent the North. If we look at the royal names from the IIIrd to the XIIth dynasty it will be seen that the Horus name, or Ka name, and the Nebti name of many of the kings are the same, *e. g.*, Tcheser has for both, Khufu has for both, Mer-en-Rā has for both, Pepi I. has for both, Menthu-ḥetep Neb-taui-Rā has for both, Sānkh-ka-Rā has for both, Ȧmen-em-ḥāt I. has for both, and so on. After the reign of Usertsen the first and second names of the king are usually different.

1. *Dizionario*, Plate LX.

The **Third** name of the king is that which is preceded by the signs, *Ḥeru nub, i. e.,* "Horus of gold". It occurs for the first time in connexion with the name of Seneferu, the last king of the IIIrd or first king of the IVth dynasty, within a cartouche thus:

We also find (vol. I, p. 20), and (vol. I, p. 33). So far back as the IIIrd dynasty we find that Rā ⊙ takes the place of Horus in the group, for in the titles of Tcheser we have (vol. I, p. 16) instead of of the later times. In the Palermo Stone, as M. Moret has already pointed out,[1] the third name of the king is called the "royal gold name". The general meaning of, when applied to the king, is that he is of, or like, the gold of Horus, *i. e.,* he is of the same substance as Horus, or Rā. Neb-taui-Rā Menthu-ḥetep called himself the "gold of the gods" (vol. I, p. 47), and gold, it is well known, has usually been associated with the gods. That the metal gold is really intended is clear from variants like, where the determinative for "metal" follows the name *nub* "gold" (vol. I, p. 77). In later times the name of Rā was added to, thus, as we find in the inscriptions of Ḥeru-em-ḥeb (vol. I, p. 154).

1. *Recueil de Travaux,* XXIII, p. 126.

The **Fourth** name is preceded by 𓇓𓏏𓆤𓏏 which, as is now known, is to be read *Suten Bàt.*[1] The first sign, *suten* 𓇓𓏏, means "king of the South", and the second, 𓆤𓏏, "king of the North", and together they indicate that the king to whom these signs are applied is "King of the South and North", *i. e.,* of Upper and Lower Egypt. The king is again held to be the successor of Rā, and therefore of every solar god, who was the lord of the two halves into which he divided the universe. The name which follows 𓇓𓏏𓆤𓏏 is commonly called the "prenomen", and is written within an oval, 𓍷, the *cartouche,* in Egyptian *shennu*; the fact that cartouches contained royal names was first pointed out by Zoëga, before the close of the XVIIIth century.[2] The oldest form of the cartouche is circular, and from the scene on the vase of king Besh it is clear that the circle with a bar attached was intended to represent a ring with a flat bezel, or seal-ring. This, of course, symbolized the *shen* 𓍶, or circular course of the sun about the universe, and when the king's name was written inside it, the meaning was that the king was the representative of the Sun god, that his rule extended to every part of the course of the sun, and that both he and his name would, like the sun,

1. A summary of the discussions on the reading is given by Moret, *op. cit.*, p. 27.

2. *De Usu et Origine Obeliscorum*, Rome, 1797, p. 465.

endure for ever. On some reliefs the cutting of the cartouche suggests that the name within it was enclosed by a rope or cord the ends of which were tied together in an elongated knot. The use of cords and knots in magical ceremonies is too well known to need description here, but if the cartouche was supposed to be formed by a rope, we may assume that the rope was intended to give magical protection to the name.

Another form of is supplied by the Palermo Stone in connexion with the name of Seneferu, where we find

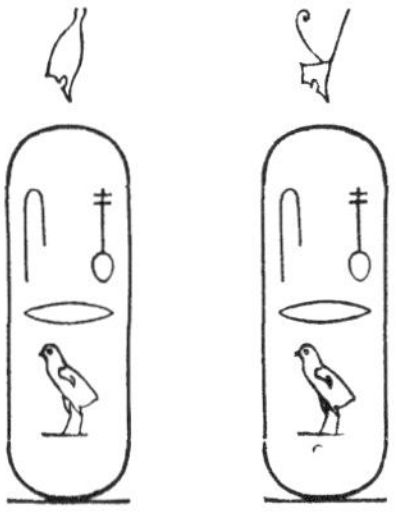

The two crowns, one of the South , and one of the North , were clearly intended to represent , and to indicate that "Seneferu" was the king's name both as Lord of the South and Lord of the North. In the early period the groups , , , and , when prefixed to the names of kings appear had much the same meaning. The title is sometimes written within the cartouche, *e.g.*, in the example quoted above, p. XVII, and it is clear that under the early dynasties any or all the titles prefixed to the royal names might be so written at times. In fact, custom had not yet definitely decided what the cartouche should or should not contain. There is no doubt that the fourth name of the king was a solar name, for the god whose name is always mentioned in it is Rā, the Sun-god; and we have proof of this from monuments from the middle of the IVth dynasty downwards. In the *Suten Bȧt* names of the earlier kings of the IVth dynasty, *e. g.*, Seneferu and Khufu, the actual name of Rā is not mentioned, but its existence seems to be implied in both.

If we examine the *Suten Bȧt* names of certain families of kings it becomes clear that a well recognized rule underlay their formation. Thus Ȧmen-ḥetep I was called "Tcheser-ka-Rā", or "Holy is the Ka of Rā"; and Thothmes I, "Āa-kheper-ka-Rā", or "The Ka of Rā becometh great"; Thothmes II, "Āa-kheper-en-Rā", or "Great is the becoming of Rā"; Ḥātshepset, "Maāt-ka-Rā", or "True is the Ka of Rā"; Thothmes III, "Men-kheper-Rā", or "Stable is he who is created by Rā"; Thothmes IV, "Men-kheperu-Rā", or "Stable are the creations of Rā"; Ȧmen-ḥetep II, "Āa-kheperu-Rā", or "Great are the creations of Rā"; Ȧi, "Kheper-kheperu-Rā-ȧri-Maāt", or "The Creator of creations is Rā, the maker of Maāt"; Tut-ānkh-Ȧmen, "Neb-kheperu-Rā", or "Lord of creations is Rā"; Ḥeru-em-ḥeb, "Tcheser-kheperu-Rā", or "Holy are the creations of Rā"; Ȧmen-ḥetep III, "Neb-Maāt-Rā", or "Lord of Maāt is Rā". The subjects chosen in these prenomens are the Ka of

Rā, Maāt, *i. e.*, Right or Truth, and the created one, or creations, of Rā. The formation of the prenomen of Ȧmen-ḥetep IV is different from that of all the other kings of his dynasty, but this is not to be wondered at, seeing that he held theological opinions different from those of the other kings. Moreover, in his prenomen as Khu-en-Ȧten he added the words "Beloved of the Disk", *meri Ȧten.*

It seems too that the prenomens of the kings of one dynasty influenced the formation of those of the kings of another. Thus the prenomen of Ȧāḥmes I, the first king of the XVIIIth dynasty, is "Neb-peḥti-Rā", and that of Rameses I, the first king of the XIXth dynasty, is "Men-peḥti-Rā". The prenomen of Ȧmen-ḥetep III is "Neb-Maāt-Rā", and that of Seti I is "Men-Maāt-Rā". The "User-Maāt-Rā" of Rameses II is repeated in the prenomens of Rameses III, Rameses IV, Rameses V, Rameses VII, Ȧmen-em-ȧp, Thekeleth I, Uasarken II, Uasarken-sa-Ȧst, Thekeleth-sa-Ȧst, Shashanq III, P-ānkhi, a Nubian, etc. Another example of the above-mentioned fact is supplied by the prenomens of the kings of the XXVIth dynasty. Thus Psammetichus I is called "Uaḥ-ȧb-Rā", or "Rā maketh prosperous the heart"; Nekau, "Nem-ȧb-Rā", or "Rā reneweth the heart"; Psammetichus II, "Nefer-ȧb-Rā", or "Rā is the beauty of the heart"; Uaḥ-ȧb-Rā, "Ḥāā-ȧb-Rā", or "Rā rejoiceth the heart"; Ȧāḥmes, "Khnem-ȧb-Rā", or "Rā uniteth himself to the heart". Finally it may be noted that although the name of Rā is always the first sign in the cartouche containing the Suten Båt name, it is to be read last, except in some few names, *e. g.*, Rā-messu, or Rameses, and Ῥατοίσης in Manetho's IVth Dynasty, which must represent some name beginning with Rā. This fact is proved by Assyrian, Greek, and Hebrew transcriptions of Egyptian royal names. Thus in the Tell al-Amarna Tablets *Men-kheper-Rā* 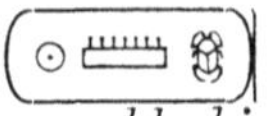 (Thothmes III) is transcribed by *Ma-na-akh-bi-ir-ya*; *Neb-Maāt-Rā*  (Åmen-ḥetep III) is transcribed by *Ni-im-mu-u-ri-ya*; and *Nefer-kheperu-Rā-uā-en-Rā* 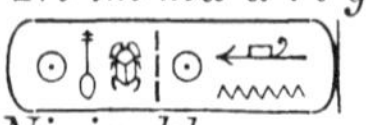 (Åmen-ḥetep IV) is transcribed by *Ni-ip-khu-ur-ri-ri-ya.* Again, *Ṭeṭ-ka-Rā*  is transcribed in Greek by Τανχέρης, and where the name Horus occurs instead of Rā it comes last also, as in Μενχερης = 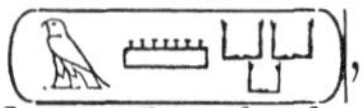, and *Uaḥ-åb-Rā* 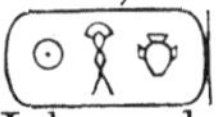 is transcribed in Greek by Ἀπρίης, and in Hebrew by *Khophr'ā* חָפְרַע.

The **Fifth** name of the king was the "son of Rā", , name, which was, like the Suten Båt name, written inside a cartouche. The title "son of Rā" was sometimes written with the name, inside the cartouche, as in the cases of Unås, 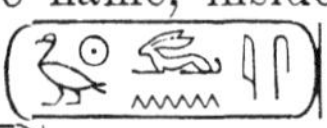 (vol. I, p. 31), and Åntef-āa 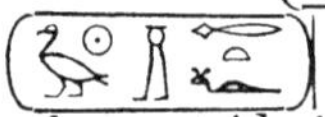 (vol. I, p. 44), sometimes *after* the cartouche, outside it, as in the case of Pepi II, 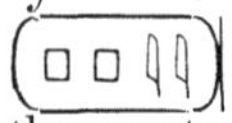  (vol. I, p. 36), but more usually *before* the cartouche, immediately after that containing the Suten Båt name. Thus the fourth and fifth names of the king were "solar names", but the fifth did not necessarily carry with it sovereignty. The fifth name of the king seems to have been his private name, or that which was given him at his birth, but though it appears to be certain that every king must have had such a name, the "son of Rā" names of many of the early kings have not come down to us. This is the case with the great kings Tcheser, Seneferu, Khufu, Khāfrā, Menkau-Rā, and others, and it is not until the end of the Vth or beginning of the VIth dynasty that "son of Rā" names become general. The first "son of Rā" name known to us seems to be Ȧssȧ 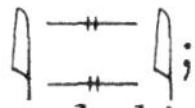; the fourth and fifth names of Unȧs are alike, and this is also the case with Tetȧ (vol. I, pp. 30, 31). The various foreign kings who ruled Egypt usually adopted Egyptian titles for their Suten Bȧt names, and had transcriptions of their own names placed in their second cartouche; compare the names of Cambyses and Darius, vol. II, pp. 91, 92. On the other hand, Xerxes used his private name for both his fourth and fifth names (*ibid.*, p. 94), and Artaxerxes prefixed  to his private name. The Macedonians and Ptolemies adopted Egyptian titles for their fourth names, and their own private names became their fifth names. Alexander the Great added to his fifth name the words "son of Ȧmen" (vol. II, p. 107), and every Ptolemy, with the exception of Soter and Philadelphus, added the titles "ever-living", and "beloved of Ptaḥ", or "beloved of Isis", or "beloved of Ptaḥ and Isis", to his private name in his second cartouche.

Several of the Roman Emperors dispensed with Egyptian titles in their first cartouches, and as Suten Bȧt names they employed first "Autokrator", and later "Autokrator Caesar". Their "son of Rā" names were their private names, after which they added titles, like the Ptolemies. Thus in the second cartouche of Caesar Augustus was inscribed "Caesar, ever-living, beloved of Ptaḥ and Isis"; in that of Tiberius, "Tiberius Caesar, ever-living"; in that of Caligula, "Caius Caesar Germanicus, ever-living"; in that of Claudius, "Claudius Tiberius", or "Germanicus Autokrator"; in that of Nero, "Autokrator Nero"; etc.

The Nubian kings of the Northern Kingdom whose capital was at Napata (Gebel Barkal) usually followed the custom of the Egyptians in placing their private names in their second cartouche, *e. g.*, Senka-Ȧmen-seken, Athlenersa, Amathel, etc.; on the other hand, one of them adopted for his fourth name the title "Sa-meri-Ȧmen", and for his fifth, "Ḥeru-sa-ȧtef" (vol. II, p. 203). The kings of the Southern Kingdom, who had their capital at Meroë, used cartouches in a somewhat irregular way. A few of them followed the custom of the Egyptians and inscribed titles in their first cartouche, and their private names in their second cartouche. Thus the first cartouche of Netek-Ȧmen contains the title "Kheper-ka-Rā", and the second his private name "Netek-Ȧmen" (vol. II, p. 209); and his queen placed in her first cartouche "Mer-ka-Rā", and in her second her private name "Ȧmen-tari", or "Ȧmentarit". We also find one queen with "Ȧmentarit" as her prenomen, and "Kenthȧḥebit" as her nomen (vol. II, p. 206). Arkenkherl had three cartouches: in the first he placed his prenomen "Ānkh-ka-Rā", in his second, "Second priest of Osiris, lord of the South", and in his third, "Arkenkherl", his private name. One king made "Kalka" his Suten Bȧt name, and "Karterȧ", or "Kalterȧ" his "son of Rā" name (vol. II, p. 207).

It now remains to note the other titles which were prefixed to the cartouches of kings. These were:—

1. (=) *Neb taui* "Lord of the Two Lands", either the two halves of the universe, *i. e.,* the North and the South, or Upper and Lower Egypt, or the two lands, one on each side of the Nile, (vol. I, p. 50.) This title was sometimes placed inside the cartouche.

2. *Neter nefer,*[1] (vol. II, p. 76), *i. e.,* "Beautiful god", or "Well-doing god".

3. *Neb ȧri khet, i. e.,* "Lord, creator of things", or "Lord who created the world".

4. *Tā ānkh Rā mȧ tchetta, i. e.,* "Giver of life, like Rā, for ever" (vol. I, p. 59).

1. Fem. (vol. I, p. 121).

5.  *Neb khāu, i. e.,* "Lord of crowns" (vol. I, p. 103).

6.  *Ānkh utcha senb, i. e.,* "Life, strength, health [be to him]" (vol. I, p. 113).

7.  =  *Suten Bȧt, i. e.,* King of the South and North (vol. I, p. 130).

8.  =  *sa Rā, i. e.,* "Son of Rā" (vol. I, p. 151).

9.  *Per āa, i. e.,* "Great House", the "Pharaoh" פַּרְעֹה of the Bible; we also have *Per-āa pa āa* , "The great Pharaoh" (vol. II, p. 94).

10. Many of the titles of the Ptolemies were translated into Egyptian thus:—

Ptolemy I. NETCH  "Divine Avenger" = SOTER.

Ptolemy II. NETER MER-SEN  "Divine loving brother" = PHILADELPHUS. , or 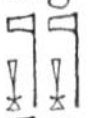 = the two brother-loving gods. The fem. is .

Ptolemy III. P-NETER-MENKH 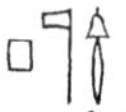 "The beneficent god" = EUERGETES. The fem. is 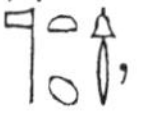, and the dual .

Ptolemy IV. NETER MER-TEF-F , or  "God loving his father" = PHILOPATOR.

The fem. is , and the dual , or .

Ptolemy V. P-NETER PER "The god who appeareth" = EPIPHANES. The fem. is , and the dual , .

Ptolemy VI (?). P-NETER-SHEPS (?)-TEF-F, "The god who sanctifies (?) his father" = EUPATOR.

Ptolemy VII (?). P-NETER-MUT-F-MERI , or , or , "The god loving his mother". The dual is .

In Roman times the following variants are found:

For we have , , , .

For we have , , , , .

For we have , , , , , etc.

For we have , , , , , , , .

CHAPTER II.

EGYPTIAN CHRONOLOGY.

Egyptian chronology has, at intervals, during the last six thousand years, formed a subject of curiosity and study among the learned, but in spite of this the matter is full of difficulties, and at the present time no general agreement, even as to fundamental questions, has been arrived at. The "Palermo Stone"[1] shews that under the Ancient Empire the Egyptians possessed a series of Annals of the kings of the early dynasties, and that they had traditions, of a more or less historical character, which preserved the names of some of the kings who reigned before the union of the Kingdoms of the South and North by Menȧ, or Menes. The evidence of this monument makes it clear that the principal events of each year were carefully noted from the beginning of the 1st Dynasty downwards, and the fragment of the Stone which has come down to us gives valuable indications as to the probable length of the period that must be assigned to the first five dynasties. Up to the present no similar monument recording the Annals of the later dynasties has been found, but certain lists of kings, which are more or less complete, are available, and these may be briefly mentioned.

1. First published by Pellegrini in *Archivio storico Siciliano*, N. S., tome XX, pp. 297—316, with plates.

The most complete of these is contained in the famous "**Royal Papyrus of Turin**", which is now in the Museum of Turin.[1] Its value was first recognized by Champollion le Jeune, who described it as a "tableau chronologique, un vrai canon royal". The papyrus was despatched in a box to Turin, but without packing, and when it arrived at its destination it was found to be broken into scores of little pieces, which lay in a heap at the bottom of the box. In 1826 Seyffarth went to Turin and undertook the work of rejoining the fragments, and he reconstructed a roll of papyrus of twelve columns or pages, each column containing 26 to 30 names of divine or human kings. The "restoration" of the Papyrus by Seyffarth was condemned by Rosellini, Birch, de Rougé, and others, and it seems quite certain that in some places at least the rejoining of the fragments was directed by guesswork. The text of the papyrus is written in the hieratic character and, when complete, may have, as Dr. Birch calculated, contained the names of about three hundred and thirty kings, which he thought coincided with the three hundred and thirty kings mentioned by Herodotus (Bk. II, § 100). The lengths of the reigns of certain kings were given in years, months, and days. Recently the Papyrus has been carefully studied by Dr. Eduard Meyer, who declares that he has derived from his examination of it some indications of importance chronologically.

1. See Lepsius, *Auswahl*, plates 3—6.

The next King List of importance is that which is commonly known as the TABLET OF ABYDOS; it was discovered by Dümichen in the Temple of Osiris at Abydos in 1864. On the Tablet we see Seti I, accompanied by his son and successor Rameses II, addressing 75 of his predecessors, whose cartouches are arranged in chronological order before him; the list is ended by Seti's own name. A third King List is known as the TABLET OF SAḲḲÂRAH; it was found in the tomb of Thunurei, , a royal scribe and "chief reader", who flourished in the reign of Rameses II. It contains 50 royal names, including the name of Rameses II; when complete the number of royal names on the Tablet was 58. Here also may be mentioned a second King List from Abydos, made for Rameses II, the remains of which are in the British Museum (Northern Egyptian Gallery, No. 61), and the TABLET OF KARNAK.[1] Of the arrangement of the kings' names on the latter no satisfactory explanation has yet been given, but it is of value because it gives the names of several kings of the XIth and XIII–XVIIth dynasties.

The following are the royal names on the TABLET OF ABYDOS and TABLET OF ṢAḲḲÂRAH:[2]—

1. See Lepsius, *Auswahl*, plate 1; the most recent copy of this monument is that published by Sethe.

2. The readings of some names are corrected by the new collations of the Lists made for Prof. Meyer.

Tablet of Abydos.	Tablet of Ṣaḳḳârah.
1 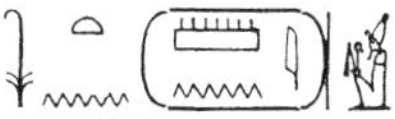 Menȧ	—
2  Tetȧ	—
3 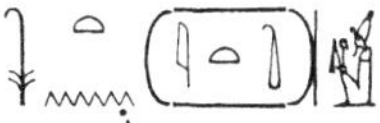 Ȧteth	—
4  Ȧta (Ȧtti?)	—
5 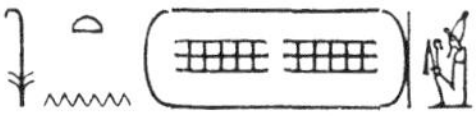 Ḥesepti (Semti)	—
6  Merbap	1  Merbapen
7 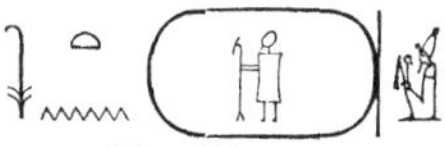 Ḥu (?)	—
8  Qebḥ	2  Qebḥu
—	3  Baiuneter
9  Betchau	—

Tablet of Abydos.

10 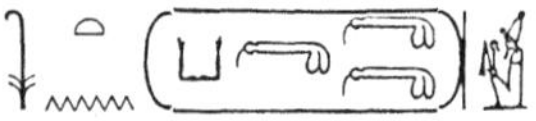

Kakau

11 

Baneteren

12 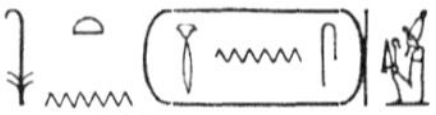

Uatchnes

13 

Senṭȧ

14 

Tchatchai

15 

Nebka

16 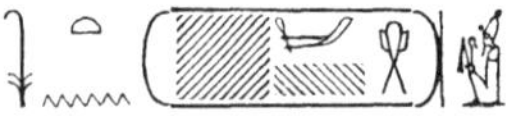

Ṯcheseṛ

Tablet of Ṣaḳḳârah.

4 

Kakau

5 

Baneteru

6 

Uatchnes

7 

Senṭȧ

8 

Neferkarā

9 

Neferka-Seker

10 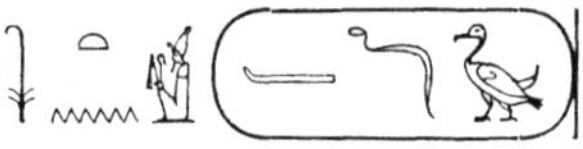

Ḥutchefa

11 

Bebi

12 

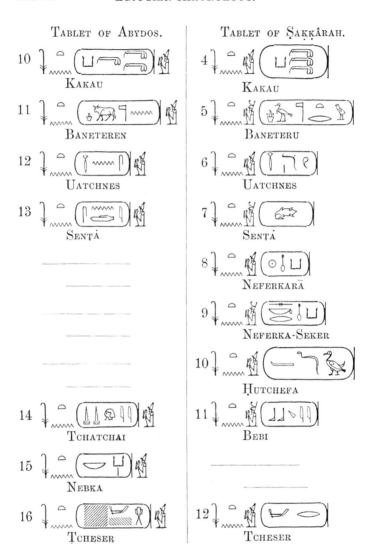

Tcheser

Tablet of Abydos.

17 

Tetà

18 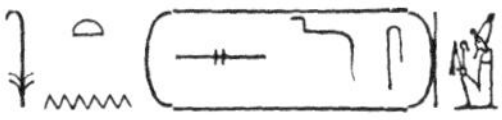

Setches

19 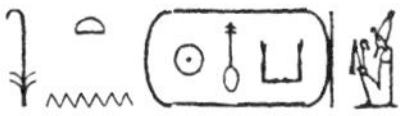

Neferkarā

20 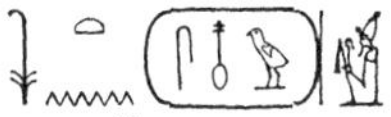

Seneferu

21 

Khefu

22 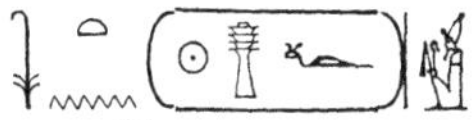

Ṭeṭfrā

23 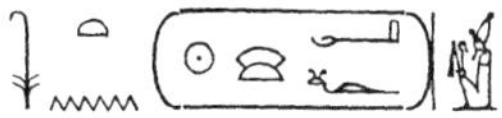

Khāfrā

24 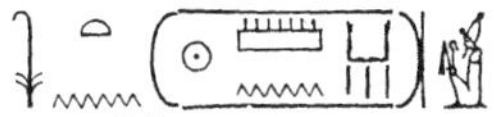

Menkaurā

Tablet of Ṣaḳḳârah.

13 

Tcheser-Tetà

14 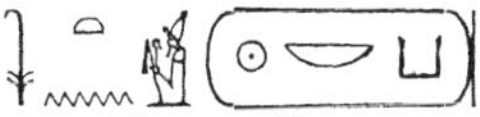

Nebkarā

15 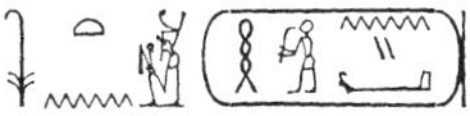

Ḥuni

16 

Seneferu

17 

Khefuf

18 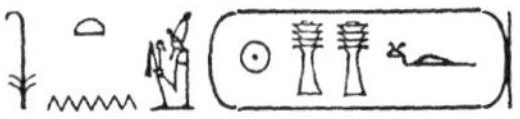

Ṭeṭfrā

19 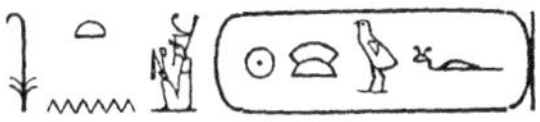

Khāufrā

20 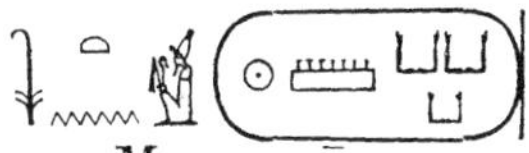

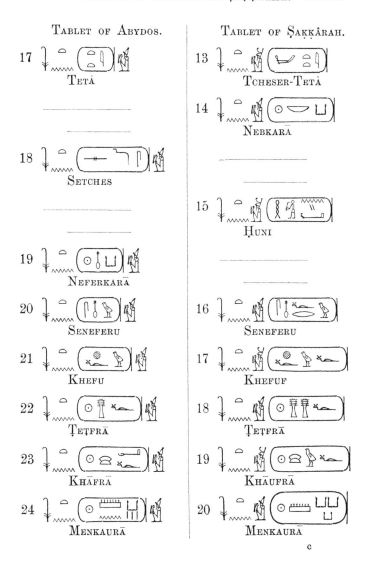

Menkaurā

Tablet of Abydos.

25 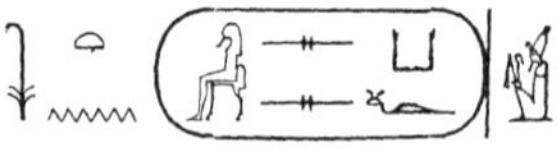

Shepseskaf

---

26 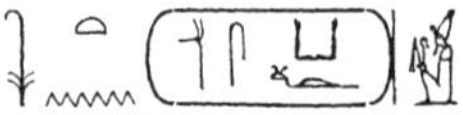

Userkaf

27 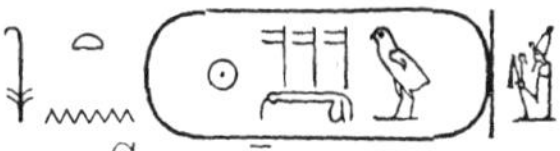

Saḥurā

28 

Kakaȧ

29 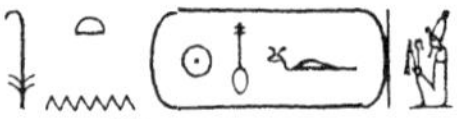

Neferfrā

---

30 

Usrenrā

Tablet of Ṣaḳḳârah.

21 [Name broken away]

22 [Name broken away]

23 [Name broken away]

24 [Name broken away]

25 

Userkaf

26 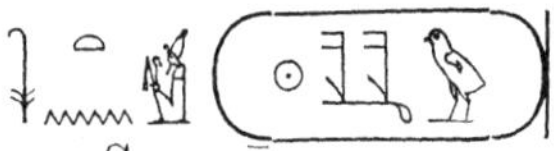

Saḥurā

27 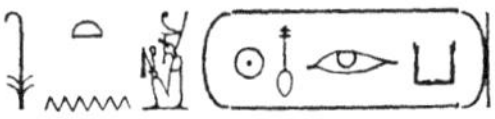

Neferȧrikarā

28 

Shepseskarā

29 

Khāneferrā

Tablet of Abydos.

31 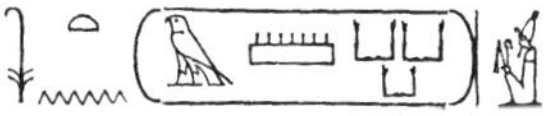
Menkau-Ḥeru

32 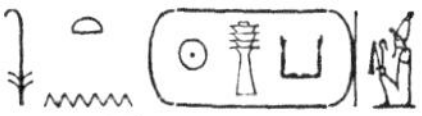
Ṭeṭkarā

33 
Unȧs

34 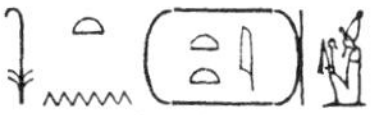
Tetȧ

35 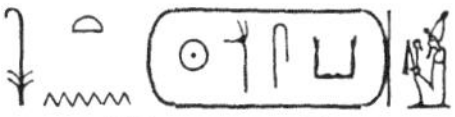
Userkarā

36 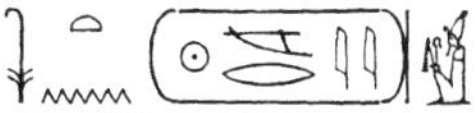
Merirā

37 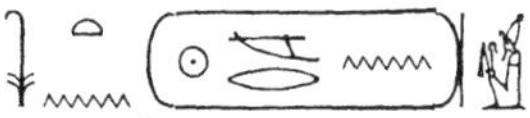
Merenrā

38 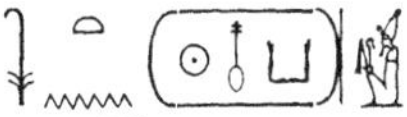
Neferkarā

39 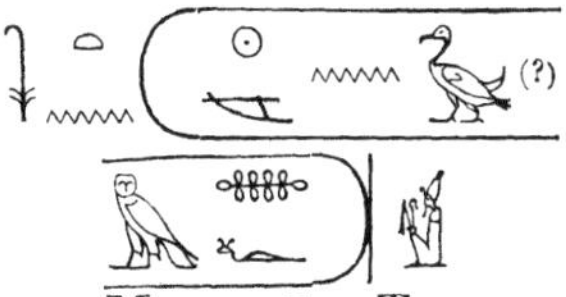
Merenrā - Tchefa-emsaf

Tablet of Ṣaḳḳârah.

30 
Menka-Ḥeru

31 

Ṭeṭkarā

32 
Unȧs

33 
Tetȧ

34 
Pepi (I)

35 
Merenrā

36 
Neferkarā (Pepi II)

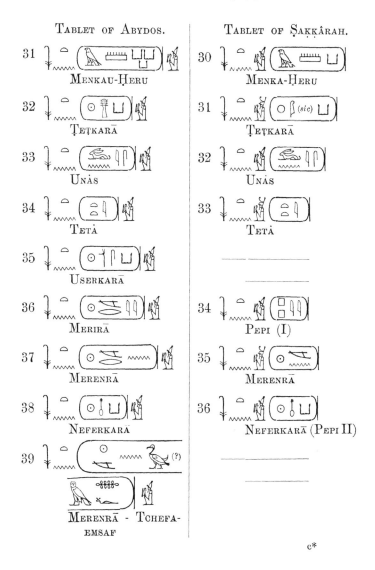

	Tablet of Abydos.	Tablet of Ṣaḳḳârah.
40	 Neterkarā	
41	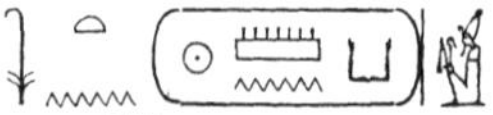 Menkarā	
42	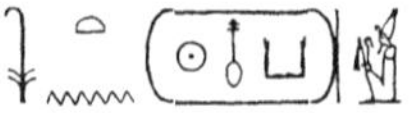 Neferkarā	
43	 Neferkarā-Nebi	
44	 Ṭeṭkarā-Maā...	
45	 Neferkarā-Khenṭu	
46	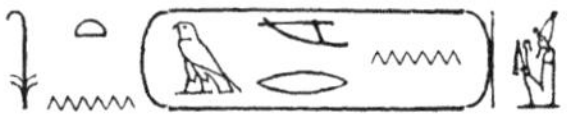 Meren-Ḥeru	
47	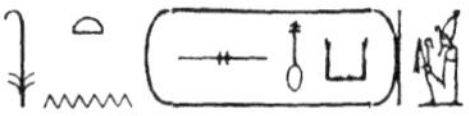 Seneferka	
48	 Kaenrā, or Nekarā	
49	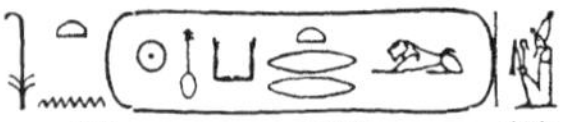 Neferkarā Tererl (?)	

Tablet of Abydos.

50 
Neferka-Ḥeru

51 
Neferkarā Pepi senb

52 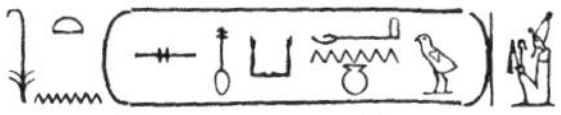
Seneferka-Ānnu

53 
... kaurā

54 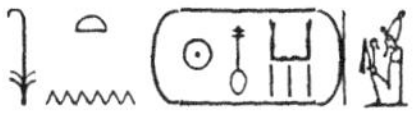
Neferkaurā

55 
Neferkau-Ḥeru

56 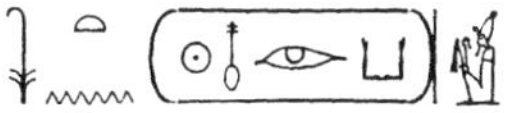
Neferȧrikarā

57 
Nebḥaprā

58 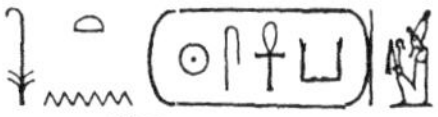
Sānkhkarā

59 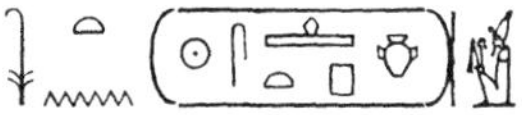
Seḥetepȧbrā

Tablet of Ṣaḳḳârah.

37 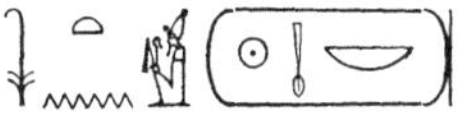
Nebḥaprā

38 
Sānkhkarā

39 
Seḥetepȧbrā

Tablet of Abydos.

60 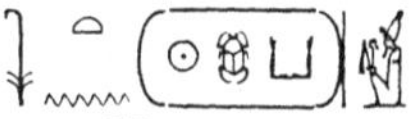

Kheperkarā

61 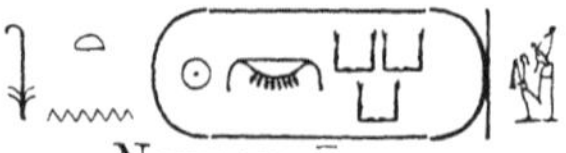

Nubkaurā

62 

Khākheperrā

63 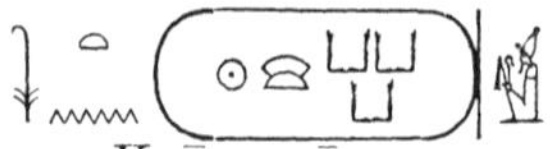

Khākaurā

64 

Maātenrā

65 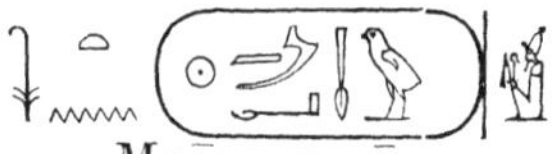

Maākherurā

———

———

66 

Nebpeḥtirā

67 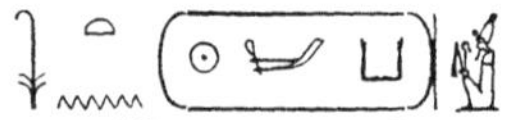

Tcheserkarā

68 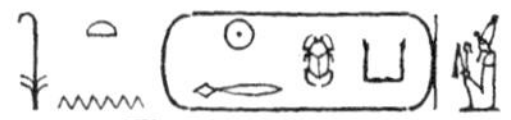

Āakheperkarā

Tablet of Ṣaḳḳârah.

40 

Kheperkarā

41 

Nubkarā

42 

Khākheperrā

43 

Khakarā

44 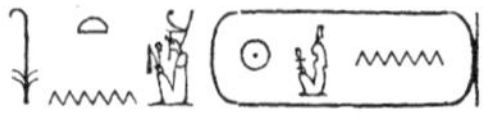

Maāt-en-Rā

45 

Maākherurā

46 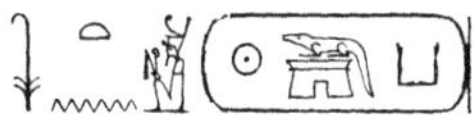

Sebekkarā

47 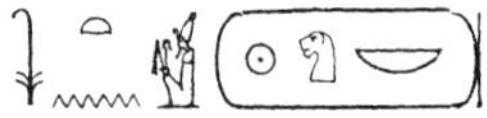

Nebpeḥrā

48 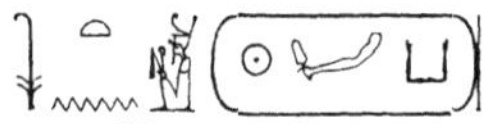

Tcheserkarā

49 

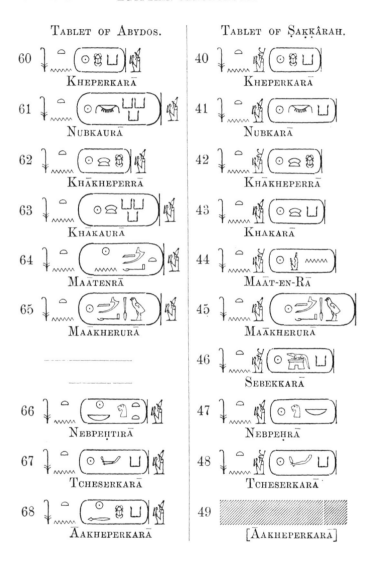

[Āakheperkarā]

Tablet of Abydos.

69 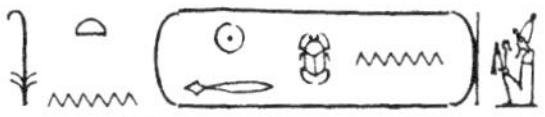

Āakheperenrā

70 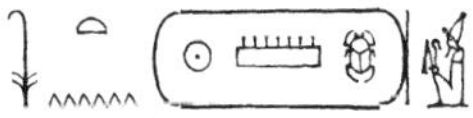

Menkheperrā

71 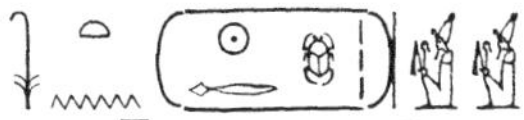

Āakheperurā

72 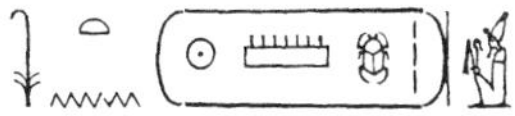

Menkheperurā

73 

Nebmaātrā

74 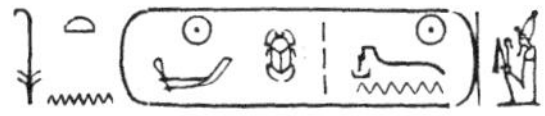

Tcheserkheperurā-setep-en-rā

75 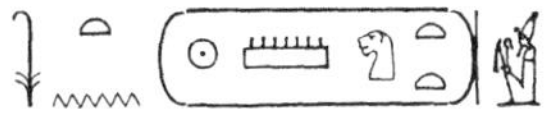

Menpeḥtirā

76 

Menmaātrā

Tablet of Ṣaḳḳârah.

50 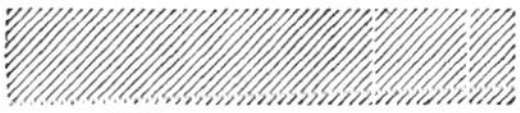

[Āakheperenrā]

51 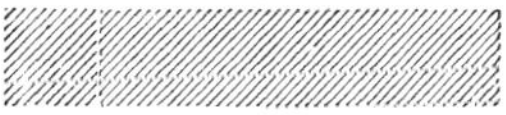

[Menkheperrā]

52 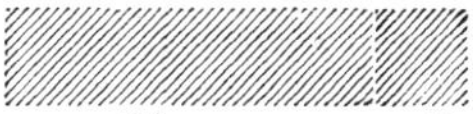

[Āakheperurā]

53 

[Menkheperurā]

54 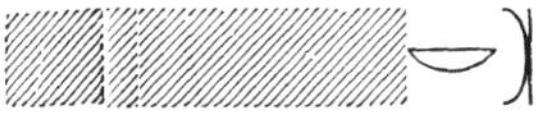

Neb[-maāt-rā]

55 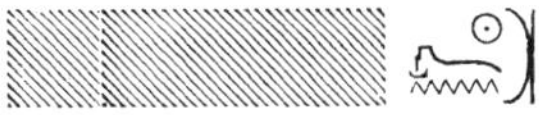

... setepenrā

56 

Men[peḥtirā]

57 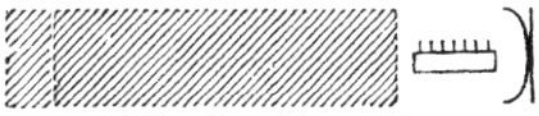

Men[maātrā]

58 

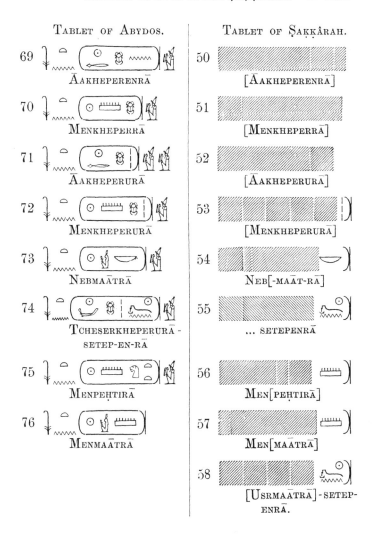

[Usrmaātrā]-setep-enrā.

Now if we compare these lists of kings with each other, it becames at once clear that, although they are both supposed to cover the same ground, they differ considerably in many places. Thus the Tablet of Ṣaḳ-ḳârah opens with the name of Merbapen, which is the sixth in the Tablet of Abydos, and the Tablet of Abydos contains a batch of eighteen names for which there is no equivalent in the Tablet of Ṣaḳḳârah. We are therefore obliged to conclude that those who drew up these lists have only given us series of selected names. Moreover, monuments bearing numbers of royal names which are not included in either list are well known to Egyptologists. The order of the names is substantially the same in each list, but we may note that in the Tablet of Ṣaḳḳârah names Nos. 37—46 are written in reverse order. Each list stops at the beginning of the XIXth dynasty, and therefore we can obtain no help from either in constructing a list of the remaining kings of that dynasty, or of the following dynasties. For help in this difficulty recourse must be had to the famous List of Kings, which tradition says was drawn up for Ptolemy Philadelphus in the third century before Christ by Manetho of Sebennytus. This List formed part of his Αἰγυπτιακά, and in it he divided the kings of Egypt into thirty Dynasties. The first section dealt with the mythological part of the history of Egypt, and with Dynasties I—XI; the second with Dynasties XII—XIX, and the third with Dynasties XX—XXX. His work is lost, but four versions of the King List are extant,[1] and are found in the "Chronography" of George the Monk, the Syncellus of Tarasius, Patriarch of Constantinople, who flourished in the VIIIth century of our era. The oldest version of the King List is that of the Chronicle of Julius Africanus, a Libyan who flourished early in the IIIrd century A. D., which is preserved in the Chronicle of Eusebius, Bishop of Caesarea (born A. D. 264, died about 340). Eusebius himself gives a King List, which contains many interpolations. If the versions of the King List of Manetho according to Africanus and Eusebius be compared, it will be seen that they do not agree in the arrangement of the dynasties, or in the lengths of the reigns of the kings, or in the total number of kings assigned to the different dynasties. Thus Africanus makes 561 kings reign in 5524 years, while Eusebius gives the number of kings as 361, and he says their total reigns amount only to 4480, or 4780 years. The version of Africanus agrees better with the monuments than that of Eusebius. It is probable that Manetho drew on the writings of the best authorities available in his time, but it is very doubtful if the sources of his information were complete or wholly trustworthy. We may, however, be quite sure that his compilation was generally regarded as a valuable work for some centuries after his death, and that he was held to be a great authority

1. See *Fragmenta Historicorum Graecorum*, vol. II, ed. Didot; Bunsen, *Egypt's Place*, vol. I, Appendix; Lepsius, *Königsbuch*, Berlin, 1858.

on Egyptian history and chronology, or we should not find literary impostors of ancient days endeavouring to obtain circulation for their own pseudo-historical works by issuing them under his name. Manetho must not be blamed for the mistakes which his editors and copyists made, but, on the other hand, he can at best only have repeated Ptolemaic traditions, based, no doubt, on King Lists which were as incomplete as the Tablet of Abydos and the Tablet of Ṣaḳḳârah.

In dealing with Egyptian Chronology it must always be remembered that, comparatively speaking, little is known about it. Many writers on the subject have spent much time and ingenuity in trying to make facts derived from the monuments square with Manetho's King List, and the result of their torturing of the figures and their manipulation of the names has frequently obscured the truth. Some investigators have misused facts in their endeavours to frame a system of Egyptian Chronology, which should harmonize with Archbishop Ussher's dates given in our Bibles, and others, with more ingenuity than knowledge, have framed schemes which the monuments now available contradict on most points. To construct a perfectly complete series of the kings of Egypt, with their dates, we need a complete set of monuments which would tell the order of the succession of the kings, and the length of each king's reign. Such a set of monuments does not exist, and therefore no complete system of Egyptian Chronology can be formulated. A sufficient number of royal monuments does exist to justify the making of a general assumption as to the probable length of the period of Dynastic Civilization, but not to make a detailed scheme of its chronology; these facts are proved by the differences that exist in the various systems of Egyptian Chronology which have been proposed in recent years. A system which is, however, *approximately* correct can be framed, and to make this recourse must be had to the monuments.

Now, we find in the Pyramid Text[1] of Pepi II, a king of the VIth dynasty, an allusion to the "gods who were born on the five days which are added to the year". This shews at once that the Egyptians were at that time using, for the ordinary purposes of daily life, a year to which they were in the habit of adding five days[2] in order to make it equal to the length of the true year, as they understood it. In other words, they had a vague year, or wandering year, or calendar year, of 365 days.[3] This year was divided into three seasons, each of which contained four months. The first season was that of the Inundation which was called  SHAT(?), or AKHET, and began in July; the second

1. Ed. Maspero, *Pyramides de Saqqarah,* p. 394, line 754.

2. , or , or . Brugsch, *Thesaurus*, pp. 231—233, 479.

3.  "The 365 days of the year". Brugsch, *Thesaurus,* p. 249.

season was called  PERT, and began in November; the third season was called 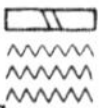 SHEMU (coptic ϣⲱⲙ), and began in March.[1] Roughly speaking, these seasons corresponded to Winter, Spring, and Summer. Each month of these seasons contained 30 days. The four months of each season were called the first, second, third, and fourth month of that season. In late times the Copts gave to the twelve months names which were derived from the names of old Egyptian gods, festivals, etc., thus:—

	EGYPTIAN.			COPTIC.
1st	month	of the Inundation	(Winter)	Thoth.
2nd	"	"	"	Paophi.
3rd	"	"	"	Athyr.
4th	"	"	"	Khoiak.
1st	"	"	Spring	Tybi.
2nd	"	"	"	Mekhir.
3rd	"	"	"	Phamenoth.
4th	"	"	"	Pharmuthi.
1st	"	"	Summer	Pakhon.
2nd	"	"	"	Payni.
3rd	"	"	"	Epiphi.
4th	"	"	"	Mesore.

The calendar containing twelve months of 30 days each survived for magical purposes until the beginning

1. According to Meyer (*Aeg. Chron.*, p. 43) Akhet began on July 19 and ended Nov. 15; Pert on Nov. 16 and ended March 15; and Shemu on March 16 and ended July 13; then followed the "five days over the year".

of the New Empire at least. Thus on the back of a papyrus in the British Museum there is a complete 360-day calendar containing twelve months, each of thirty days, and each day is supposed to be divided into three parts, which are marked lucky , or unlucky . It may be noted in passing that the Babylonians possessed a similar calendar, a fact proved by tablet No. 32641 in the British Museum, which contains a list of twelve months, each of 30 days, lucky and unlucky, etc. The text is published by Rawlinson in *Cuneiform Inscriptions of Western Asia*, vol. V, plate 48.

Now, it is clear that since the wandering, or calendar, year of 365 days was shorter than the true year by nearly a quarter of a day, every fourth wandering year would be shorter than the true year by nearly a whole day, and that given a sufficient number of years, the wandering year would work backward through all the months of the year until at length the first day of the wandering year would coincide with the first day of the solar year. This fact was discovered by the Egyptians at a very early period, and they found it necessary to employ another year which more closely resembled the true year in length. This second year began about the time of the Inundation, and its first day was declared to be that on which the star Sirius, or Sothis,[1] rose heliacally, *i. e.*, with the Sun. This year

1. In Egyptian *Sept* .

began on July 19 or 20; it is called the "Sothic Year", and contained $365\frac{1}{4}$ days, *i. e.*, a few minutes more than the true solar year. The Egyptians found the wandering, or calendar, year sufficiently accurate for all the general purposes of life, but, unfortunately, it does not help the modern investigator to ascertain chronological data with sufficient exactitude for historical purposes. It is therefore necessary to look in the inscriptions for mentions of the risings of the star Sothis, expressed in terms of the wandering, or calendar, year, and if these can be found it is possible to arrive at fixed points in Egyptian chronology, for 1461 wandering, or calendar, years are equal to 1460 Sothic years, *i. e.*, one Sothic period, provided that it can be stated when the Sothic period referred to ended or began. Now the inscriptions do, fortunately, contain mentions of risings of the star Sirius expressed in terms of the wandering year, but they do not state when any Sothic period ended or began, indeed it is doubtful if the Egyptians know of the existence of the Sothic period.[1] Mr. Torr, after pointing out that Sirius did not really rise at intervals of exactly $365\frac{1}{4}$ days, that the cycle of Sirius did not really amount to four times $365\frac{1}{4}$ years, or 1461, that a Sothic period which ended at Alexandria A. D. 139 would really have begun there in B. C. 1318, and that further south the beginning and the ending would both have been considerably later, as the date of rising varies

1. See Brugsch, *Thesaurus*, p. 203.

with the latitude, comes to the conclusion that the Sothic period, or cycle of Sirius, was invented by the later Greeks at Alexandria.[1] Further, he thinks that "there "is very little hope of correcting any dates in history "by reference to the cycles of the phoenix and the dog-"star, or other things pertaining to the calendar".[2]

The facts brought forward by those who think that a correct system of Egyptian Chronology can be founded on the notices of the risings of Sirius mentioned in the inscriptions may now be briefly noticed. The ablest supporter of this view is Prof. E. Meyer, who assumes the existence of three Sothic Periods which began respectively [3] on

July 19 B. C. 1321-20 — 1318-17
July 19 B. C. 2781-80 — 2778-77
July 19 B. C. 4241-40 — 4238-37

The date of the ending of the Period which began B. C. 1321-20 is obtained from the statement of Censorinus [4] who, writing A. D. 238 about the Egyptian year, says that it is reckoned from the first day of the Egyptian month of Thoth. He then goes on to say that the first day of the year in which he was writing was the first of Thoth, and that its equivalent was the

1. *Memphis and Mycenae*, p. 57.
2. *Ibid*, p. 60.
3. *Aegyptische Chronologie*, p. 28.
4. *De die natali*, XVIII. 10.

VIIth day of the Kalends of July, or June 25, and adds that this was also the case one hundred years before (B. C. 139), when the equivalent of the first of Thoth was the XIIth day of the Kalends of August, or July 21, on which day the Dog-star (Sirius) is wont to rise. According to Professor Meyer, Censorinus made a mistake in the last statement, since in 139 Sirius rose heliacally on July 20, not July 21.[1] Assuming that the statement of Censorinus is correct, the Sothic period preceding that in which he lived ended in B.C. 1321-20, the one before that in 2781-80, and so on. The whole theory of the existence of a system of Sothic periods rests in fact upon the words of Censorinus.

Having assumed that Censorinus is a credible witness Prof. Meyer goes on to give three instances in the inscriptions in which the risings of Sirius are expressed in terms of the years of the wandering year. The first is found in the Ebers Papyrus, the second is in a fragment of a calendar, said to be of the time of Thothmes III, inscribed on a block of stone at Elephantine,[2] and the third is in the Kahun papyri.[3] The first mention states that the rising of Sirius, *pert Sepṭ* , took place on the day of the festival of the New Year which was celebrated on the 9th day of the third month of the season of the Inundation, *i. e.*, the 9th of the

1. *Op. cit.*, p. 24.
2. Lepsius, *Denkmäler*, III, plate 4 *c*; Brugsch, *Thesaurus*, p. 363 *a*.
3. *Aeg. Zeit.*, vol. XXXVII, p. 99 ff.

eleventh month of the year, in the 9th year of king Tcheserkarā, or Àmen-ḥetep I

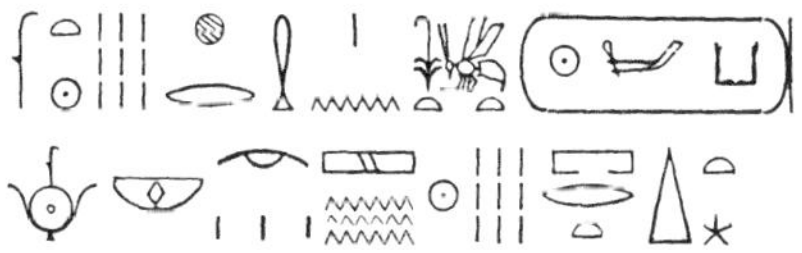

According to the calculations of Prof. Meyer, the 9th year of the reign of Àmen-ḥetep I fell on one of the four years B. C. 1550—49 to 1547—46, and the first year of his reign fell in the period B. C. 1558—57 to 1555—54. Now this passage was discussed by Mr. Torr twelve years ago,[1] and he argued thus: "Had there been "365 days to the year, day 9 of month 11 would have "57 days from day 1 of month 1 in the year after; "and then year 9 of king Ser-ka-Rā would have been "assignable to 1550 B. C., that being four times 57 years "before 1322 B. C., the supposed date of the rising of "the dog-star on day 1 of month 1. But this calendar "proceeds from day 9 of month 12 to day 9 of month 1 "just as it proceeds from day 9 of any other month to "day 9 of the next; so that it clearly is intended for "the year of 360 days with twelve months of thirty days "apiece and nothing added." His conclusion is: "And "thus it will not serve to fix the date of Ser-ka-Rā "Àmen-ḥetep, as there is nothing to fix the date at which "the dog-star rose on day 1 of month 1 in these years "of 360 days apiece."

1. *Memphis and Mycenae*, p. 57.

The second mention of the rising of Sirius given by Prof. Meyer is in these words:   *i. e.*, the appearance of Sirius took place on the 28th day of the third month of the season of the Inundation, that is, on the 28th day of the 11th month of the year, and on this day the customary offerings were made. Here there is given neither the name of a king, nor the year of his reign. It is, however, asserted boldly that the mention belongs to the reign of Thothmes III, because this king's name is found on another fragment (published by Lepsius, *Denkmäler*, III, 43*f*) which is said to belong to it. As a result of his calculations Prof. Meyer has concluded that Thothmes III reigned from 3rd May B.C. 1501 to 17th March 1447. This rising of Sirius has also been discussed by Mr. Torr, who says: "With a year of "365 days this would put the rising 38 days before "day 1 of month 1; and thus it might be taken to refer "to 1474, that being four times 38 years before 1322 B.C. "But there is nothing in the fragments of this calendar "to show whether the year had 365 days, or only 360; "and as the fragments came from Elephantine, the ca-"lendar was probably intended for a southern latitude "in which the time would not be reckoned from 1322. "In any case, however, this calendar is useless as a "guide to history, since it cannot be assigned with cer-"tainty to any king. It doubtless was inscribed upon "a building of king Men-cheper-Ra Thothmes: but it "may have been inscribed there by one of his successors."[1]

From the third mention of the rising of Sirius discussed in his work Prof. Meyer concludes that the 7th year of the reign of Usertsen III fell in the period B. C. 1882—81 to 1879—78, and the first year in the period B. C. 1888—87 to 1885—84.[2] From what has been said above it is clear that the three risings of Sirius quoted by Prof. Meyer took place in the Sothic period which began according to him B. C. 2778—77 and ended B. C. 1318—17. In the preceding Sothic period, *i. e.*, that which began B. C. 4241—40 and ended B. C. 2778—77, no point is fixed by him, but he assumes that Menȧ, the first dynastic king of Egypt, began to reign about B. C. 3315, and that the first year of this Sothic period (B. C. 4241—40) witnessed the introduction of the Calendar. His general results are thus tabulated:

		B. C.
Menȧ, or Menes		3315
Dynasties 1 and 2,	18 kings in 420 years	3315—2895
Dynasty 3,	4 kings in 55 „	2895—2840
Dynasty 4,	160 years	2840—2680
Dynasty 5,	140 „	2680—2540
Dynasties 6—8,	181 „	2540—2360
Dynasties 9 and 10,	200 „	2360—2160
Dynasty 12 begins		2000

1. *Op. cit.*, p. 58.
2. See also *Nachträge zu ägyptischen Chronologie*, Berlin, 1908, p. 18.

	B. C.
Dynasty 12 ends	1791
Dynasties 13—17, about 200 years	1789—1589
Dynasty 18 begins	1580
„ „ ends	1321
The Era of Menophreôs (Rameses I) begins	1321, July 19
Dynasty 19	1320
Dynasty 20	1200—1179.

Omitting for the moment any mention of the lengths of the reigns of the kings of dynasties 21—31, we may compare Prof. Meyer's results with the systems of Egyptian Chronology proposed by other Egyptologists, which are tabulated on pp. LIV, LV.

A glance at the table there given will shew how greatly the authors of these systems vary in their estimates of the length of the period of dynastic civilization, and in the dates which they assign to the reign of Menes, the first dynastic king. Champollion Figeac, Boeckh, Mariette, and Petrie give the highest dates, Bunsen, Lepsius, and Lieblein give the lowest, and Brugsch takes a middle course. The obvious deduction which may fairly be made from this array of conflicting figures is that Egyptian Chronology is either a very inexact science, or that very little is known about it. The greater number of these systems we may now disregard, for they were formulated at a time when Egyptology was, comparatively speaking, in its infancy, but all are instructive as illustrating the difficulties which beset the subject. The systems which agree most closely with the results of modern investigators are those of Bunsen, Lepsius and Lieblein, and after them comes the system of Brugsch. This distinguished scholar assigned to Menes the date B. C. 4400, to the VIth dynasty B. C. 3300, to the XIIth B. C. 2466, to the XVIIIth B. C. 1700, and to the XIXth B. C. 1400, whilst those of Prof. Meyer are B. C. 3315, 2540, 2000, 1580, 1320, respectively. In fixing his earliest date Brugsch was probably influenced to some extent by Manetho's King List. It seems clear that he made the interval between the VIth and the XIIth, and that between the XIIth and XVIIIth dynasties too long, that he allowed too few generations to a century, and that his dates for the kings of the XVIIIth dynasty must be modified. In spite of all this, however, it seems to me that the period of 4400 years which he assigned to dynastic civilization agrees more closely with the general facts of Egyptian chronology and history than the 5867 years of Champollion Figeac, or the 3315 years of Prof. Meyer. In arriving at conclusions about a subject like Egyptian Chronology where, comparatively, so few exact data exist, wide and general knowledge of every branch of Egyptology and mature judgment count for a great deal, and in these respects Brugsch had no rival, except in Professor Maspero. It is impossible to think that Brugsch did not consider carefully the mentions of the risings of Sirius in the Ebers Papyrus and on the calendar fragment from Elephantine, and also what conclusions could be drawn from them for the purposes of chronology. The state-

Dynasty	Champollion-Figeac	Boeckh	Bunsen	Lepsius	Unger
1	5869	5702	3623	3892	5613
2	5615	5449	3433	3639	5360
3	5318	5147	3433	3338	5058
4	5121	4933	3209	3124	4845
5	4673	4650	3054	2840	4568
6	4426	4402	3054	2744	4310
7	4222	4199	2947	2592	4107
8	4147	4198	—	2522	4107
9	4047	4056	—	2674	3967
10	3947	3647	—	2565	3558
11	3762	3462	—	2423	3374
12	3703	3404	2755	2380	3315
13	3417	3244	2634	2136	3315
14	3004	2791	2260	2267	2702
15	2520	2607	2547	2101	2518
16	2270	2323	2287	1842	2258
17	2082	1806	1776	1684	2007
18	1822	1655	1625	1591	1796
19	1473	1326	1410	1443	1404
20	1279	1183	1293	1209	1195
21	1101	1048	1109	1091	1060
22	971	934	979	961	930
23	851	814	829	787	810
24	762	725	740	729	721
25	718	719	734	716	715
26	674	658	(684)	685	663
27	524	529	525	525	525
28	404	405	405	525	424
29	398	399	399	399	399
30	377	378	378	378	382
31	339	340	340	340	346

Lieblein	Mariette	Brugsch	Brugsch	Petrie (1906)
3893	5004	4455	4400	5510
3630	4751	4202	4133	5247
3328	4449	3900	3966	4945
3114	4235	3686	3733	4731
2830	3951	3402	3566	4454
2612	3703	3204	3300	4206
2414	3500	"	3100	4003
2414	3500	3001	—	3933
2862	3358	"	—	3787
2506	3249	"	—	3687
2321	3064	2855	—	3502
2268	2851	2812	2466	3459
2108	—	2599	2233	3246
2108	2398	2599	—	2793
1925	2214	2146	—	2533
2108	—	1896	—	2249
1641	—	2115	—	1731
1490	1703	1706	1700	1580
1231	1462	1464	1400	1322
1022	1288	1288	1200	1202
887	1110	1110	1100	1102
950 (?)	980	980	966	952
773	810	810	766	755
684	721	721	733	721
728 (?)	715	715	700	—
678	665	665	666	—
527	527	527	527	—
404	406	527	—	—
398	399	399	399	—
378	378	378	378	—
340	340	340	340	—

ment of Censorinus was well known to him, and he himself discussed[1] the effort made to reform the calendar by Euergetes I, B. C. 238, but still we do not find that he attempted to form a system of Egyptian chronology by means of the mentions of the risings of Sirius. In his *Thesaurus*[2] he states boldly that the monuments contain no mention either of the Sothic period or the Phoenix period,[3] and that he thought the use of the wandering year by the Egyptians was inseparable from the knowledge of a fixed solar year.[4] These facts suggest that Brugsch believed the Sothic period to have been invented at a late period, and thought that the Egyptians knew the solar year, and employed it to check the progress of the wandering year, and as he did not make use of the mentions of the risings of Sirius in his chronological scheme, it is difficult to think that he attached to them the importance which has been assigned to them by some recent investigators. The present writer has no wish to belittle in any way the importance of the help which astronomical calculations

1. *Aegyptologie*, p. 353.

2. "Weder die eine noch die andere Ueberlieferung des Alter-"thumes hat bis jetzt durch die Denkmäler ihre überzeugende Be-"stätigung gefunden." (P. 203.)

3. It contained 500, or 540, or 654, or 972, or 1000, or 7006, or 12,954 years; for the authorities see Torr, *Memphis and Mycenae*, p. 54.

4. "Unter allen Umständen ist so viel sicher, dass der Gebrauch "des Wandeljahres unzertrennlich von der Kenntniss eines festen "Sonnenjahres gewesen sein musste." (*Aegyptologie*, p. 353.)

may afford the Egyptologist in his chronological difficulties, or to deny their general accuracy, but the variations in the results obtained by the different authorities[1] from the same data must tend to make every one hesitate to accept blindly dates which are declared by their advocates to have been ascertained astronomically, and to be "absolutely certain".[2]

After the system of Brugsch the only other scheme of Egyptian Chronology worthy of serious thought is that of Prof. Meyer. His work, to which reference has already been made, is undoubtedly a valuable contribution to the subject, and he has stated his case with the skill, learning, and moderation which we should expect from him. Some of his conclusions, however, it is impossible to accept, *e. g.*, the date of B. C. 3315 for the beginning of the reign of Menà, and the date which he is inclined to assign to the introduction of the calendar, B. C. 4241, is open to many objections. On the other hand, he appears to be correct in shortening the interval between the VIth and the XIIth dynasties, and that between the XIIth and the XVIIIth dynasties, but his shortening of the latter interval is probably too great. It seems to be almost impossible, or at least extremely difficult, to crowd the reigns of five dynasties of kings into

1. See Nicklin in *Classical Review*, vol. XIV, 1900, p. 148.

2. The Rev. F. A. Jones as a result of his examination of the whole precessional cycle of 25,920 years has come to the conclusion that the Great Pyramid was built B. C. 2170 (!). *Athenaeum*, No. 4195, March 21, 1908.

about 200 years, which is what must be done if his dates are accepted, and this fact alone will shake the confidence of many in his general conclusions. If Professor Meyer makes the interval too short, Professor Petrie makes it too long — 1666 years — an estimate which need not be seriously considered.

The true reason of such extreme and opposed views on such points of chronology is the absence of facts, coupled with the desire of framers of systems of chronology to explain every thing. The scheme of the XIth dynasty proposed by Mr. Breasted in Prof. Meyer's work, and elsewhere, can hardly be maintained in the light of the results which have been derived from the excavations made at Dêr al-Baḥarî by Prof. Naville. The lowering of the dates of kings of the XVIIIth dynasty may be accepted provisionally, especially as it seems to agree with the general trend of the evidence which has been deduced from the Cuneiform Inscriptions.[1] Finality in such matters cannot be expected for some time to come. Throughout Prof. Meyer's work there appears to be a tendency to rely too much on the King List in the Turin Papyrus, which, after all, only represents XVIIIth dynasty tradition. At that period probably less was known about the early

1. See L. W. King, *Chronicles concerning early Babylonian Kings*, vol. I, p. 19. Basing his conclusion on the materials published by Mr. King, Prof. Meyer asserts that no monument found in Babylonia is as old as B. C. 3000. This conclusion agrees with his preconceived belief.

kings than now, and it is clear from the misreading of the names of kings Semti and Sen that the scribes, like modern investigators, were sometimes unable to arrive at right conclusions. Prof. Meyer's monograph contains the ablest statement of Egyptian Chronology which has appeared since the masterpiece of Lepsius, and it merits the study of all those who are interested in the subject.

It is unnecessary to discuss here the period which lies between the reign of Rameses III and Psammetichus I, for the facts will be found in all the Histories of Egypt. The period between Psammetichus I and Alexander the Great is well known, and the admirable work of Prof. Strack[1] has settled the chronology of the Ptolemies.

1. *Die Dynastie der Ptolemäer,* Berlin, 1897.

THE GREEK LISTS.

I. MYTHICAL PERIOD.

Gods.

			Manetho.		Panodorus.	
Dynasty	I	Hephaistos	9000	years	$727\frac{3}{4}$	years
„	II	Helios	992	„	$80\frac{1}{6}$	„
„	III	Agatho-daimon	700	„	$56\frac{7}{12}$	„
„	IV	Kronos	501	„	$40\frac{1}{2}$	„
„	V	Osiris and Isis	433	„	35	„
„	VI	Typhon	359	„	29	„
			11985	years	969	years.

Demi-gods.

Dynasty	VII	Horus	100	years	25	years
„	VIII	Ares	92	„	23	„
„	IX	Anubis	68	„	17	„
„	X	Herakles	60	„	15	„
„	XI	Apollo	100	„	25	„
„	XII	Ammon	120	„	30	„
„	XIII	Tithoes	108	„	27	„
„	XIV	Sosos	128	„	32	„
„	XV	Zeus	80	„	20	„
	Years wanting		2	„	$-\frac{1}{2}$	„
			858	years	$214\frac{1}{2}$	years.

Summary.

Gods	11985	years	969	years
Demi-gods	858	„	$214\frac{1}{2}$	„
Total	12843	years	$1183\frac{1}{2}$	years.

II. MANETHO (BOECKH).

Dynasty I of Gods.

Hephaistos	9000 years	
Helios and others, Typhon	2985 "	11985 years

Dynasty II of Gods.

Horus, Others, Zeus	858 years	858 years

Dynasty III of Gods.

..., Bytes	1056 years	1056 years

Dynasty I of Demi-gods	1255	"
Dynasty II of Demi-gods	1817	"
Dynasty III of Demi-gods (Memphis)	1702	"
Dynasty IV of Demi-gods (This)	350	"
Dynasty of Manes	5813	"
Total	24836	years.

III. THE KING LIST OF MANETHO.[1]

Book I.

Dynasty I at This.

	Africanus	Years	Eusebius	Years	Eusebius (A. v.)	Years
			8 kings in 263 years.			
1.	Menes	62	Menes	60	Menes	30
2.	Athothis	57	Athothis	27	Athothis	25
3.	Kenkenes	31	Kenkenes	39	Kenkenes	39
4.	Uenephes	23	Uenephes	42	Vavenephis	42
5.	Usaphais	20	Usaphais	20	Usaphaes	20
6.	Miebis	26	Miebaes	26	Niebaes	26
7.	Semempses	18	Semempses	18	Mempses	18
8.	Bieneches	26	Bienthes	26	Vibestes	26
	Total	263		258		226

Dynasty II at This.

9 kings in 302 years.

		Years		Years		Years
1.	Boethos	38	Bochos	—	Bochus	—
2.	Kaiechos	39	Choos	—	Cechous	—
3.	Binothris	47	Biophis	—	Biophis	—
4.	Tlas	17	...	—	...	—
5.	Sethenes	41	. .	—	...	—
6.	Chaires	17	...	—	...	—
7.	Nephercheres	25	...	48	...	—
8.	Sesochris	48	Sesochris	—	Sesochris	48
9.	Chenneres	30	...	—	...	—
		302				

1. See *Fragmenta Historicorum Graecorum*, ed. C. Müller, Paris, 1848, p. 539.

Dynasty III at Memphis.

Africanus		Eusebius		Eusebius (Armenian version)	
		9 kings in 214 years.			
	Years		Years		Years
1. Necherophes	28	Nechcrochis	—	Necherochis	—
2. Tosorthos	29	Sesorthos	—	Sesorthos	—
3. Tyreis	7	...	—	...	—
4. Mesochris	17	...	—	...	—
5. Soyphis	16	...	—	...	—
6. Tosertasis	19	...	—	...	—
7. Aches	42	...	—	...	—
8. Sephuris	30	...	—	...	—
9. Kerpheres	26				
	214				

Dynasty IV at Memphis.

8 kings in 274 (*sic*) years.		17 kings in 448 years.			
	Years		Years		Years
1. Soris	29	...	—	...	—
2. Suphis I	63	...	—	...	—
3. Suphis II	66	Suphis	—	Suphis	—
4. Menkheres	63	...	—	...	—
5. Ratoises	25	...	—	...	—
6. Bicheris	22	...	—	...	—
7. Sebercheres	7	...	—	...	—
8. Thamphthis	9	...	—	...	—
	284				

Dynasty V at Elephantine.

Africanus		Eusebius		Eusebius (Armenian version)	
8 kings in 248 years.		31 kings in — years.			
	Years		Years		Years
1. Usercheres	28	Othoes	—	Othius	—
2. Snephres	13	...	—	...	—
3. Nephercheres	20	...	—	...	—
4. Sisires	7	Phiops	—	Phiops	—
5. Cheres	20	27 others	—	27 others	—
6. Rathures	44				
7. Menkheres	9				
8. Tatcheres	44				
9. Onnos	33				
	218				

Dynasty VI at Memphis.

6 (?) kings in 203 years.		-- kings in 203 years.			
	Years				
1. Othoes	30	[Names and number of kings unknown]		[Names of kings unknown]	
2. Phios	53				
3. Methusuphis	7				
4. Phiops	100				
5. Menthesuphis	1		Years		Years
6. Nitokris	12	Nitokris	—	Nitokris	—
	203				

Dynasty VII at Memphis.

Africanus	Eusebius	Eusebius (Armenian version)
70 kings in 70 days.	5 kings in 75 days.	5 kings in 75 years.

Dynasty VIII at Memphis.

27 kings in 146 years.	5 kings in 100 years.	9 (or 19) kings in 100 years.

Dynasty IX at Herakleopolis.

19 kings in 409 years. 4 kings in 100 years.

	Years		Years		Years
1. Akhthoes	—	Akhthoes	—	Akhthoes	—
18 others	—	3 others	—	3 others	—

Dynasty X at Herakleopolis.

19 kings in 185 years.

Dynasty XI at Thebes.

16 kings in 43 years.

Ammenemes 16 years.

Summary of Kings in Book I:

Dynasties	Africanus
I—XI	200 kings in 2293 years, or in 2289 years and 70 days.
	Eusebius
	192 kings in 1842 years and 75 days.

Book II.

Dynasty XII at Thebes.

Africanus		Eusebius		Eusebius (Armenian version)	
7 kings in 160 years.		7 kings in 182 years.			
	Years		Years		Years
1. Sesonchosis	46	Sesonkhosis	46	Sesonchosis	46
2. Ammanemes	38	Ammanemes	38	Ammanemes	38
3. Sesostris	48	Sesostris	48	Sesostris	48
4. Lamaris	8	Lamaris	8	Lampares	8
5. Ammeres	8	...		...	
6. Amenemes	8	...	42	...	42
7. Skemiophris	4	...		...	
	160		182		182

Dynasty XIII at Thebes.

60 kings in 453 years.

Dynasty XIV at Xoïs.

76 kings in 184 years. 76 kings in 184 years. 76 kings in 484 years.

Dynasty XV Shepherds.

Africanus			Eusebius		Eusebius (Armenian version)
6 kings in 284 years.			6 Theban kings in 250 years.		
	Years		Years		Years
1. Saïtes	19	...	—	...	—
2. Bnon	44	...	—	...	—
3. Pachnan	61	...	—	...	—
4. Staan	50	...	—	...	—
5. Archles	49	...	—	...	—
6. Aphobis	61	...	—	...	—
	284				

Dynasty XVI Shepherds.

32 kings in 518 years. 5 kings in 190 years.

Dynasty XVII Shepherds.

5 (?) kings in 151 years. 4 kings in 103 years.

	Years		Years
1. Saites	19	Saites	19
2. Bnon	40	Benon	40
[3]. Aphophis	14	Archles	14
4. Archles	30	Aphophis	30
	103		103

According to the emended text in Müller's edition, p. 570, the Shepherd kings of Dynasties XV—XVII were 43 in number, and the Theban kings 53 in number; total number of kings 96.

e*

Dynasty XVIII at Thebes.

Africanus		Eusebius		Eusebius (Armenian version)	
16 kings in 263 years.		16 kings in 376 years, or 14 kings in 321 or 351 years.		14 kings in 317 years.	
	Years		Years		Years
1. Amos	—	1. Amosis	25	Amoses	25
2. Khebros	13	2. Khebron	13	Chebron	13
3. Amenoph-		3. Ammen-		Amophis	21
this	21	ophis	21		
4. Amensis	22	4. Miphres	12	Mephres	12
5. Misaphris	13	5. Misphrag-		Mispharmu-	
6. Misphrag-		muthosis	26	thosis	26
muthosis	26	6. Tuthmosis	9	Tuthmosis	9
7. Tuthmosis	9	7. Amenophis	31	Amenophis	31
8. Amenophis	31	8. Oros	36	Orus	28
9. Oros	37	9. Achencher-		Achencheres	16
		ses	12		
10. Acherres	32	[Athoris 39 or 9]		Ancheres	8
11. Rathos	6	[Kencheres 16]		Cheres	15
12. Khebres	12	10. Acherres	8	Armais	5
13. Akherres	12	11. Cherres	15	Ramesses	68
14. Armesses	5	12. Armais	5	Menophis	40
15. Ramesses	1	13. Ramesses	68		317
16. Amenoph-		14. Ammen-			
ath	19	ophis	40		
	259		346		

Dynasty XIX at Thebes.

	Africanus		Eusebius		Eusebius (A. v.)	
	7 (*sic*) kings in 209 years.		5 kings in 194 years.			
		Years		Years		Years
1.	Sethos	51	Sethos	55	Sethus	55
2.	Rapsakes	61	Rampses	66	Rampses	66
3.	Ammenephthes	20	Ammenephthes	40	Amenephthis	40
4.	Ramesses	60	Ammenemes	26	Ammenemes	26
5.	Ammenemnes	5	Thuoris	7	Thuoris	7
6.	Thuoris	7		194		194
		204				

Summary of Kings in Book II:

Dynasties	
	Africanus
XII—XIX	289, or 290 kings in 2222 years
	Eusebius
	171, or 173 kings in 1967, or 1904, or 2294, or 2267 years.

Book III.

Dynasty XX at Thebes.

12 kings in 135 years. 12 kings in 178 years.

Dynasty XXI at Tanis.

7 kings in 114 or 130 years.

		Years		Years		Years
1.	Smendes	26	Smendis	26	Smendis	26
2.	Psusennes	46	Psusennes	41	Psusennes	41
3.	Nephercheres	4	Nephercheres	4	Nephercheres	4
4.	Amenophthis	9	Amenophthis	9	Amenophthis	9
5.	Osochor	6	Osochor	6	Osochor	6
6.	Psinaches	9	Psinaches	9	Psinnaches	9
7.	Psusennes	14	Psusennes	35	Psusennes	35
		114		130		130

Dynasty XXII at Bubastis.

Africanus		Eusebius		Eusebius (A. v.)	
9 kings in 120 years.		3 kings in 49 years.			
	Years		Years		Years
1. Sesonchis	21	Sesonchosis	21	Sesonchosis	21
2. Osorthon	15	Osorthon	15	Osorthon	15
3. ...	} 25	...	—	...	—
4. ...		...	—	...	—
5. ...		...	—	...	—
6. Takelothis	13	Takelothis	13	Takelothis	13
7. ...	} 42	...	—	...	—
8. ...		...	—	...	—
9. ...		...	—	...	—
	116		49		49

Dynasty XXIII at Tanis.

4 kings in 89 years.		3 kings in 44 years.			
	Years		Years		Years
1. Petubastes	40	Petubastis	25	Petubastis	25
2. Osorcho	8	Osorthon	9	Osorthon	9
3. Psammus	10	Psammus	10	Psammus	10
4. Zet	31		44		44
	89				

Dynasty XXIV.

Bocchoris 6 years Bocchoris 44 years Bocchoris 44 years.

Dynasty XXV of Ethiopians.

3 kings in 40 years.		3 kings in 44 years.			
	Years		Years		Years
1. Sabakon	8	Sabakon	12	Sabakon	12
2. Sebichos	14	Sebichos	12	Sebichos	12
3. Tarkos	18	Tarakos	20	Tarakos	20
	40		44		44

Dynasty XXVI at Saïs.

	Africanus 9 kings in $150\frac{1}{2}$ years.	Years	Eusebius 9 kings in 168 years.	Years	Eusebius (A. v.) 9 kings in 167 years.	Years
1.	Stephinates	7	Ammeris	12	Ammeres	12
2.	Nechepsos	6	Stephinatis	7	Stephinathis	7
3.	Nechao I	8	Nechepsos	6	Nechepsos	6
4.	Psammetichos	54	Nechao I	8	Nechaus I	8
5.	Nechao II	6	Psammetichos	45	Psammetichus	44
6.	Psammuthis	6	Nechao II	6	Nechaus II	6
7.	Uaphris	19	Psammuthis	17	Psammuthes	17
8.	Amosis	44	Uaphris	25	Vaphres	25
9.	Psammeche-rites	$-\frac{1}{2}$	Amosis	42	Amosis	42
		$150\frac{1}{2}$		168		167

Dynasty XXVII of Persians.

	8 kings in $124\frac{1}{3}$ years.	Years	8 kings in $120\frac{1}{3}$ years.	Years		Years
1.	Cambyses	6	Cambyses	3	Cambyses	3
2.	Darius Hys-taspes	36	Magoi	$\frac{7}{12}$	Magi	$-\frac{7}{12}$
3.	Xerxes the Great	21	Darius	36	Darius	36
4.	Artabanus	$-\frac{7}{12}$	Xerxes I	21	Xerxes I	21
5.	Artaxerxes	41	Artaxerxes	41	Artaxerxes	40
6.	Xerxes II	$-\frac{1}{6}$	Xerxes II	$-\frac{1}{6}$	Xerxes II	$-\frac{1}{6}$
7.	Sogdianus	$-\frac{7}{12}$	Sogdianus	$-\frac{7}{12}$	Sogdianus	$-\frac{7}{12}$
8.	Darius Xer-xes	19	Darius Xer-xes	19	Darius Xer-xes	19
		$124\frac{1}{3}$		$121\frac{1}{3}$		$120\frac{1}{3}$

Dynasty XXVIII at Saïs.

Amyrtaeus 6 years.

Dynasty XXIX at Mendes.

Africanus		Eusebius		Eusebius (Armenian version)	
4 kings in $20\frac{1}{3}$ years.		5 kings in $21\frac{1}{3}$ years.			
	Years		Years		Years
1. Nepherites	6	Nepherites	6	Nepherites	6
2. Achoris	13	Achoris	13	Achoris	13
3. Psammuthis	1	Psammuthis	1	Psammuthis	1
4. Nepherites	—$\frac{1}{3}$	Nepherites	—$\frac{1}{3}$	Muthes	1
	$20\frac{1}{3}$	Muthis	1	Nepherites	—$\frac{1}{3}$
			$21\frac{1}{3}$		$21\frac{1}{3}$

Dynasty XXX at Sebennytus.

3 kings in 38 years.		3 kings in 20 years.			
	Years		Years		Years
1. Nektanebes	18	Nektanebes	10	Nectanebis	10
2. Teos	2	Teos	2	Teos	2
3. Nektanebos	18	Nektanebos	8	Nectanebis	8
	38		20		20

Dynasty XXXI of Persians.

3 kings in 9 years.		3 kings in 16 years.			
	Years		Years		Years
1. Ochus	2	Ochus	6	Ochus	6
2. Arses	3	Arses	4	Arses	4
3. Darius	4	Darius	6	Darius	6
	9		16		16

SUMMARY OF KINGS IN BOOK III:

Dynasties	
	AFRICANUS
XX—XXXI	64 kings in $868\frac{1}{6}$ years.
	EUSEBIUS
	58 kings in $801\frac{2}{3}$, or $803\frac{2}{3}$ years.
Total number of kings in Manetho:	AFRICANUS
	553, or 554 kings in 5380 years.
	EUSEBIUS
	421, or 423 kings in 4547, or 4939 years.

IV. TABLE OF ERATOSTHENES.

(*Frag. Hist. Graec.*, II, ed. Didot, p. 340 ff.)

	Years	Anno Mundi
1. Menes	62	2900
2. Athothes	59	2962
3. Athothes	32	3021
4. Diabaes	19	3053
5. Pemphos	18	3072
6. Momcheiri	79	3090
7. Stoichos	6	3169
8. Gosormies	30	3175
9. Mares	26	3205
10. Anoyphis	20	3231
11. Sirios	18	3251
12. Chnubos Gneuros	22	3269

		Years	Anno Mundi
13.	Ragosis	13	3291
14.	Bigres	10	3304
15.	Saophis I	29	3314
16.	Saophis II	27	3343
17.	Moscheres	31	3370
18.	Masthes	33	3401
19.	Pammes	35	3434
20.	Apappus	100	3469
21.	Ekheskososokaras	1	3570
22.	Nitokris	6	3571
23.	Murtaios	22	3576
24.	Thuosimares	12	3598
25.	Sethinilos	8	3610
26.	Semphrukrates	18	3618
27.	Khouther	7	3636
28.	Meures	12	3643
29.	Khomaephtha	11	3655
30.	Soikuniosokho	60	3666
31.	Peteathyres	16	3726
32.	Ammenemes	26	3742
33.	Stammenes	23	3768
34.	Sesortosis	55	3791
35.	Mares	43	3846
36.	Siphthas	5	3889
37.	Phruaro	19	3894
38.	Amuthartaios	63	3913—3976
	THIRTY-EIGHT KINGS in	1076	

V. THE OLD CHRONICLE.

(*Frag. Hist. Graec.*, II, ed. Didot, p. 534.)

Dynasty				Years
I–XV				443
XVI	at Tanis	8	kings, or dynasties, in	190
XVII	at Memphis	4	„ „ „	103
XVIII	„	14	„ „ „	348
XIX	Thebes	5	„ „ „	194
XX	„	8	„ „ „	228
XXI	Tanis	6	„ „ „	121
XXII	„	3	„ „ „	48
XXIII	Thebes	2	„ „ „	19
XXIV	Saïs	3	„ „ „	44
XXV	of Ethiopians	3	„ „ „	44
XXVI	Memphis	7	„ „ „	177
XXVII	of Persians	5	„ „ „	124
XXVIII	...	...	„ „ „	...
XXIX	Tanis	...	„ „ „	39
XXX	„	1	„ „ „	18
		69	kings, or dynasties, in	2140

VI. THE BOOK OF THE SOTHIS.

(*Frag. Hist. Graec.*, II, p. 607.)

	Years	Anno Mundi
1. Mestraim (Menes)	35	2776
2. Kurodes	63	2811
3. Aristarkhos	34	2874
4. Spanios	36	2908
5. ... } 6. ...	72	2944

		Years	Anno Mundi
7.	Osiropis	23	3016
8.	Sesonkhosis	49	3039
9.	Amenemes	29	3088
10.	Amasis	2	3117
11.	Akesephthres	13	3119
12.	Ankhoreus	9	3132
13.	Armiyses	4	3141
14.	Khamois	12	3145
15.	Miamus	14	3157
16.	Amesesis	65	3171
17.	Uses	50	3236
18.	Rameses	29	3286
19.	Ramessomenes	15	3315
20.	Usimare	31	3330
21.	Ramesseseos	23	3361
22.	Ramessameno	19	3384
23.	Ramesse Iubasse	39	3403
24.	Ramesse Uaphru	29	3442
25.	Kankharis	5	3471
26.	Silites	19	3477
27.	Baion	44	3496
28.	Apakhnas	36	3540
29.	Aphophis	61	3576
30.	Sethos	50	3637
31.	Kertos	29	3687
32.	Asseth	20	3716
33.	Amosis (Tethmosis)	26	3736
34.	Khebron	13	3762

	Years	Anno Mundi
35. Anemphis	15	3775
36. Amenses	11	3790
37. Misphragmuthosis	16	3801
38. Misphres	23	3817
39. Touthmosis	39	3840
40. Amenophthis	34	3879
41. Oros	48	3913
42. Akhenkheres	25	3961
43. Athoris	29	3986
44. Khenkheres	26	4015
45. Akherres	8	4011
46. Armaios	9	4049
47. Ramesses	68	4058
48. Amenophis	8	4126
49. Thuoris	17	4134
50. Nekhepsos	19	4151
51. Psammuthis	13	4170
52. ...	4	4183
53. Kertos	16 (20)	4187
54. Rampsis	45	4207
55. Amenses (Ammenemes)	26	4252
56. Okhuras	14	4278
57. Amendes	27	4292
58. Thuoris	50	4319
59. Athothis (Phusanos)	28	4369
60. Kenkenes	39	4397
61. Uennephis	32 (42)	4436
62. Susakeim	34	4478

	Years	Anno Mundi
63. Psuenos	25	4512
64. Ammenophis	9	4537
65. Nepherkheres	6	4546
66. Saïtes	15	4552
67. Psinakhes	9	4567
68. Petubastes	44	4576
69. Osorthon	9	4620
70. Psammos	10	4629
71. Konkharis	21	4639
72. Osorthon	15	4660
73. Takalophis	13	4675
74. Bokkhoris	44	4688
75. Sabakon, the Ethiopian,	12	4732
76. Sebekhon	12	4744
77. Tarakes	20	4756
78. Amaes	38	4776
79. Stephinathes	27	4814
80. Nekhepsos	13	4841
81. Nekhao I	8	4854
82. Psamitikhos	14	4862
83. Nekhao II Pharao	9	4876
84. Psamuthis	17	4885
85. Uaphris	34	4902
86. Amosis	50	4936

VII. JOSEPHUS.

(*Contra Apion,* I, 15.)

Dynasty XV of Shepherds.

		Years
1.	Salatis	19
2.	Beon	44
3.	Apachnas	36 $\frac{7}{12}$
4.	Apophis	61
5.	Jannas	50 $\frac{1}{12}$
6.	Assis	49 $\frac{1}{6}$
	6 Kings in	259 $\frac{5}{6}$

Dynasty XIX.

	Years
Sethosis	59
Rampses	66
Amenophis	—
Sethos	—

Dynasty XVIII at Thebes.

		Years
1.	Tethmosis	25 $\frac{1}{3}$
2.	Chebron	13
3.	Amenophis	20 $\frac{7}{12}$
4.	Amessis	21 $\frac{3}{4}$
5.	Mephres	12 $\frac{3}{4}$
6.	Mephramuthosis	25 $\frac{5}{6}$
7.	Thmosis	9 $\frac{2}{3}$
8.	Amenophis	30 $\frac{5}{6}$
9.	Orus	36 $\frac{5}{12}$
10.	Acencheres I	12 $\frac{1}{12}$
11.	Rathotis	9
12.	Acencheres II	12 $\frac{5}{12}$
13.	Acencheres III	12 $\frac{1}{4}$
14.	Armais	4 $\frac{1}{12}$
15.	Ramesses	1 $\frac{1}{3}$
16.	Armesses Miammi	66 $\frac{1}{6}$
17.	Amenophis	19 $\frac{1}{2}$
	17 Kings in	333

List of Papers bearing on Egyptian Chronology.

BORCHARDT, L. Das Grab des Menes. *Aeg. Zeit.*, XXXVI. 1898. 87.

Der zweite Papyrusfund von Kahun und die zeitliche Festlegung des mittleren Reiches der Ägyptischen Geschichte. *Ibid.*, XXXVII. 1899. 89.

BREASTED, J. H. Chronology. *Ancient Records*, I. 25 ff.

The Eleventh Dynasty. Meyer, *Aeg. Chron.*, 156; and see *American Jnl. of Semitic Languages*, XXI. (April.)

BRUGSCH, H. Die Grossen Zeitperioden. *Thesaurus, Kalendarische Inschriften*, 1883. 203.

CHASSINAT, É. Les Νέκυες de Manéthon et la troisième ennéade Héliopolitaine. *Recueil de Travaux*, XIX. 23.

DARESSY, G. Les Rois Psusennès. *Ibid.*, XXI. 9.

GARSTANG, J. The Tablet of Mena. *Aeg. Zeit.*, XLII. 1905. 61.

Mahasna and Bet Khallaf. London. 1902.

GRIFFITH, F. L. Zum Ägyptischen Namen des Usaphais. *Aeg. Zeit.*, XXXVI. 1898. 142.

HOLLINGSWORTH, E. W., The Hyksos and the Twelfth Dynasty. *P. S. B. A.*, XXX. 1908, 155.

JONES, F. A. The Ancient Year and the Sothic Cycle. *Proc. Soc. Bibl. Arch.*, XXX. 95.

LEGGE, F. Recent Discoveries at Abydos. *P. S. B. A.*, XXI. 183.

The carved slates from Hieraconpolis and elsewhere. *Ibid.*, XXII. 125.

LEGGE, F. The Kings of Abydos. *Ibid.*, XXVI, 125, 144.

New carved slate. *Ibid.*, XXVI. 262; XXVIII. 87.

Early Monarchy of Egypt. *Ibid.*, XXVIII. 14.

Tablets of Negadah and Abydos. *Ibid.*, XXVIII. 252, 263; XXIX. 18, 70, 150, 243.

Titles of the Thinite Kings. *Ibid.*, XXX. 86, 121—128.

LIEBLEIN, J. Les VIIe—XIe dynasties Égyptiennes. *Recueil de Travaux*, XXI. 216.

Thotmès III, était-il le fils de Thotmès I. *P. S. B. A.*, XX. 93.

Le lever héliaque de Sothis le 16 Pharmouti. *Ibid.*, XXII. 352.

Observations on the Ancient History of Egypt. *Ibid.*, XXVIII. 29.

Eine chronologische Bestimmung. *Aeg. Zeit.*, XLIV. 1907, p. 101.

MAHLER, E. Chronologische Bestimmung. *Aeg. Zeit.*, XXVII. 1889. 97.

Materialien zur Chronologie der alten Aegypter. *Ibid.*, XXXII. 1894. 99.

Das Mittlere Reich der Aegyptischen Geschichte. *Ibid.*, XL. 1902. 79.

MASPERO, G. Sur la XVIIIe et la XIXe dynasties de Manéthon. *Recueil de Travaux*, XXVII. 13.

Sur la XIIe dynastie de Manéthon. *Ibid.*, XXVIII. 8.

Meyer, E. Aegyptische Chronologie. Berlin. 1904.

Nachträge zur Ägyptischen Chronologie, Berlin, 1908.

Moret, A. Le Titre Horus d'or. *Recueil de Travaux*, XXIII. 23.

Müller, M. Bemerkung über einige Königsnamen. *Ibid.*, IX. 176.

Naville, É. Les plus anciens Monuments Égyptiens. *Ibid.*, XXI. 105; XXIV. 19; XXV. 199.

La Pierre de Palerme. *Ibid.*, XXV. 34.

La succession des Thoutmès d'après un mémoire récent. *Aeg. Zeit.*, XXXV. 1897. 30.

Un dernier mot sur la succession des Thoutmès. *Ibid.*, XXXVI. 1898. 48.

À propos du groupe . *Ibid.*, XXXVI. 1898. 132.

Petrie, W. F. Note on a carved slate. *P. S. B. A.*, XXII. 140.

Les plus anciens rois de l'Égypte. *Recueil de Travaux*, XXIV. 214.

Notes on the XIXth and XXth dynasties. *P. S. B. A.*, XXVI. 36—41.

Notes on later Egyptian Dynasties. *Ibid.*, XXVI. 283.

The Early Monarchy of Egypt. *Ibid.*, XXVII. 279.

Revision of Chronology. *Researches in Sinai*, 163 ff.

Quibell, J. E. Hierakonpolis. London. 1900.

Riehl, C. Das Sonnen- und Siriusjahr der Ramessiden mit dem Geheimniss der Schaltung. Leipzig. 1875.

Robiou, F. Observations sur une date astronomique du haut Empire Égyptien. *Recueil de Travaux*, III. 86—102.

Sethe, K. Zur zeitlichen Festlegung der zwölften Dynastie und zur Benutzung Ägyptischer Sothisdaten überhaupt. *Aeg. Zeit.*, XLI. 1904. 38.

Zur Königsfolge der 11. Dynastie. *Ibid.*, XLII. 1905. 131.

Die ältesten geschichtlichen Denkmäler der Ägypter. *Ibid.*, XXXV. 1897. 1.

Beiträge zur ältesten Geschichte Ägyptens.

Steindorff, G. Die Könige Mentuhotep und Antef. Zur Geschichte der 11. Dynastie. *Aeg. Zeit.*, XXXIII. 1895. 77.

Stern, L. Die XXII. manethonische Dynastie. *Ibid.*, XXI. 1883. 15.

Torr, C. Egyptian Chronology. *Memphis and Mycenae,* 53.

Weill, R. Notes sur les monuments de la période thinite. *Recueil de Travaux*, XXIX. 26.

Wiedemann, A. On a monument of the First Dynasties. *P. S. B. A.*, IX. 180.

Zur XXI. Dynastie Manetho's. *Aeg. Zeit.*, XX. 1882. 86.

ADDITIONS.

Tcheser-nub.

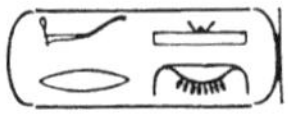

Jéquier, *Recueil*, XXX, p. 45.

Khāu-f-Rā, a prince of the time of *Neb-ka*.

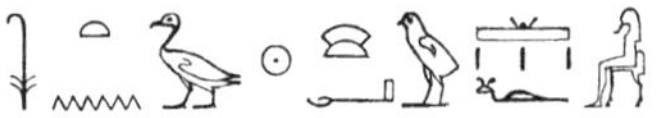

Westcar Papyrus, I, 17.

Shaȧru.

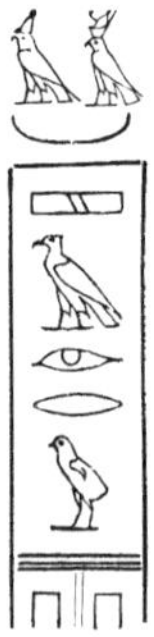

The predecessor of Khufu, the Σῶρις of Manetho.

Inscription at Al-Kâb. Sayce, *P. S. B. A.*, vol. XXI, p. 111.

Baiu-f-Rā, a prince.

He lived in the time of Khufu. *Westcar Papyrus*, IV, 17.

Rā-nefer-f.

I. Horus name NEFER-KHĀU.
IV. Suten Bāt name NEFER-F-RĀ.
V. Son of Rā name RĀ-SHEPSES-KA.

I. 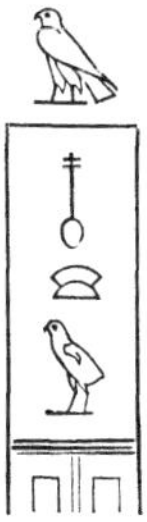

Petrie, *Abydos*, II, p. 42. For the two other names see vol. I of this work, pp. 26, 27.

Ḥeru-àkau, or *Àkau-Ḥeru.*

I. Horus name SEKHEM-KHĀU.
IV. Suten Bāt name RĀ-KHĀ-NEFER.
V. Son of Rā name ḤERU-ÀKAU.

I. 

Clay seal in the Berlin Museum, No. 16277 (Meyer, *op. cit.*, p. 149). For the two other names see vol. I of this work, pp. 26, 27.

Rā-nefer-àri-ka.

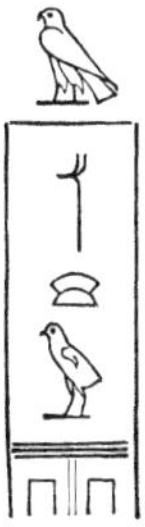

His Horus name was USR-KHĀU.

See Mariette, *Mon. Div.*, 54*f*; Sethe, *Aeg. Zeit.*, XXX, 1892, p. 63; Petrie, *Abydos*, II, plate XIV.

Ḥeru-sa-nefer.

, or 

Daressy, *Recueil*, XX, 72.

Ḥeru-nefer-Khnem.

Daressy, *Recueil*, XX, 72.

Semu (?).

Stobart Stele. See Stobart, *Egyptian Antiquities*, Berlin, 1855.

Usertsen IV (?).

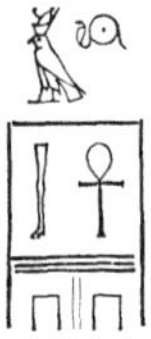

His Horus name was NEM-ĀNKH.

See Legrain, *Recueil*, XXX, 16; and Legrain, *Catalogue*, Cairo, 1906, p. 15.

Åmen-em-ḥāt-senb-f.

I. Horus name	MEḤ-ÅB-TAUI.
II. N-U name	THET-SESHESH-F.
III. Golden Horus name	...
IV. Suten Båt name	RĀ-SESHESH-KA.
V. Son of Rā name	ÅMEN-EM-ḤĀT-SENB-F.

I. 

From a cylinder in the Amherst Collection (*P. S. B. A.*, XXI, p. 282).

II.

Ibid.

III.  ...

IV. 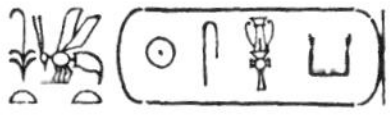 *Ibid.*

V. 

Ibid.

Meḥ-àb-taui Rā-seshesh-ka.

Scarab in Lord Percy's Collection.

Rā-neb-ḥap Menthu-ḥetep.

His Horus of gold name is QA-SHUTI.

Naville, *XIth Dynasty Temple*, p. 3.

Rā-mer-ānkh Menthu-ḥetep.

Legrain, *Catalogue*, p. 12.

Āa-peḥ.

Scarab in the British Museum, No. 32368.

Ṭu-ā (?)-*n-r-ā* (?) (Hyksos Period).

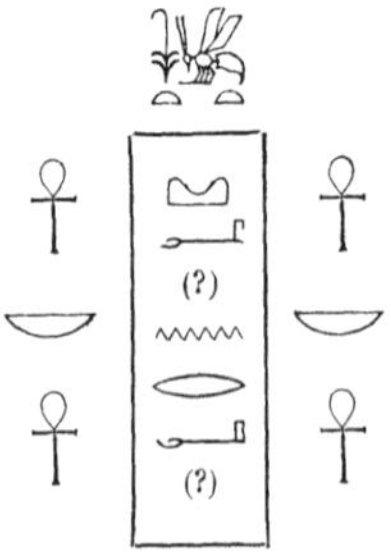

Scarab in Lord Percy's Collection.

Merseḳer, queen.

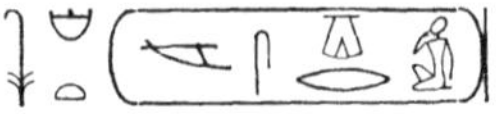

Stele in the British Museum, No. 846.

Ȧmen-ḥetep-ȧbui (?).

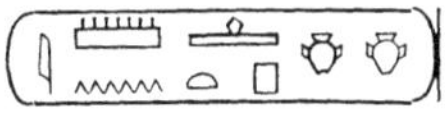

British Museum, No. 36378.

ERRATA.

Page 8. For  read .

„ 46. For 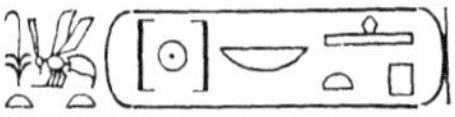 read 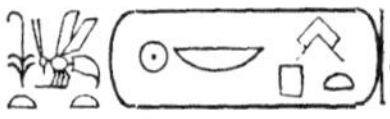.

„ 86. For  read .

PREDYNASTIC PERIOD.

I. Kings of Upper Egypt.—Names wanting.

II. Kings of Lower Egypt:—

[Name No. 1 is wanting.]

1. . . . u.

Palermo Stele,[1] No. 2.

2. Seka.

Palermo Stele, No. 3.

3. Khaȧu.

Palermo Stele, No. 4.

4. Tȧu.

Palermo Stele, No. 5.

5. Thesh.

Palermo Stele, No. 6.

1. See A. Pellegrini, *Archivio Storico Siciliano*, N. S. Anno XX, Palermo, 1896; Naville, *Recueil*, XXI, p. 112; XXV, p. 64.

6. Neheb.

Palermo Stele, No. 7.

7. Uatch-nār, or *Uatch-Ȧnt.*

Palermo Stele, No. 8.

8. Mekha.

Palermo Stele, No. 9.

9. . . . a.

Palermo Stele, No. 10.

[Names No. 10 ff. are wanting.]

DYNASTIC PERIOD.

ANCIENT EMPIRE.

FIRST DYNASTY. FROM THIS.

1. Men, Menȧ (Menes).

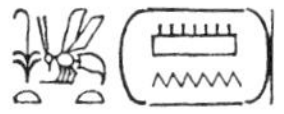

Limestone stele of the priest Unnefer (Louvre, No. 421, or 328). See E. de Rougé, *Recherches,* Paris, 1866, p. 31.

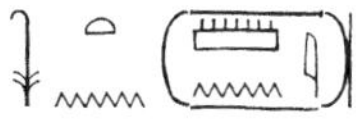

Abydos List, No. 1.

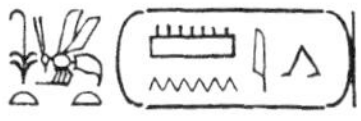

Turin Papyrus. (Published in Lepsius, *Auswahl,* plates 3—6.)

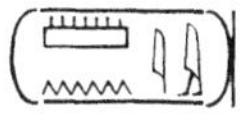

Turin Papyrus.

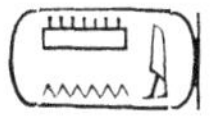

Prisse d'Avennes, *Monuments,* plate 47.

2. Ȧ-Teḥuti, Thetet, or *Tetȧ.*

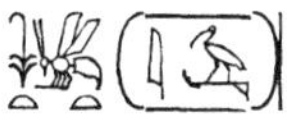

Turin Papyrus.

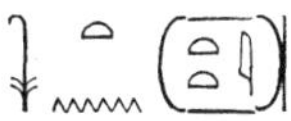

Abydos List, No. 2.

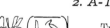

Ebers Papyrus, plate 66, line 16.

Limestone stele of the priest Unnefer (Louvre, No. 421, or 328). See E. de Rougé, *Recherches*, Paris, 1866, p. 31.

Shesh, mother of Tetȧ Ȧ-Teḥuti.

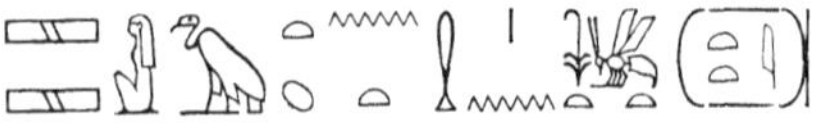

Ebers Papyrus, plate 66, line 15.

3. *Ȧteth.*

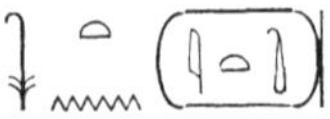

Abydos List, No. 3.

4. *Ȧta.*

Abydos List, No. 4.

5. *Semti.*

I.	Horus name	Ṭen.
II.	N-U[1] name	...
III.	Golden Horus name	...
IV.	Suten Bȧt name	Semti.
V.	Son of Rā name	...

I. 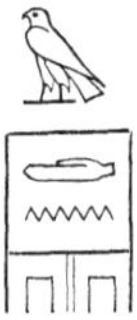

British Museum, Plaque, No. 32650.

IV. 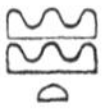

Fragments of bowls, vases, etc., found at Abydos. (British Museum, No. 32664, etc.)

1. N-U = Nekhebit-Uatchit name, .

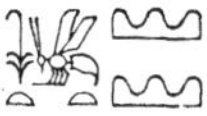 Fragments of bowls, etc., found at Abydos.

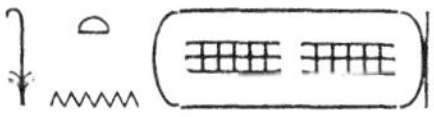 Abydos List, No. 5.

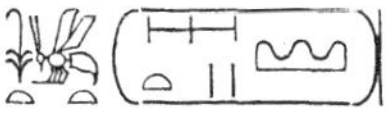 Papyrus of Nu (sheet 13).

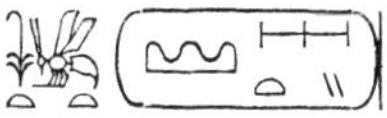 Lepsius, *Königsbuch.*

 Lepsius, *Todtenbuch*, Bl. 53.

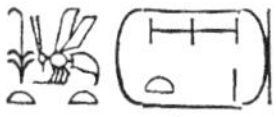 Medical Papyrus at Berlin, ed. Brugsch, *Recueil*, II, pl. XCIX.

 Ebers Papyrus, plate 103, l. 2.

 Papyrus at Berlin (Lepsius, *Todtenbuch*, p. 12.

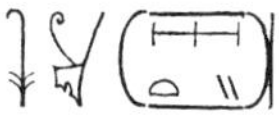 Naville, *Todtenbuch*, II, p. 139.

6. Merpeba.

I. Horus name	Āṭ-Ȧb.
II. N-U name	...
III. Golden Horus name	...
IV. Suten Bȧt name	Merbap, or Merbapen.
V. Son of Rā name	...

I. 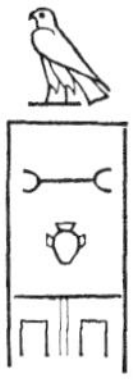 Fragment of alabaster bowl in the British Museum (No. 32667).

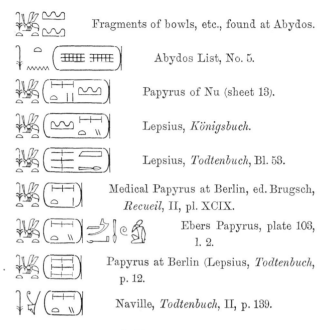

IV. 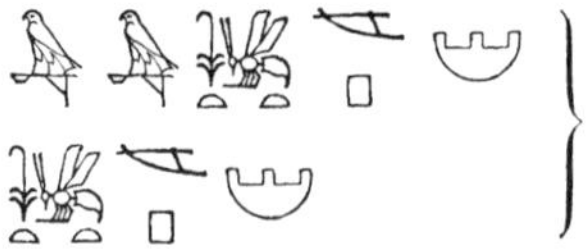

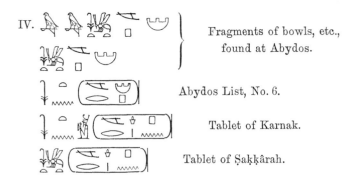

Fragments of bowls, etc., found at Abydos.

Abydos List, No. 6.

Tablet of Karnak.

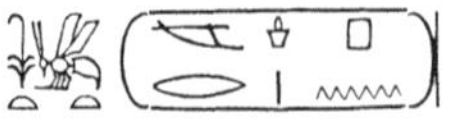

Tablet of Ṣaḳḳârah.

That MERPEBA succeeded SEMTI is proved by the following inscription on a piece of limestone found at Abydos.

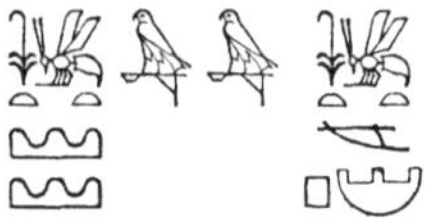

7. *Ḥu,* or *Nekht,* or *Semsu.*

I. Horus name	SMERKHA.
II. N-U name	...
III. Golden Horus name	...
IV. Suten Bât name	ḤU, or NEKHT, or SEMSU.
V. Son of Rā name	...

I. 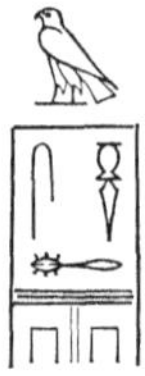

Sculpture at Wâdî Maghârah (Weill, *Recueil*, Paris, 1904, p. 97).

IV.  Ivory plaque. British Museum, No. 32668.

 Abydos List, No. 7.

8. Sen (Qebḥ, or Qebḥu).

I.	Horus name	Qā, or Qa-ā.
II.	N-U name	Sen, or Qā, or Qa-ā.
III.	Golden Horus name	...
IV.	Suten Bȧt name	Qebḥ, or Qebḥu.
V.	Son of Rā name	...

I. 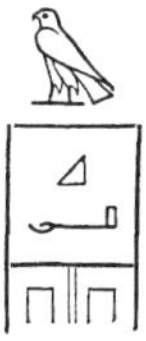 Ivory plaque, jar-sealings, etc., found at Abydos.

II.  Ivory plaque, found at Abydos.

IV. 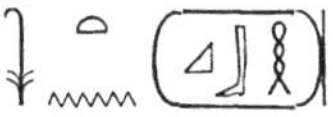 Abydos List, No. 8.

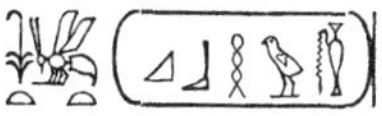 Tablet of Ṣaḳḳârah.

 Bowl fragment, British Museum, No. 32672.

The kings whose Horus names, etc., follow here probably reigned during the First Dynasty.

1. Āḥa.

I. 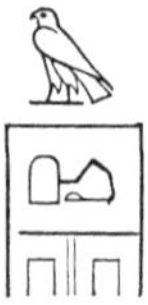

Ivory plaques (No. 1410, 1412) in the Egyptian Museum at Cairo (Maspero, *Guide*, p. 533 ff.). King Āḥa has been by some identified with Menes (see also British Museum, No. 38010).

II. 

Ivory plaque in Cairo (No. 1410).

2. Tcha.

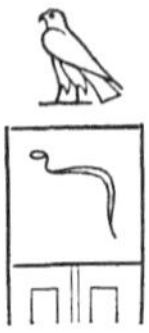

Stele in the Louvre (see J. de Morgan, *Recherches*, Paris, 1897, p. 238), and British Museum, No. 32641. On some jar-sealings found at Abydos this Horus name is followed by the signs  and therefore king TCHA has, by some, been identified with king  of the Tablet of Abydos.

3. Khent.

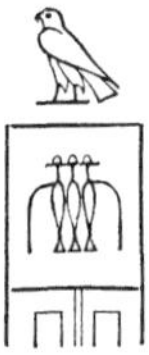

From objects found by Amélineau (*Les nouvelles fouilles d'Abydos*, Paris, Leroux, 1896 ff., see also British Museum, No. 35607). King KHENT has been, by some, identified with the TETȦ (or Ȧ-TEḤUTI) of the Tablet of Abydos.

4. Mer-Net, or *Mer-Neith.*

Stele in the Museum at Cairo; British Museum, No. 32645; etc. MER-NET has, by some, been identified with the ȦTA of the Tablet of Abydos.

THE SECOND DYNASTY. FROM THIS.

1. Betchau.

I. Horus name	Nārmer.
I *a*. Horus-Set name	Khā-Sekhemui.
II. N-U name	...
III. Golden Horus name	...
IV. Suten Bȧt name	1. 2. Neter-Baiu.
	3. Betchau.
	4. Besh.
V. Son of Rā name	...

I. 

From a fragment of an alabaster jar found at Abydos; the green slate object of this king in the Museum at Cairo (Quibell, *Aeg. Zeit.*, vol. XXXVI, p. 81); etc.

I *a*. 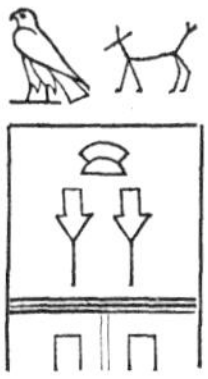

From a cylinder-seal (J. de Morgan, *Recherches*, Paris, 1897, p. 243).

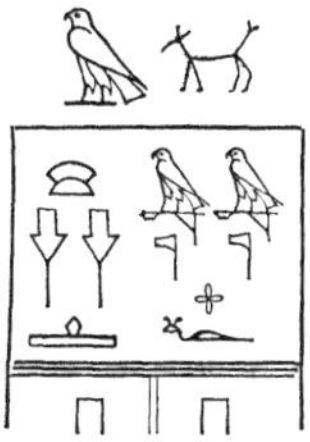

From a cylinder-seal (J. de Morgan, *Recherches*, Paris, 1897, p. 243).

IV. 1. 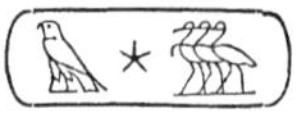 From a cylinder-seal (J. de Morgan, *Recherches*, Paris, 1897, p. 243).

2.  Tablet of Ṣaḳḳârah.

3.  Abydos List, No. 9.

4.  From a granite vase (Quibell, *Hierakonpolis*, plate 37).

2. Ḥetep-Sekhemui.

I.	Horus name	Ḥetep-sekhemui.
II.	N-U name	Ḥetep.
III.	Golden Horus name	...
IV.	Suten Bȧt name	Ḥetep.
V.	Son of Rā name	...

I. 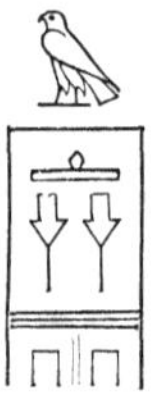 Statue No. 1 at Cairo (J. de Morgan, *Recherches*, p. 253; Grébaut, *Le Musée Égyptien*, plate XIII). See the stone fragment, British Museum, No. 35559.

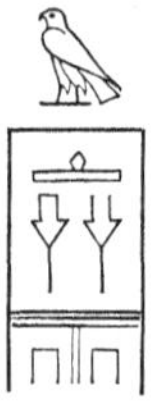 II. IV.  From a cylinder-seal (Maspero, *Annales du Service*, III, 1902, p. 187).

3. *Ka-kau.*

I.	Horus name	RĀ-NEB.
II.	N-U name	...
III.	Golden Horus name	...
IV.	Suten Bȧt name	KA-KAU.
V.	Son of Rā name	...

I. 

Statue No. 1 at Cairo. See the fragments in the British Museum, Nos. 35556—58, and Maspero, *Annales*, III, p. 188.

IV. 

Abydos List, No. 10.

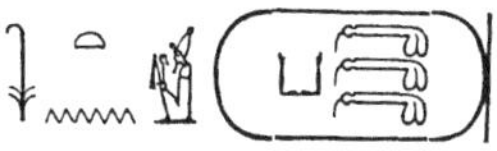

Tablet of Ṣaḳḳârah.

4. *Ba-en-neter.*

I.	Horus name	EN-NETER.
II.	N-U name	...
III.	Golden Horus name	...
IV.	Suten Bȧt name	BA-EN-NETER, or BA-NETRU.
V.	Son of Rā name	...

I. 

Statue No. 1 at Cairo; fragment of a stone bowl in the British Museum (No. 35556). See the fragments in the British Museum, Nos. 35556—58.

IV. 

Abydos List, No. 11.

Tablet of Ṣaḳḳârah.

The order of kings Nos. 2—4 is given by statue No. 1 at Cairo, on which their Horus names appear thus :—

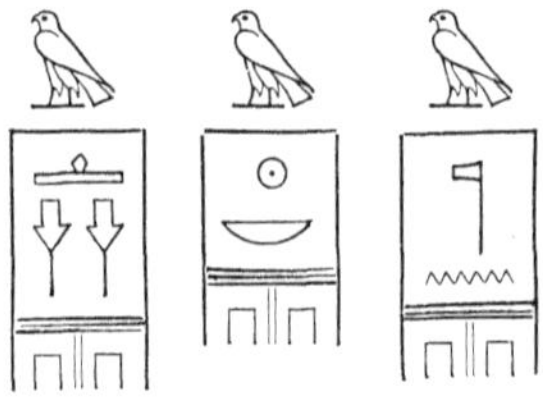

5. *Uatchnes.*

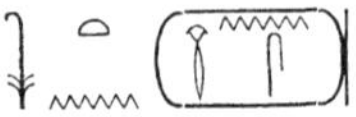

Abydos List, No. 12.

Tablet of Ṣaḳḳârah.

6. *Per-àb-sen.*

I. Horus name	Sekhem-Àb.
Set name	Per-Àb-sen.
II. N-U name	...
III. Golden Horus name	...
IV. Suten Bàt name	Per-Àb-sen, or Per-Àb-s.
V. Son of Rā name	...

I. 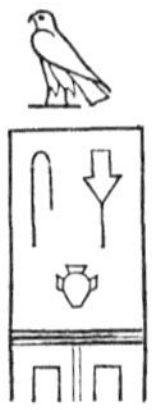

Jar-sealing, British Museum, No. 35596.

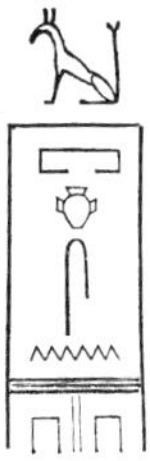

Granite stele in the British Museum, No. 35597.

IV.  Jar-sealings from Abydos.

 Mariette, *Mastabas*, p. 93.

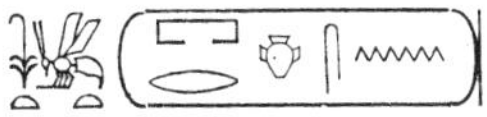 Mariette, *Mastabas*, p. 92.

7. *Senṭ*, or *Senṭȧ*.

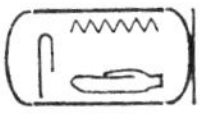

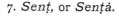

Tomb of Sheri , Mariette, *Mastabas*, pp. 92, 93; Lepsius, *Auswahl*, plate 9; British Museum, No. 1192; Brugsch, *Recueil*, tome II, plate 99 (page 15, line 2), Leipzig, 1863.

 Abydos List, No. 13.

 Medical papyrus at Berlin, ed. Brugsch, *Recueil*, vol. II, plate 99, line 2.

 Tablet of Ṣaḳḳârah.

8. *Rā-ka.*

 Cylinder-seal (J. E. Quibell, *El-Kab*, plate XX, No. 29).

9. *Rā-nefer-ka.*

 Tablet of Ṣaḳḳârah.

10. Seker-nefer-ka, or *Nefer-ka-Seker.*

Tablet of Ṣaḳḳârah.

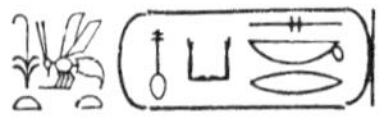

Papyrus of Turin.

11. Ḥetchefa.

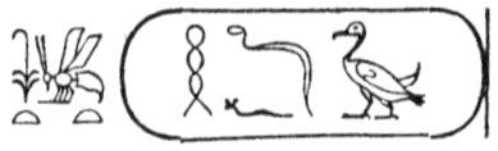

Turin Papyrus.

Tablet of Ṣaḳḳârah.

THIRD DYNASTY. FROM MEMPHIS.

1. Sa-Nekht.

Jar-sealings from Bêt Khallâf (see Garstang, *Mahâsna*, London, 1902, plate XIX); fragment in the British Museum, No. 691; he is identified by Jéquier (*Recueil*, XXIX, p. 1) with .

2. Bebi, or *Tchatchai.*

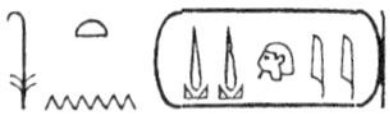

Abydos List, No. 14, and Turin Papyrus.

Tablet of Ṣaḳḳârah.

3. Neb-ka, or *Neb-ka-Rā.*

Abydos List, No. 15; Lepsius, *Denkmäler*, II, 39 *a*, *b*.

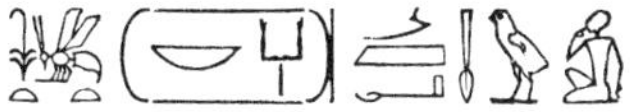 Westcar Papyrus, I, 19, etc.

 *Aeg. Zeit.*, 1864, p. 103.

 Tablet of Ṣaḳḳârah.

4. *Tcheser*, or *Tcheser-sa*.

I. Horus name — NETER-KHA, or NETER-KHAT.
II. N-U name — NETER-KHA, or NETER-KHAT.
III. Golden Horus name (?) — TCHESER.
IV. Suten Bât name — TCHESER, or TCHESER-SA.
V. Son of Rā name — ...

I. 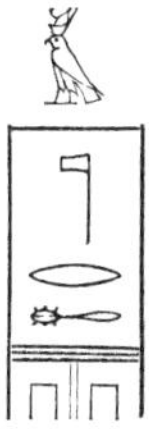 Pyramid at Ṣaḳḳârah (Lepsius, *Auswahl*, plate 7); jar-sealings from Bêt Khallâf, ed. Garstang, pl. VIII.

 Stele of Sâḥal, line 1.

II.  Stele of Sâḥal, line 1.

 Stele of Sâḥal, line 1.

III. 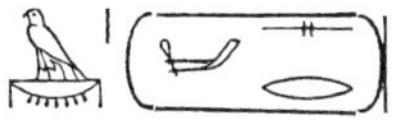 Stele of Sâḥal, line 1.

IV.  Tablet of Ṣaḳḳârah.

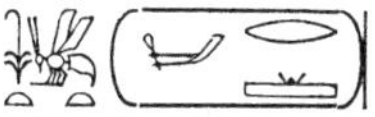 Westcar Papyrus, I, 14.

 Ivory fragment from Abydos in the British Museum.

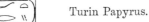

 Abydos List, No. 16. Probably a different king from Tcheser.

 Jar-sealing from Bêt Khallâf, ed. Garstang, plate VIII.

 Pyramid of Ṣaḳḳârah (Lepsius, *Auswahl*, pl. 7).

5. *Tetȧ.*

 Abydos List, No. 17.

6. *Setches.*

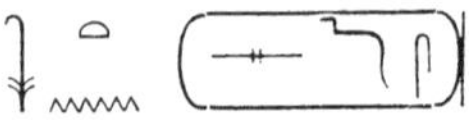 Abydos List, No. 18.

7. *Tcheser-Tetȧ.*

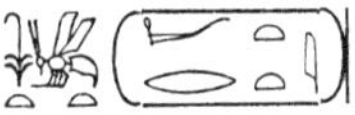 Turin Papyrus.

 Tablet of Ṣaḳḳârah.

 Turin Papyrus.

8. *Ȧḥtes.*

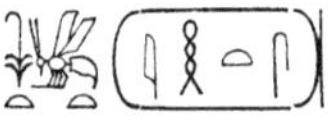 Palermo Stele (Brugsch and Bouriant, No. 24).

9. *Rā-nefer-ka Ḥuni.*

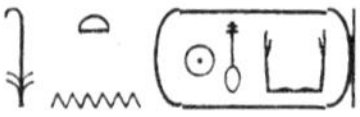 Abydos List, No. 19.

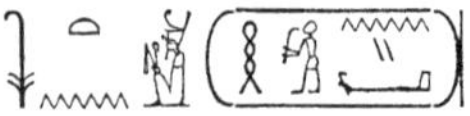 Tablet of Ṣaḳḳârah.

 Prisse Papyrus, plate I, line 7.

FOURTH DYNASTY. FROM MEMPHIS.

1. Seneferu.[1]

I.	Horus name	NEB MAĀT.
II.	N-U name	NEB MAĀT.
III.	Golden Horus name	SENEFERU.
IV.	Suten Bất name	SENEFERU.
V.	Son of Rā name	...

I. 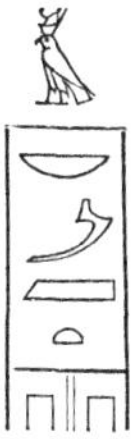 Wâdî Maghârah, L. D., II, 2; Weill, *Sinai*, p. 103.

II.  Wâdî Maghârah, L. D., II, 2.

III.  Wâdî Maghârah, L. D., II, 2.

IV. 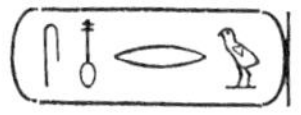 Palermo Stele.

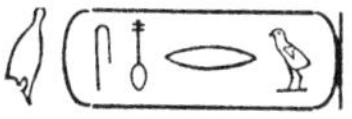 Palermo Stele.

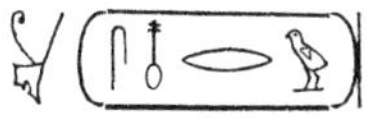 Palermo Stele.

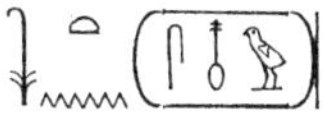 Abydos List, No. 20.

1. The order of the reigns of the first three kings of this Dynasty is fixed by the stele of Queen Mertet-tefs, who was a contemporary of them all.

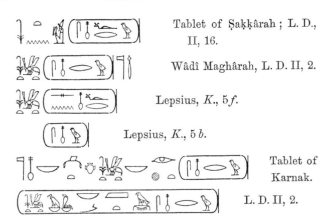

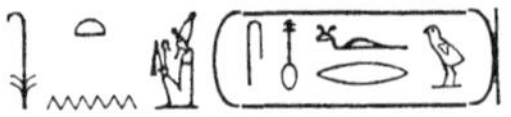 Tablet of Ṣaḳḳârah; L. D., II, 16.

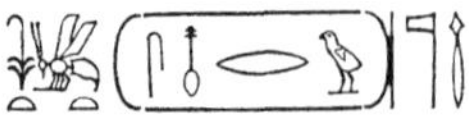 Wâdî Maghârah, L. D. II, 2.

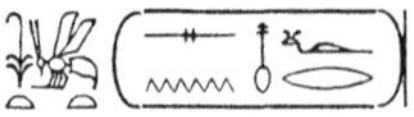 Lepsius, *K.*, 5*f*.

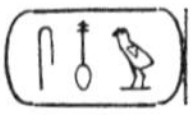 Lepsius, *K.*, 5*b*.

 Tablet of Karnak.

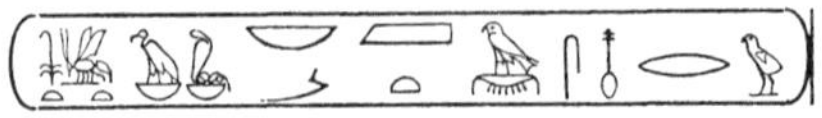 L. D. II, 2.

Mertet-tef-s, wife of *Seneferu.*

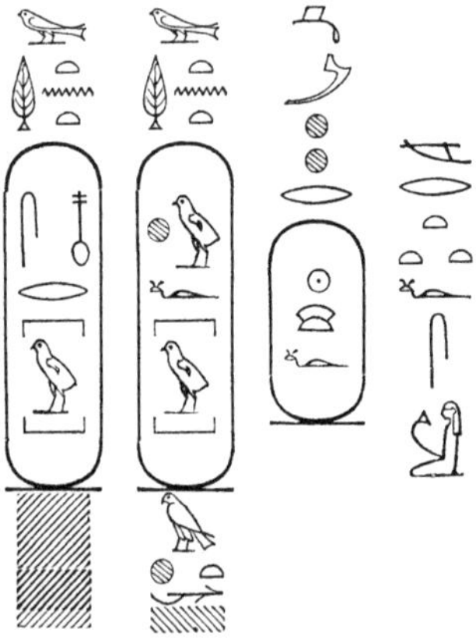

Her titles were  and 

Stele in the Egyptian Museum at Cairo. (Mariette, *Mastabas*, p. 565; de Rougé, *Six Premières Dynasties*, p. 37; *Inscrip. hiér.*, I, plate 62.)

Ḥāp-en-Maāt, a royal mother.

 L. D. II, 6.

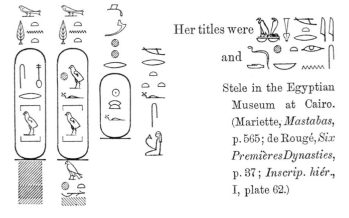

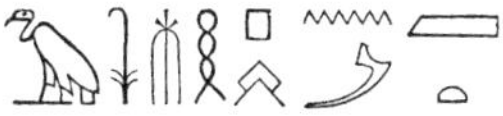 With the title 
Cylinder-seal at Cairo. See Borchardt, Naville, and Sethe in *Aeg. Zeit.*, XXXVI, 1898, p. 142—144; Maspero, *Rev. Crit.*, Dec. 15, 1897.

Nefert-kau, daughter of Seneferu (?).

 L. D. II, 16.

Nefer-Maāt, a prince.

 L. D. II, 16.

Seneferu-khā-f, a prince.

 L. D. II, 16.

2. *Khufu* (Kheops).

I. Horus name	METCHERU (?).
II. N-U name	METCHERU (?).
III. Golden Horus name	KHUFU.
IV. Suten Bȧt name	KHUFU.
V. Son of Rā name	...

I.  Wâdî Maghârah, L. D. II, 2.
 *Aeg. Zeit.*, 1904, 87.

II.  Wâdî Maghârah, L. D. II, 2.

 *Aeg. Zeit.*, 1904, 87.

III.  L. D. II, 2; *Aeg. Zeit.*, 1904, 87.

IV.  Schäfer, *Aeg. Zeit.*, 1904, 87.

 Abydos List, No. 21.

 Westcar Papyrus.

 L. D., II, 55.

 Tablet of Ṣaḳḳârah.

 Lepsius, *Auswahl*, VII. B.

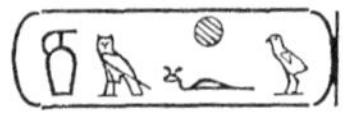 Lepsius, *Auswahl*, VII. C.

 Mariette, *Mastabas*, p. 521.

Ḥeru-ṭāṭā-f, a son of *Khufu.*

 Westcar Papyrus (ed. Erman, pl. 6).

 Papyrus of Nu. Chap. LXIV. Rubric (ed. Budge, *Text*, p. 141, line 9; and p. 309, line 12).

Ḥentsen, daughter of Khufu.

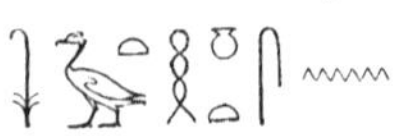 Stele of Khufu (Mariette, *M. D.*, plate 53).

Ḥetep-ḥer-s, daughter of Khufu (?).

 De Rougé, *Recherches*, p. 50.

Mer-ānkh-s, daughter of Khufu (?).

 De Rougé, *Recherches*, p. 50.

3. *Rā-ṭeṭ-f.*

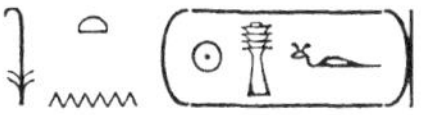 Abydos List, No. 22.

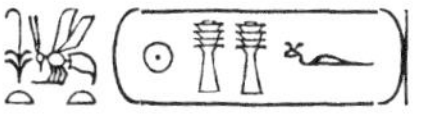 Tablet of Ṣaḳḳârah.

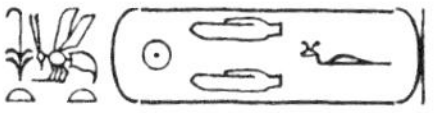 Lepsius, *K.* 44 *a*.

4. *Rā-khāf* (Khephren).

I.	Horus name	USR-ÅB.
II.	N-U name	USR-EM...
III.	Golden Horus name	SEKHEM.
IV.	Suten Båt name	RĀKHĀF.
V.	Son of Rā name	...

I. 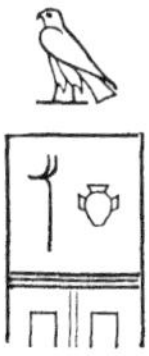  *Aeg. Zeit.*, 1904, 87.

II.  *Aeg. Zeit.*, 1904, 87.

III.  (?) *Aeg. Zeit*, 1904, 87.

IV. 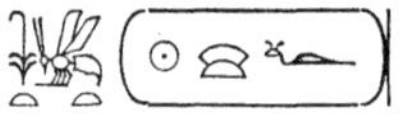 L. D. II, 41; *Aeg. Zeit.*, 1904, 87.

 Tablet of Ṣaḳḳârah.

 Abydos List, No. 23.

Mer-ānkh-s, a queen, mother of Neb-em-khut.

 De Rougé, *Recherches*, p. 50.

Neb-em-khut, an Erpā and prince.

 De Rougé, *Recherches*, p. 57; L. D., II, 12.

5. *Rā-men-kau* (Mykerinos).

I.	Horus name	KA-KHA.
II.	N-U name	KA.
III.	Golden Horus name	...
IV.	Suten Bȧt name	RĀ-MEN-KAU.
V.	Son of Rā name	...

I.  Statue of the king in the Museum in Cairo, and a cylinder-seal (Legrain, *Annales*, IV, 134).

II.  Cylinder-seal (Legrain, *Annales*, IV, 134).

IV. 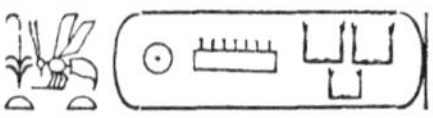 L. D. II, 41.

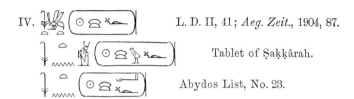

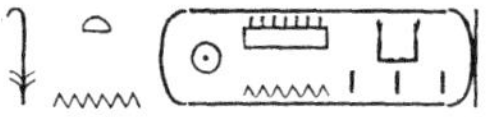 Abydos List, No. 24.

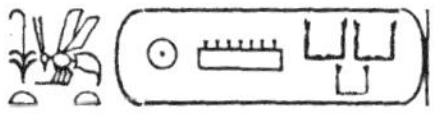 Papyrus of Nu (sheet 5).

 Coffin of Men-kau-Rā, British Museum, No. 6647.

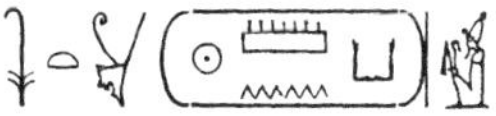 Second Abydos List, No. 15.

6. Shepses-ka-f.

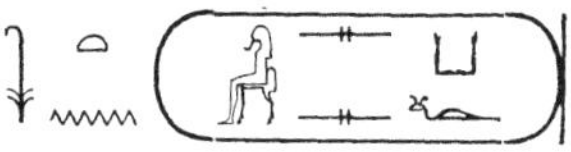 Abydos List, No. 25.

 Palermo Stele; L. D. II, 41, etc.

Maāt-khā, daughter of Shepses-ka-f.

 De Rougé, *Recherches*, p. 68.

Ptaḥ-shepses, husband of Maāt-khā.

 Mariette, *Mastabas*, p. 112.

7. Rā-Sebek-ka.

 Tablet of Ṣaḳḳârah.

8. I-em-ḥetep.

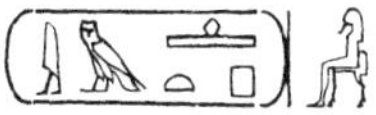 Wâdî Ḥammâmât, L. D. II, 115.

FIFTH DYNASTY. FROM ELEPHANTINE.

1. Userkaf.

I. Horus name	Ȧri-Maāt.
II. N-U name	...
III. Golden Horus name	...
IV. Suten Bȧt name	Userkaf.
V. Son of Rā name	...

I. 

Cylinder-seal. (Mariette, *Mon. Divers*, pl. 54.)

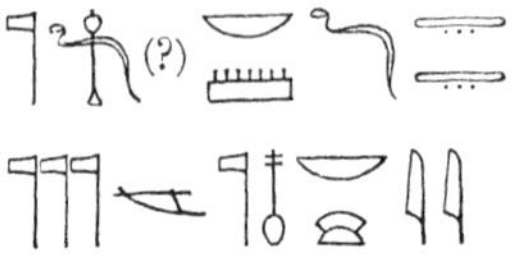

IV.  Abydos List, No. 26.

 Tablet of Ṣaḳḳârah.

 Palermo Stele; L. D. II, 41, etc.

 Mariette, *Mon. Divers*, pl. 54.

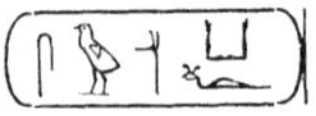 Mariette, *Mon. Divers*, pl. 54.

 Stele in the British Museum, No. 1143.

2. Rā-Saḥu.

I. Horus name	NEB-KHĀU.
II. N-U name	...
III. Golden Horus name	...
IV. Suten Bȧt name	RĀ-SAḤU.
V. Son of Rā name	...

I.  Wâdî Maghârah, L. D. II, 39; vase in the British Museum, No. 29330.

IV. 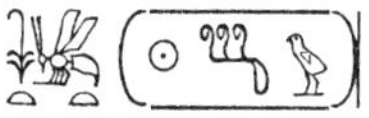 Palermo Stele; Wâdî Maghârah, L. D. II, 39 *g*.

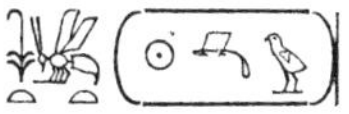 L. D. II, 41.

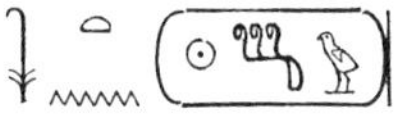 Abydos List, No. 27.

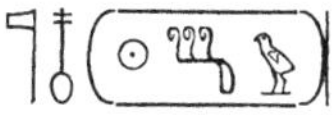 Tablet of Karnak.

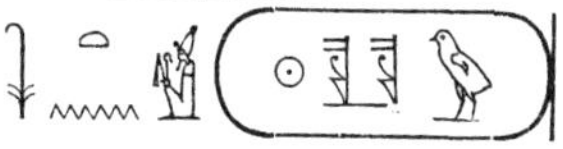 Tablet of Ṣaḳḳârah.

 L. D. II, 55; statue at Cairo, No. 42004.

3. Rā-nefer-ȧri-ka.

I. Horus name	SEKHEM-KHĀU, or USR-KHĀU.
II. N-U name	KHĀ-EM-SEKHEMU-NEBU (?).
III. Golden Horus name	...
IV. Suten Bȧt name	RĀ-NEFER-ȦRI-KA.
V. Son of Rā name	...

I.  Cylinder-seal. (Mariette, *Mon. Divers*, plate 54 *e*.)

 Palermo Stele (Naville, *Recueil*, XXV. Plate II *B*).

II.  Palermo Stele (*Ibid.*).

IV. 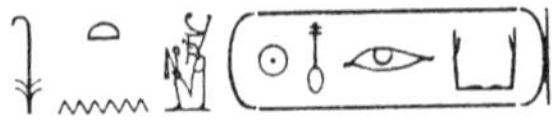 Tablet of Ṣaḳḳârah.

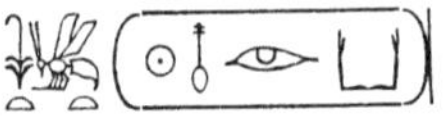 Palermo Stele; L. D. II, 55.

4. *Kaka-à.*[1]

 Abydos List, No. 28.

 De Rougé, *Recherches*, p. 97.

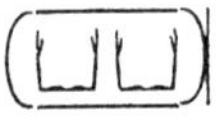 Scarab in the British Museum, No. 22954.

5. *Rā-shepses-ka.*

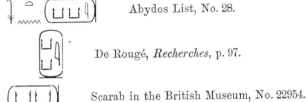

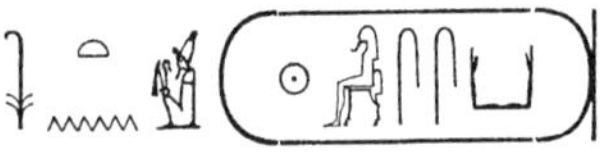 Tablet of Ṣaḳḳârah.

6 (?). Suḥtes.[2]

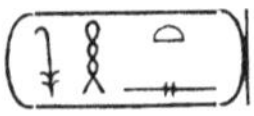 Palermo Stele.

1. Some think that this is the 'Son-of-Rā' name of Rā-nefer-àri-ka.
2. Position doubtful. The reading may be 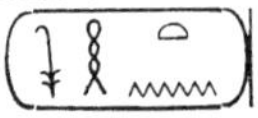 SUḤTEN;

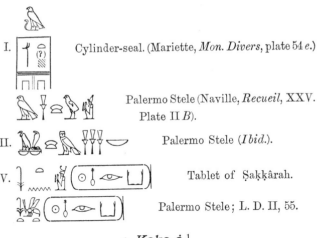

6. Rā-nefer-f.

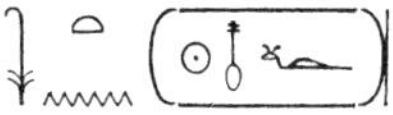

Abydos List, No. 29.

7. Rā-khā-nefer.[1]

Tablet of Ṣaḳḳârah.

Tablet of Karnak.

8. Rā-User-en Ȧn.

I. Horus name	ȦST-ȦB-TAUI.
II. N-U name	ȦST-ȦB.
III. Golden Horus name	NETER (?)
IV. Suten Bȧt name	RĀ-USER-EN.
V. Son of Rā name (?)	ȦN.

I. 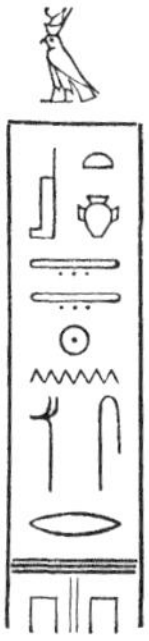

Wâdî Maghârah (L. D., II, 152*a*; Weill, *Sinai*, p. 107).

compare 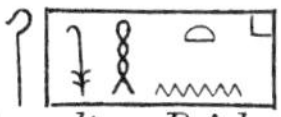 in the Inscription of Methen, Sethe, *Urkunden des alten Reiches*, p. 2, line 17.

1. His 'Son-of-Rā' name is thought by some to be 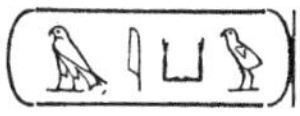 L. D., II, 76.

II.  L. D., II, 152 *a*.

III.  (?) L. D., II, 152 *a*.

IV. 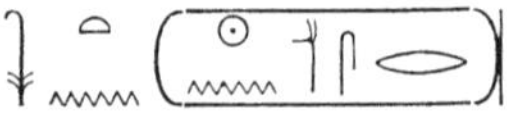 Abydos List, No. 30.

 Tablet of Karnak.

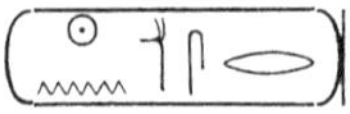 L. D., II, 55, 152 *a*.

 Statue in the British Museum, No. 870; L. D., II, 39 *c*; statue in Cairo, No. 42003; vase in the British Museum, No. 32620.

V. 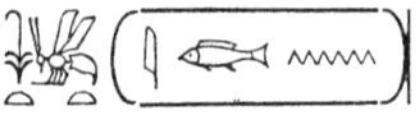 Statue in the British Museum, No. 870; Lepsius, *Auswahl*, IX *b*.

 Tablet of Karnak.

9. Ḥeru-men-kau.

I. Horus name	Men Khāu.
II. N-U name	...
III. Golden Horus name	...
IV. Suten Bāt name	Ḥeru-men-kau.
V. Son of Rā name	...

I.  Wâdî Maghârah (L. D., II, 39 *e*; Weill, *Sinai*, p. 109.)

IV. 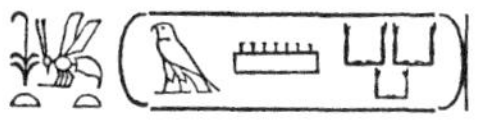 Wâdî Maghârah, L. D., II, 39 *e*.

 Abydos List, No. 31.

 Tablet of Ṣakkârah.

 E. de Rougé (*Six Premières Dynasties*, plate VI.)

10. Rā-ṭeṭ-ka Åssà.

I. Horus name	ṬEṬ-KHĀU.
II. N-U name	ṬEṬ-KHĀU.
III. Golden Horus name	ṬEṬ.
IV. Suten Bàt name	RĀ-ṬEṬ-KA.
V. Son of Rā name	ÅSSÀ.

I. 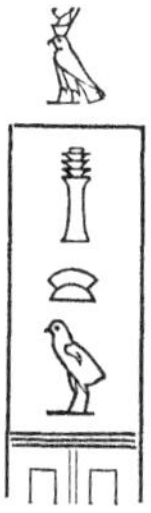 Wâdî Maghârah (L. D., II, 39 *d*, 115 *l*; and Birch, *Aeg. Zeit.*, 1869, p. 26).

II.  Wâdî Maghârah (Birch, *Aeg. Zeit.*, 1869, p. 26).

III.  Wâdî Maghârah (Birch, *Aeg. Zeit.*, 1869, p. 26).

IV. 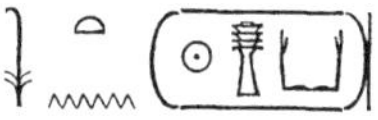 Abydos List, No. 32.

 Turin Papyrus.

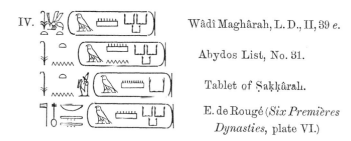

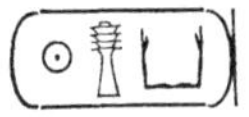 Wâdî Maghârah (Weill, *Sinai*, p. 140).

 L. D., II, 65.

 Tablet of Ṣakkârah.

V. 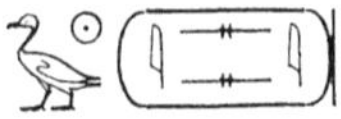 De Rougé, *Recherches*, p. 100

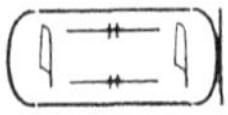 L. D., II, 75 ; de Morgan, *Catalogue*, p. 168.

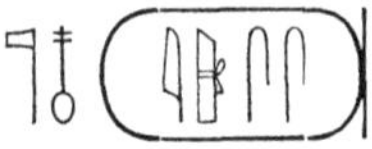 Tablet of Karnak.

Ȧssȧ-Ānkh, a prince.

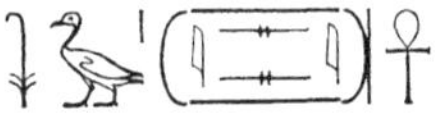 De Rougé, *Recherches*, p. 101.

11. Unȧs.

I. Horus name	UATCH TAUI.
II. N-U name	UATCH-EM-...
III. Golden Horus name	UATCH.
IV. Suten Bȧt name	UNȦS.
V. Son of Rā name	UNȦS.

I.  Pyramid of Unȧs (Barsanti, *Annales*, II, 254).

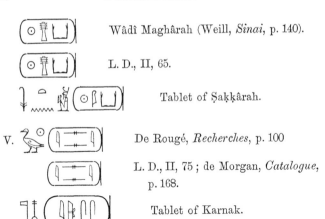

II.  Pyramid of Unȧs.

III.  Pyramid of Unȧs.

IV.  L. D. II, 75 ; Turin Papyrus.

 Abydos List, No. 33.

 Tablet of Ṣaḳḳârah.

V.  Pyramid of Unȧs.

 Pyramid of Unȧs.

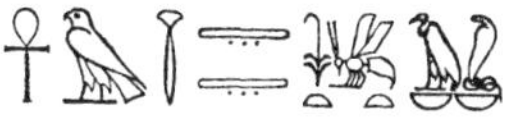

 Vase in the British Museum, No. 4603.

SIXTH DYNASTY. FROM MEMPHIS.

1. Tetȧ.

I. Horus name	SEḤETEP-TAUI.
II. Ṇ-U name	...
III. Golden Horus name	...
IV. Suten Bȧt name	TETȦ. (With the addition, under
V. Son of Rā name	TETȦ. the XIXth dynasty, of Mer-en-Ptaḥ.)

I. 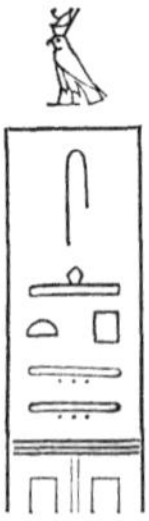

Temple at Mît Rahînah (Daressy, *Annales*, III, 29); inscription at Ḥet-nub (Fraser, *Graffiti*, plate XV).

Abydos List, No. 34.

Tablet of Ṣaḳḳârah.

IV. 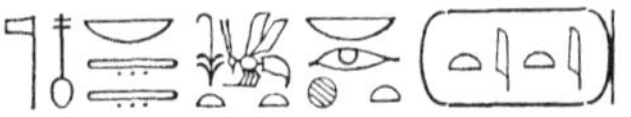

Tablet of Karnak.

V. 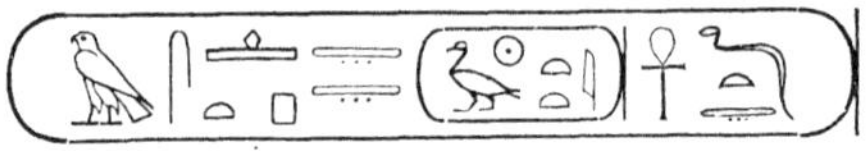

Vase in the British Museum, No. 29204.

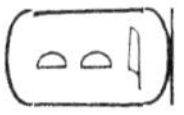

Al-Ḳâb, L. D., II, 117.

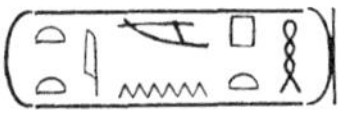

Statue in the Chateau Borély (Naville, *Aeg. Zeit.*, 1878, plate IV).

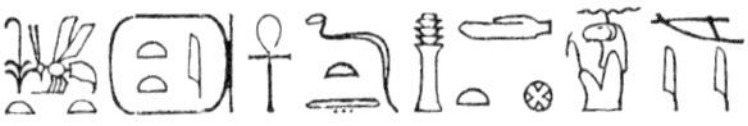

Mariette, *Catalogue*, No. 1464.

2. *Rā-user-ka Àti.*

Abydos List, No. 35.

Ḥammâmât, L. D., II, 115.

3. Rā-meri Pepi I.

I. Horus name	MERI-TAUI.
II. N-U name	MERI-KHAT, or MERI-TAUI.
III. Golden Horus name	...
IV. Suten Bȧt name	RĀ-MERI.
V. Son of Rā name	PEPI.

I.  Ḥammâmât, L. D., II, 115; British Museum, No. 22559.

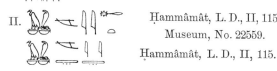

II.  Ḥammâmât, L. D., II, 115; British Museum, No. 22559.

 Ḥammâmât, L. D., II, 115.

III.  Ḥammâmât, L. D., II, 115.

IV. 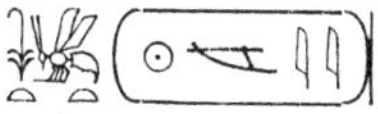 Ḥammâmât, L. D., II, 115.

 Abydos List, No. 36.

V. 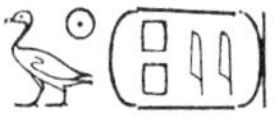 Pyramid at Ṣaḳḳârah.

 Tablet of Karnak.

 Wâdî Maghârah, L. D., II, 116.

 Tablet of Ṣaḳḳârah.

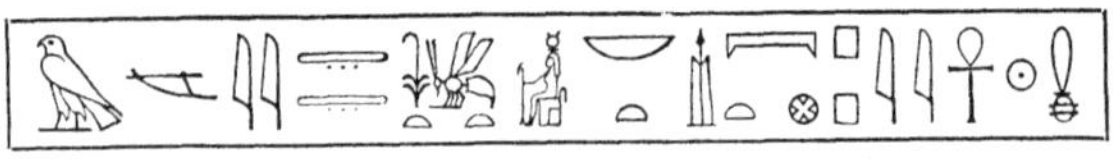

Vase in the British Museum, No. 22559, etc.

Rā-meri-ānkh-nes,[1] wife of Pepi I, daughter of Khuȧ and Nebt.

Stele in Cairo (Mariette, *Abydos*, I, pl. 2).

Tchāu, brother of Queen *Rā-meri-ānkh-nes.*

Stele in Cairo (Mariette, *Abydos*, I, pl. 2).

4. *Rā-mer-en Meḥti-em-sa-f,* eldest son of Pepi I.

I.	Horus name	ĀNKH-KHĀU.
II.	N-U name	ĀNKH-KHĀU.
III.	Golden Horus name	...
IV.	Suten Bȧt name	RĀ-MER-EN.
V.	Son of Rā name	MEḤTI-EM-SA-F (reading doubtful).

I.

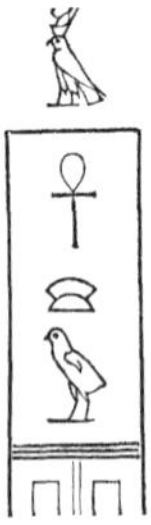

Rocks at Ḥammâmât, L. D., II, 115; vase in the British Museum, No. 4493.

1. Her father was called , and her mother .

II.  Rocks at Ḥammâmât, L. D., II, 115; vase in the British Museum, No. 4493.

III.  Rocks at Ḥammâmât, L. D., II, 115.

IV.  Ḥammâmât, L. D., II, 115; vase in the British Museum, No. 4493.

 Tablet of Karnak.

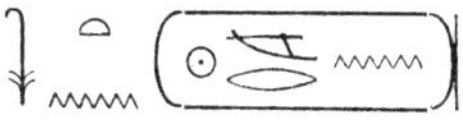 Abydos List, No. 37.

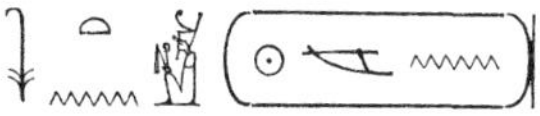 Tablet of Ṣaḳḳârah.

V.  Pyramid of Ṣaḳḳârah.

5. *Rā-nefer-ka Pepi II,* second son of Pepi I.

I. Horus name	NETER-KHĀU.
II. N-U name	NETER-KHĀU.
III. Golden Horus name	SEKHEM.
IV. Suten Bât name	RĀ-NEFER-KA.
V. Son of Rā name	PEPI.

I. 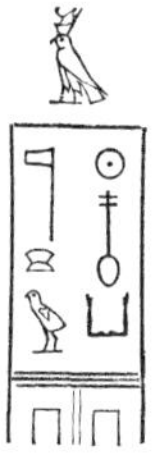 Rocks at Wâdî Maghârah, L. D., II, 116.

Vase in the British Museum, No. 4492.

II. 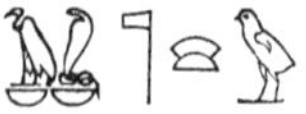 Vase in the British Museum, No. 4492.

III.  Wâdî Maghârah, L. D., II, 116.

IV. 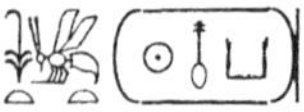 Wâdî Maghârah, L. D., II, 116.

 Abydos List, No. 38.

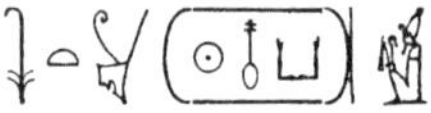 Second Abydos List, No. 16.

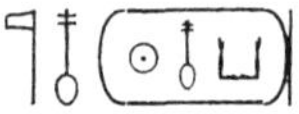 Tablet of Karnak.

V.  Pyramid at Ṣaḳḳârah.

 Sarcophagus of Pepi II.

6. *Rā-mer-en Meḥti-em-sa-f.*

 Pyramid at Ṣaḳḳârah; Abydos List, No. 39.

7. *Rā-neter-ka.*

 Abydos List, No. 40.

8. *Rā-men-ka Net-Ȧqerti.*

 Abydos List, No. 41.

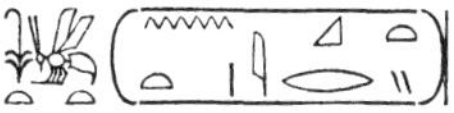 Turin Papyrus.

Rā-neb-Ṭeṭ.

 Scarab in the British Museum, No. 40283.

Rā-neb-khā.

 Scarab in the Hilton Price Collection.

Ḥeru-nefer-ḥen.

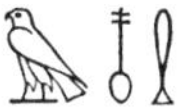 Alabaster fragment (Petrie, *H. E.*, I, p. 106).

The following names of princes and princesses are attributed to this period by Lepsius:—

Queen PER... 

Queen ...SĀNKH 

Princess SHEPSET-KAU 

Prince RĀ-EN-KAU 

Prince KA-ĀB 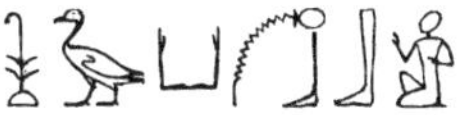

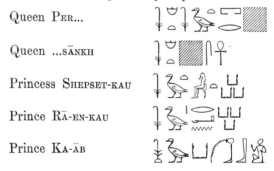

Prince Thes-ṭeṭ-f 

Prince Thes-ȧn 

Prince Rā-sekhem-ka 

Princess Khent-kau-s 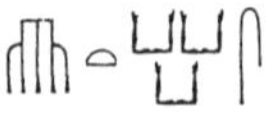

Prince Mer-ȧb 

Princess Seṭtȧ 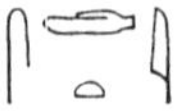

Prince Sheta-ḥetep-hetȧ 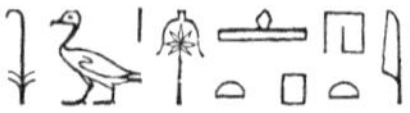

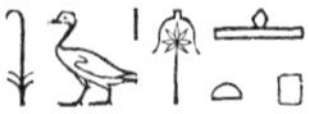

Prince Ḥer-ṭua-en 

Prince Thes-khā-f 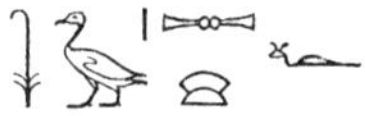

Prince Nefer-ḥetep-s 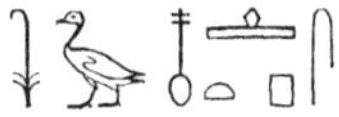

SEVENTH AND EIGHTH DYNASTIES. FROM MEMPHIS.

1. Nefer-ka.

 Turin Papyrus.

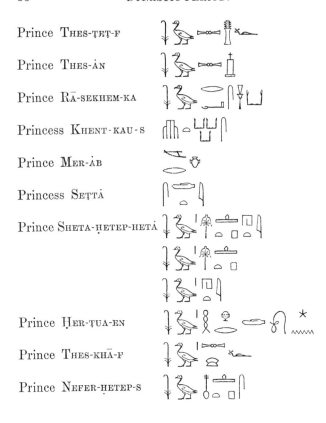

2. *Nefer-seḥ...*

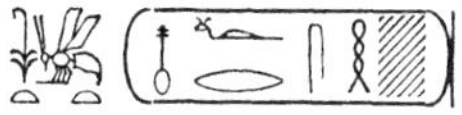

Turin Papyrus.

3. *Àb.*

Turin Papyrus.

4. *Rā-nefer-kau.*

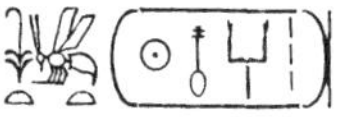

Turin Papyrus.

4. *Katthi.*

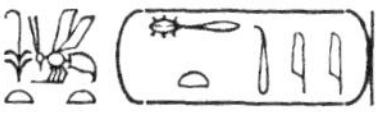

Turin Papyrus.

6. *Rā-nefer-ka.*

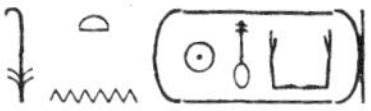

Abydos List, No. 42.

7. *Rā-nefer-ka Nebi.*

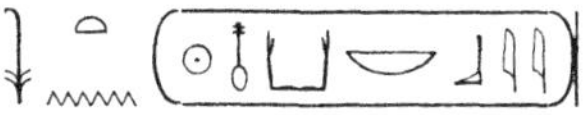

Abydos List, No. 43.

Second Abydos List, No. 17.

8. *Rā-Ṭeṭ-ka Maā-ṭua.*

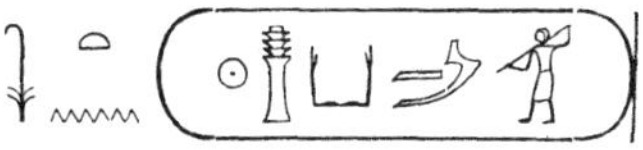

Abydos List, No. 44.

Second Abydos List, No. 18.

9. Rā-nefer-ka Khenṭu.

Abydos List, No. 45.

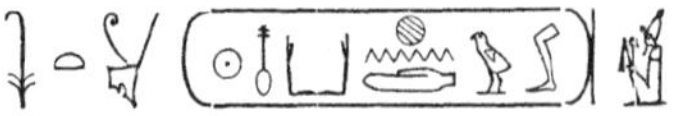

Second Abydos List, No. 19.

10. Ḥeru-mer-en.

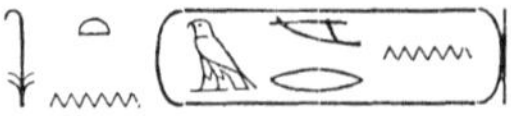

Abydos List, No. 46.

Second Abydos List, No. 20.

11. Senefer-ka, or *Rā-senefer-ka.*

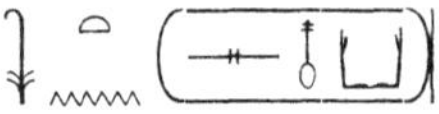

Abydos List, No. 47.

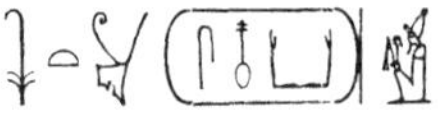

Second Abydos List, No. 21.

Tablet of Karnak.

12. Rā-en-ka.

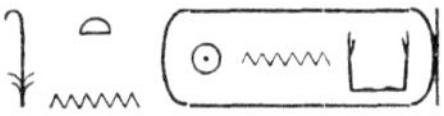

Abydos List, No. 48.

Second Abydos List, No. 22.

Plaque in the British Museum, No. 8444.

13. Rā-nefer-ka Tererl (?).

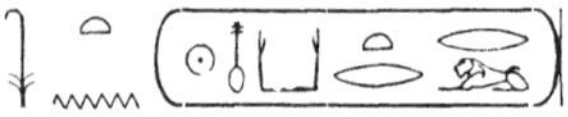

Abydos List, No. 49.

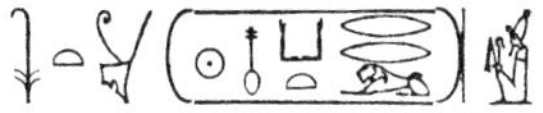 Second Abydos List, No. 23.

14. Ḥcru-nefer-ka.

 Abydos List, No. 50.

 Second Abydos List, No. 24.

15. Rā-nefer-ka Pepi-senb.

 Abydos List, No. 51.

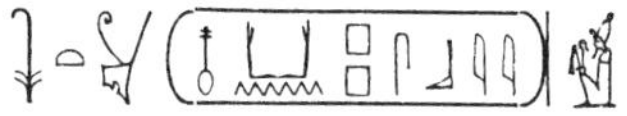 Second Abydos List, No. 25.

16. [Rā]-s-nefer-ka Ānnu.

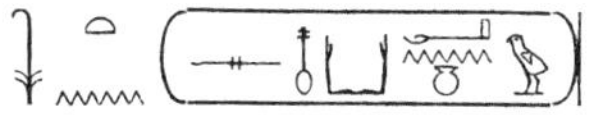 Abydos List, No. 52.

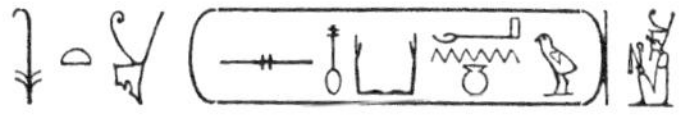 Second Abydos List, No. 26.

17. Rā-[men]-kau.

 Abydos List, No. 53.

18. Rā-nefer-kau.

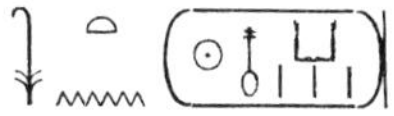 Abydos List, No. 54.

19. Ḥeru-nefer-kau.

 Abydos List, No. 55.

20. *Rā-nefer-ȧri-ka.*

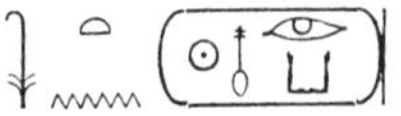

Abydos List, No. 56.

NINTH AND TENTH DYNASTIES. FROM HERAKLEOPOLIS.

Khati.

I. Horus name	MERI-ȦB-TAUI.
II. N-U name	MERI-ȦB.
III. Golden Horus name	...
IV. Suten Bȧt name	RĀ-MERI-ȦB.
V. Son of Rā name	KHATI.

I. 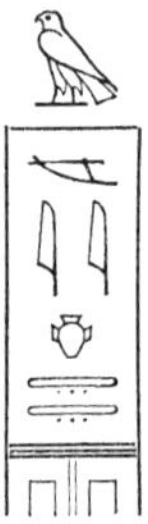

Bronze bowl in the Louvre (Maspero, *Bulletin des Musées*, t. II, p. 38).

II. 

Bronze bowl in the Louvre.

IV. 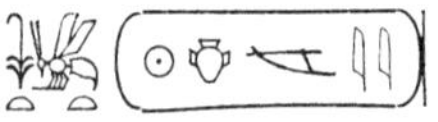

Bronze bowl in the Louvre.

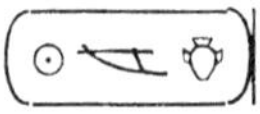

Scarab in the Louvre (Maspero, *P.S.B.A.*, XIII, p. 429).

V. 

Bronze bowl in the Louvre.

Rā-ka-meri.

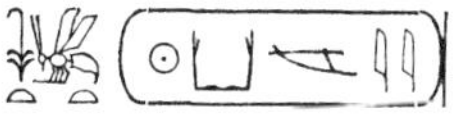

Palette in the Louvre; Tomb of Khati at Asyût.

The position of the following kings is doubtful:

RĀ-MAĀ-ȦB  Scarab B. M. 30510.

RĀ-SEKHĀ-EN 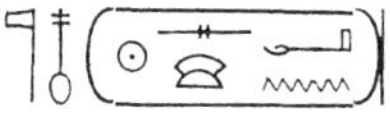 Scarab B. M. 30511.

RĀ-NUB-TAUI 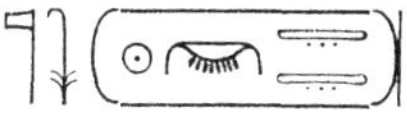 Scarab B. M. 30512.

RĀ-ĀA-ḤETEP 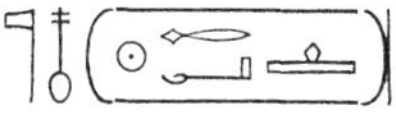 Scarab B. M. 28097.

RĀ-KHĀ-USER 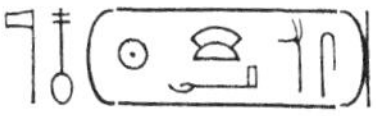 Scarab B. M. 32331.

Rā-uaḥ-ka Khati.

Coffin from Al-Barsha (Lacau, *Recueil*, XXIV, p. 90).

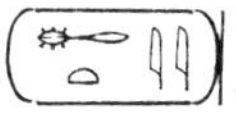

Coffin from Al-Barsha (Lacau, *Recueil*, XXIV, p. 90.

Rā-ṭeṭ-nefer Ṭāṭāumes.

Stele from Gebelên (Daressy, *Recueil*, XIV, p. 26, No. XXXI).

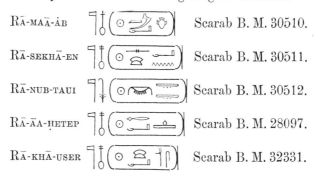

Fragment found by Mr. H. R. Hall at Dêr al-Baḥari in 1905.

ELEVENTH DYNASTY. FROM THEBES.

Ȧntef, or *Ȧntefȧ*, the *Erpā* and *Ḥā* prince.

Tablet of Karnak.

Stele in the Egyptian Museum, Cairo (Mariette, *Mon. Div.*, plate 50).

Tablet of Karnak.

Uaḥ-ānkh Ȧntef-āa.

I. Horus name — UAḤ-ĀNKH.
II. N-U name — ...
III. Golden Horus name — ...
IV. Suten Bȧt name — ȦNTEF-ĀA.
V. Son of Rā name — ȦN[TEF]-ĀA.

I. 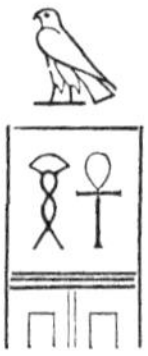

Stele in the Egyptian Museum, Cairo (Mariette, *Mon. Div.*, plate 49).

Stele in the British Museum, No. 1203.

IV. 

Mariette, *Mon. Div.*, plate 49.

V.  Mariette, *Mon. Div.*, plate 49.

 Tablet of Karnak.

Nekht-neb-ṭep-nefer Ȧntef.

I.	Horus name	NEKHT-NEB-ṬEP-NEFER.
II.	N-U name	...
III.	Golden Horus name	...
IV.	Suten Bȧt name	...
V.	Son of Rā name	ȦNTEF.

I.  Stele in the British Museum, No. 1203.

V.  Tablet of Karnak.

Ȧntef.

 Tablet of Karnak.

S-ānkh-ȧb-taui Menthu-ḥetep.

I.	Horus name	S-ĀNKH-ȦB-TAUI.
II.	N-U name	...
III.	Golden Horus name	...
IV.	Suten Bȧt name	...
V.	Son of Rā name	MENTHU-ḤETEP.

I. 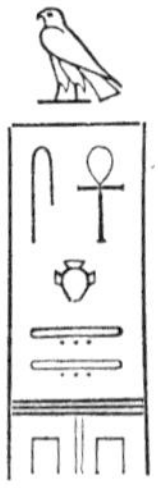 Stele in the British Museum, No. 1203.

V. 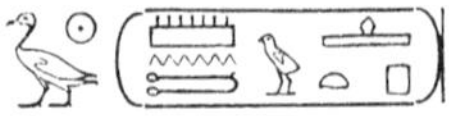 Stele in the British Museum, No. 1203.

Rā-neb-ḥetep Menthu-ḥetep.

I. Horus name	NETER ḤETCH.
II. N-U name	NETER-ḤETCH.
III. Golden Horus name	...
IV. Suten Bȧt name	RĀ-NEB-ḤETEP.
V. Son of Rā name	MENTHU-ḤETEP.

I. 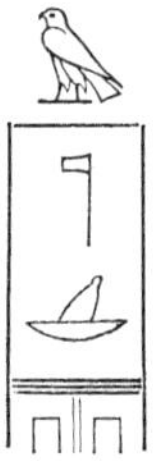 Rock sculpture on Konosso, L. D., II, 150 *b*; rock sculpture at Gebelên (Daressy, *Recueil*, XVI, 42, No. 87).

II.  Sculpture at Konosso, L. D., II, 150 *b*.

IV. 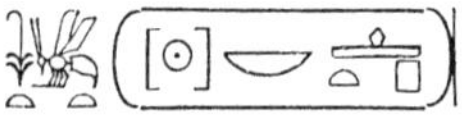 Lepsius, *K.*, 162.

 Rock on Konosso, L. D., II, 150 *b*.

V. 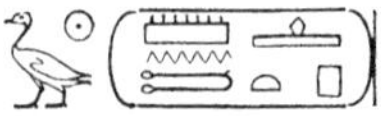 Lepsius, *K.*, 162.

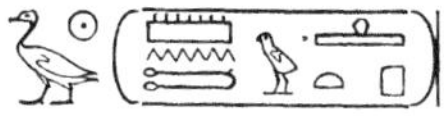

Annales, II, 203.

Rock at Ḥammâmât, L. D., II, 150 *d*.

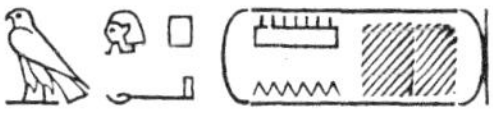

Tablet of Karnak.

Rā-neb-taui Menthu-ḥetep.

I.	Horus name	NEB-TAUI.
II.	N-U name	NEB-TAUI.
III.	Golden Horus name	NETERU.
IV.	Suten Bȧt name	RĀ-NEB-TAUI.
V.	Son of Rā name	MENTHU-ḤETEP.

I. 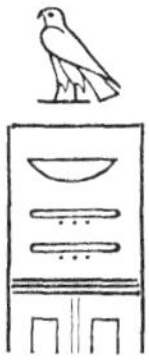

Rock inscription at Ḥammâmât, L. D., II, 149 *c*.

II. 

Rock inscription at Ḥammâmât, L. D., II, 149 *c*.

III. 

Rock inscription at Ḥammâmât, L. D., II, 149 *c*.

IV. 

Rock inscription at Ḥammâmât, L. D., II, 149 *c*.

V. 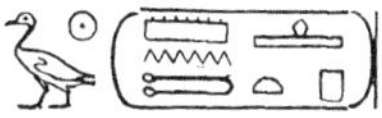

Rock inscription at Ḥammâmât, L. D., II, 149 *c*.

Ȧmām, mother of *Rā-neb-taui Menthu-ḥetep.*

Rock inscription at Ḥammâmât, L. D., II, 149 *f*.

Rā-neb-ḥapt Menthu-ḥetep.

I. Horus name	SMA-TAUI.
II. N-U name	SMA-TAUI.
III. Golden Horus name	...
IV. Suten Bȧt name	RĀ-NEB-ḤAPT.
V. Son of Rā name	MENTHU-ḤETEP.

I. 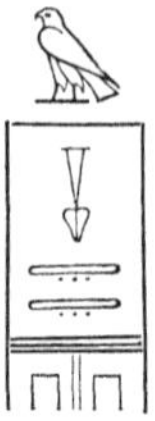 Rock inscription at Aswân, L. D., II, 149 *b*; rock inscription at Gebel Silsila.

II. 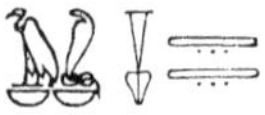 Rock inscription at Aswân, L. D., II, 149 *b*.

IV.  Rock inscription at Aswân, L. D., II, 149 *b*; rock inscription at Gebel Silsila.

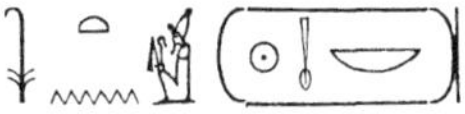 Tablet of Ṣaḳḳârah.

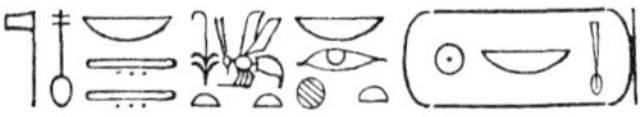 Tablet of Karnak.

 Abydos List, No. 57.

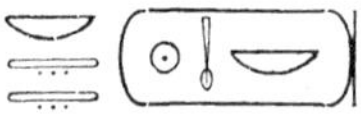 Prisse, *Monuments*, plate 3.

 Legrain, *Annales*, VII, 34.

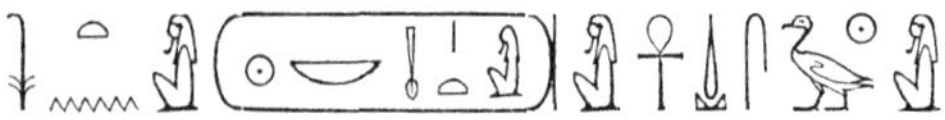

 Abbott Papyrus.

V. 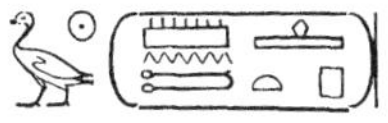 Rock inscription at Aswân, L. D., II, 149 *b*.

Åāḥet, a royal mother.

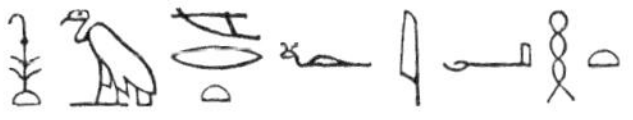 Rock at Hôsh (Eisenlohr, *P. S. B. A.*, 1881, p. 98).

Åntef, son (?) of *Rā-neb-ḥapt Menthu-ḥetep.*

 Rock sculpture at Gebel Silsila.

Āat-shet, wife of *Rā-neb-ḥapt Menthu-ḥetep.*

 Scarab in the British Museum, No. 40855.

Temem, a queen of this period.

(var. )

Sarcophagus from Dêr al-Baḥarî (Maspero, *Aeg. Zeit.*, Bd. XXI, 1883, p. 77, No. XLIII; *Mémoires de la Mission*, I, p. 134).

Rā-s-ānkh-ka Menthu-ḥetep.

I. Horus name	S-ĀNKH-TAUI-F.
II. N-U name	S-ĀNKH-TAUI-F.
III. Golden Horus name	...
IV. Suten Bȧt name	RĀ-S-ĀNKH-KA.
V. Son of Rā name	MENTHU-ḤETEP.[1]

1. The discovery that Menthu-ḥetep was the Son-of-Rā name of Rā-s-ānkh-ka was first made by Devéria.

I. 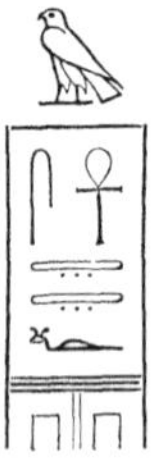 Rock inscription at Ḥammâmât, L. D., II, 150 *a*.

II.  Rock inscription at Ḥammâmât, L. D., II, 150 *a*.

III. 

IV.  Abydos List, No. 58; Turin Papyrus.

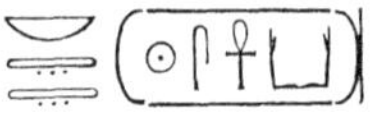 Block from Erment.

 Tablet of Ṣaḳḳârah.

V. 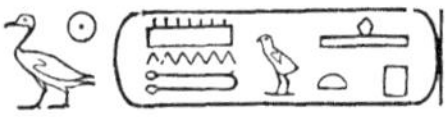 L. D., II, 150 *a*.

Rā-skhā- ... Mentu-ḥetep.

 Fragment found by Prof. Naville at Dêr al-Baḥarî.

MIDDLE EMPIRE.

TWELFTH DYNASTY. FROM THEBES.

1. *Ȧmen-em-ḥāt I.*

I. Horus name	NEM (or UḤEM) MESTU.
II. N-U name	NEM MESTU.
III. Golden Horus name	NEM MESTU.
IV. Suten Bȧt name	RĀ-SEḤETEP-ȦB.
V. Son of Rā name	ȦMEN-EM-ḤĀT.

1. 2. 3.

I. 

4. 

L. D., II, 118 *d* and *e*, and Lepsius, *Auswahl*, plate X.

II. 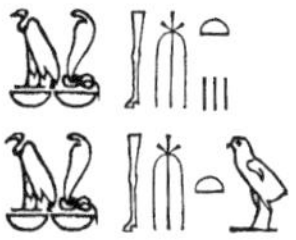

L. D., II, 118 *e*, *f*, and *i*, and Lepsius, *Auswahl*, plate X.

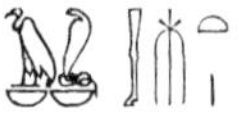

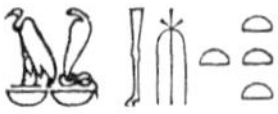

III.  L. D., II, 118.

IV. 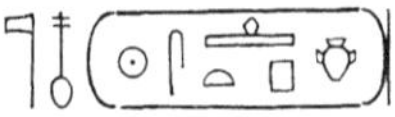 L. D., II, 118 *e*.

 Tablet of Karnak; Lepsius, *Auswahl*, plate X.

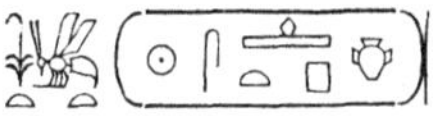 Lepsius, *Königsbuch*, No. 176 *D*.

 Lepsius, *Königsbuch*, No. 176 *f*.

 L. D., II, 118 *d*.

 Abydos List, No. 59.

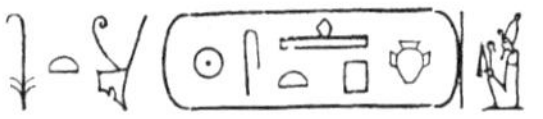 Second Abydos List, No. 33.

 Tablet of Ṣaḳḳârah.

V. 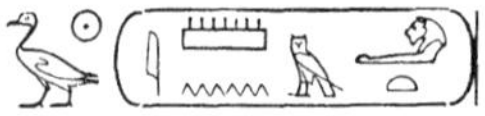 Mariette, *Catalogue*, No. 1338.

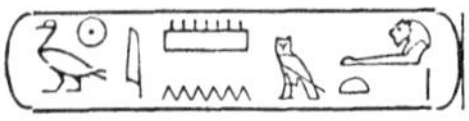 L. D., II, 118 *d*.

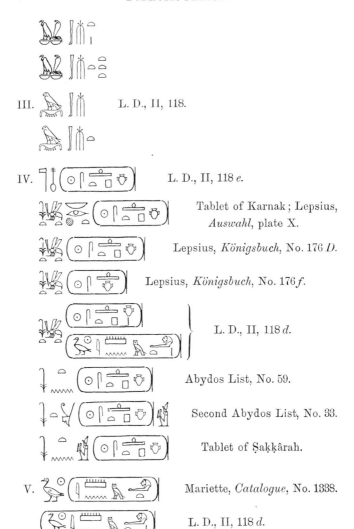

2. *Usertsen I.*

I. Horus name	Ānkh Mestu.
II. N-U name	Ānkh Mestu.
III. Golden Horus name	Ānkh Mestu.
IV. Suten Bȧt name	Rā-kheper-ka.
V. Son of Rā name	Usertsen.

1. 2. 3.

I.

L. D., II, 118.

II.

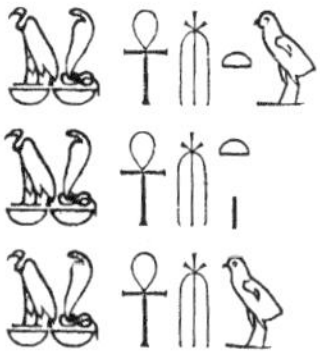

Obelisk, L. D., II, 118.

Mariette, *Abydos*, II, 23.

III.

Obelisk, L. D., II, 118.

IV.

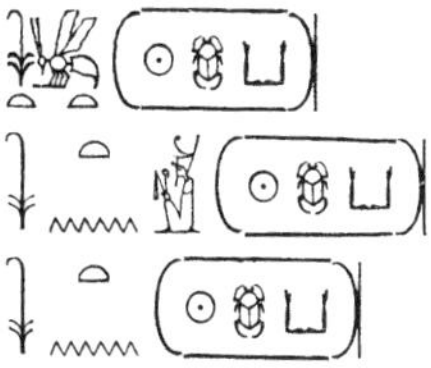

Obelisk, L. D., II, 118.

Tablet of Ṣaḳḳârah.

Abydos List, No. 60.

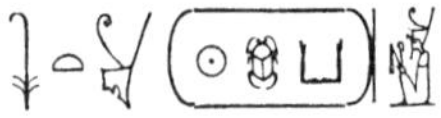 Second Abydos List, No. 34.

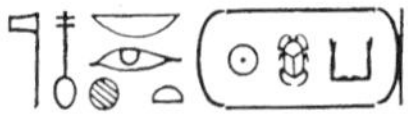 Tablet of Karnak.

 Lepsius, *K.*, 177 *c.*

 Lepsius, *K.*, 177 *d.*

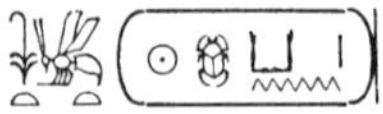 Lepsius, *K.*, 177 *e.*

V. 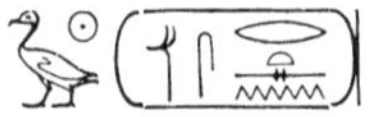 Obelisk, L. D., II, 118.

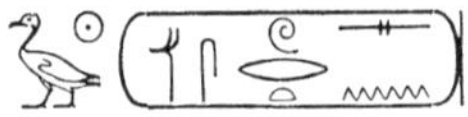 Lepsius, *K.*, 177 *f.*

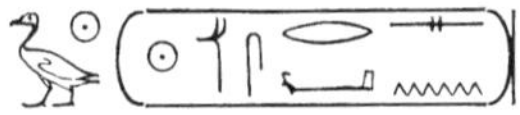 Turin Papyrus.

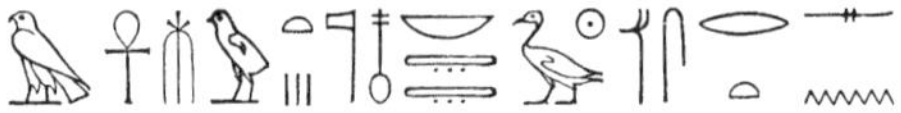 Aswân, L. D., II, 118.

Nefert-Àten-Thenen, Royal Mother.

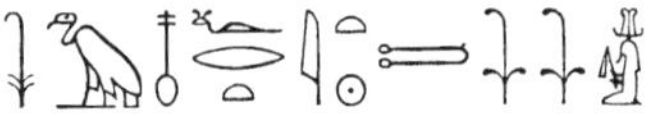 Lepsius, *K.*, 178.

Àmeni, a Prince.

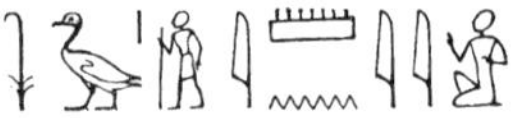 Lepsius, *K.*, 179.

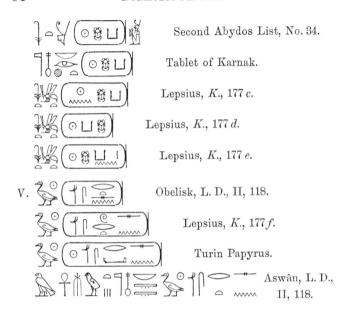

3. *Àmen-em-ḥāt II.*

I. Horus name — Ḥeken-em-Maāt.
II. N-U name — Ḥeken-em-Maāt.
III. Golden Horus name — Maāt-kheru.
IV. Suten Bȧt name — Rā-nub-kau.
V. Son of Rā name — Àmen-em-ḥāt.

I.  Rock inscription at Aswân, L. D., II, 123 *e*.

II.  Stele in Leyden, Lepsius, *Auswahl*, pl. X.

III. 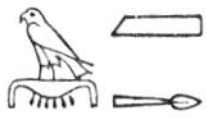 Stele in Leyden, Lepsius, *Auswahl*, pl. X.

IV. 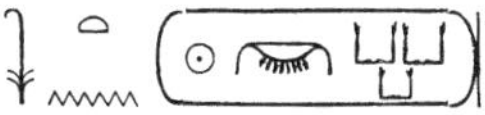 Abydos List, No. 61.

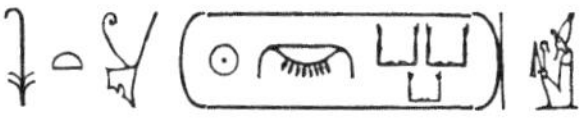 Second Abydos List, No. 35.

 Tablet of Ṣaḳḳârah.

 Tablet of Karnak.

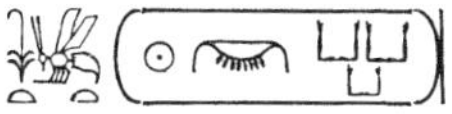 Birch, *Aeg. Zeit.*, 1874, p. 113; Lepsius, *Auswahl*, pl. X.

V. 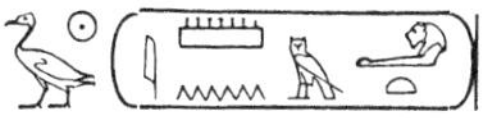 Stele in Leyden, Lepsius, *Auswahl*, pl. X.

4. *Usertsen II.*

I. Horus name	Semu-taui.
II. N-U name	Sekhā-Maāt.
III. Golden Horus name	Neteru-ḥetep.
IV. Suten Bȧt name	Rā-khā-kheper.
V. Son of Rā name	Usertsen.

I.  Stele at Alnwick Castle (Birch, *Catalogue*, p. 269); and L. D., II, 123 *d*.

II. 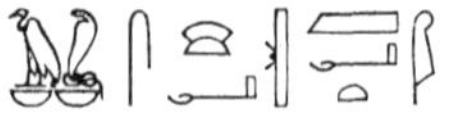 Inscription at Aswân, L. D., II, 123 *d*.

 De Morgan, *Dahshûr*, p. 60.

III.  Inscription at Aswân, L. D., II, 123 *d*.

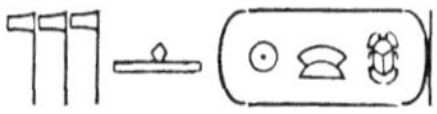 De Morgan, *Dahshûr*, p. 60.

IV.  Stele at Alnwick Castle (Birch, *Catalogue*, p. 269).

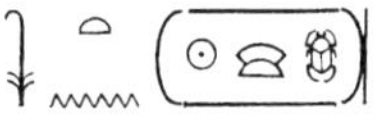 Abydos List, No. 62.

 Second Abydos List, No. 36.

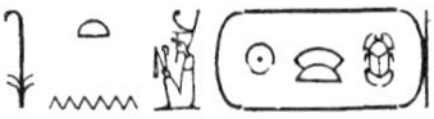 Tablet of Ṣaḳḳârah.

 Legrain, *Annales*, VII, 34.

V.  Inscription at Aswân, L. D., II, 123 *d*.

 Lepsius, *Auswahl*, plate X.

Nefert, wife of Usertsen II.

Statue from Tanis in Cairo (Petrie, *Tanis*, II, plate XI, No. 171).

5. *Usertsen III.*

I.	Horus name	NETER-KHEPERU.
II.	N-U name	NETER-MESTU.
III.	Golden Horus name	ĀNKH-KHEPER.
IV.	Suten Bāt name	RĀ-KHĀ-KAU.
V.	Son of Rā name	USERTSEN.

I. 

De Morgan, *Dahshûr*, p. 59.

II. 

De Morgan, *Dahshûr*, p. 51.

III. 

Stele in Berlin, L. D., II, 136 *h*.

IV. 

Legrain, *Annales*, VII, 34.

De Morgan, *Dahshûr*, p. 59.

Tablet of Karnak.

Brugsch and Bouriant, *Livre des Rois*, p. 18.

Abydos List, No. 63.

Tablet of Ṣaḳḳârah.

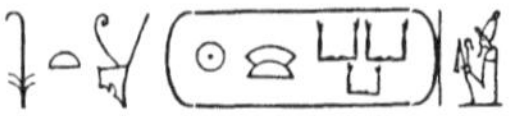

Second Abydos List, No. 37.

V. 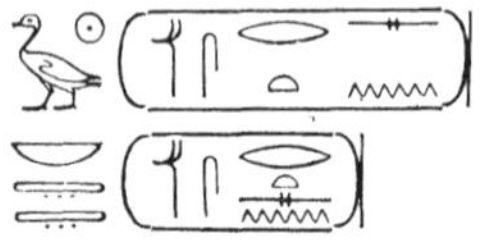

Stele in Berlin, L. D., II, 136 *h*.

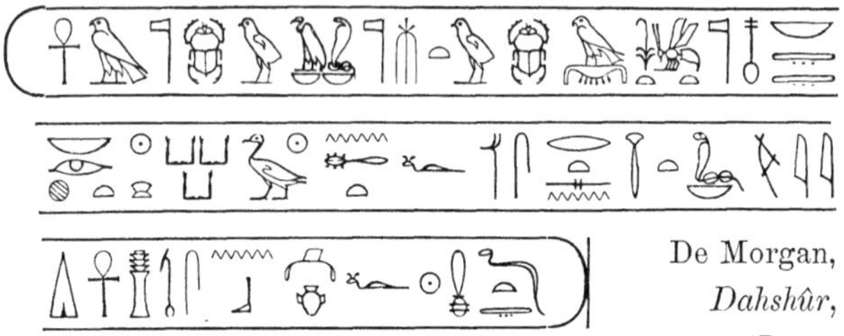

De Morgan, *Dahshûr*, p. 47.

Ḥent-taui.

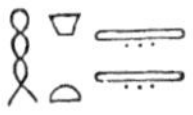

Pyramid at Dahshûr.

6. Ȧmen-em-ḥāt III.

I. Horus name	Āa-baiu.
II. N-U name	Thet-ȧuāt-taui.
III. Golden Horus name	Uaḥ-ānkh.
IV. Suten Bȧt name	Rā-en-Maāt.
V. Son of Rā name	Ȧmen-em-ḥāt.

I. 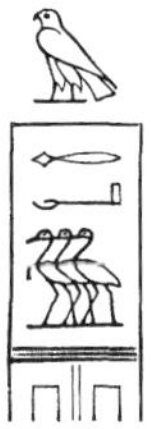 Granite slab in Cairo (Maspero, *Annales*, III, 207).

II.  Stele from Al-Ḳâb.

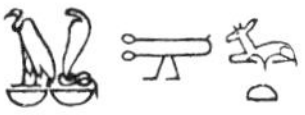 Lepsius, *K.*, No. 183 *b*.

 Granite slab in Cairo.

III.  Granite slab in Cairo.

IV. 

 Rocks at Semnah, L. D., II, 139.

 Lepsius, *K.*, No. 183 *d*.

 L. D., II, 138 *a*.

 L. D., II, 138 *e*.

 Dahshûr Jewellery.

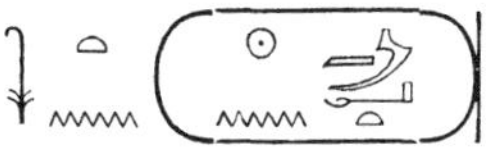 Abydos List, No. 64.

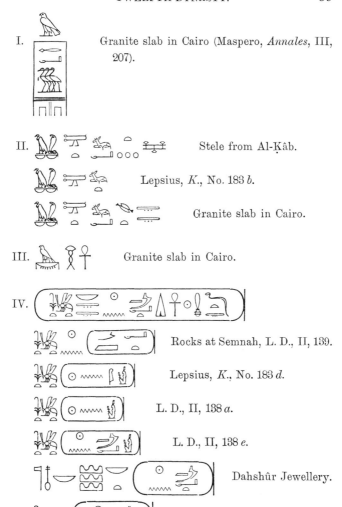

 Second Abydos List, No. 38.

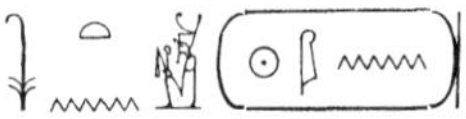 Tablet of Ṣaḳḳârah.

V. 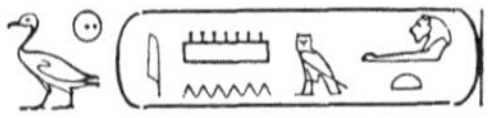 Granite slab in Cairo.

Ptaḥ-Neferu, wife of Ȧmen-em-ḥāt III.

 Black granite mortar in Cairo (Daressy, *Recueil*, X, 142; Daressy, *Catalogue*, No. 9438; Legrain, *Annales*, IV, 134).

Ḥeru.

I. Horus name	ḤETEP-ȦB.
II. N-U name	NEFER-KHĀU.
III. Golden Horus name	NEFER-NETERU.
IV. Suten Bȧt name	RĀ-ȦU-ȦB.
V. Son of Rā name	ḤERU.

I. 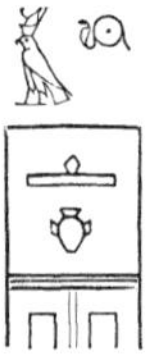 De Morgan, *Dahshûr*, p. 93.

II. 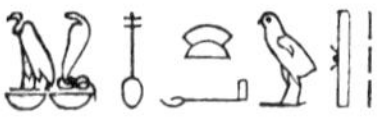 De Morgan, *Dahshûr*, p. 93.

III. 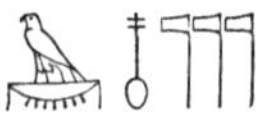 De Morgan, *Dahshûr*, p. 93.

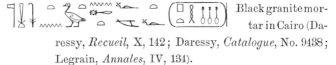

IV.  De Morgan, *Dahshûr*, p. 90.

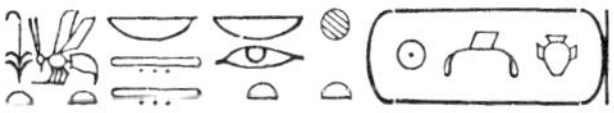 De Morgan, *Dahshûr*, p. 93.

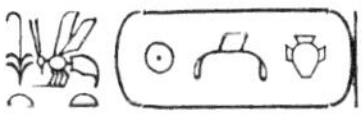 De Morgan, *Dahshûr*, p. 94.

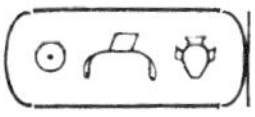 Scarab in Cairo (Legrain, *Annales*, VI, 137).

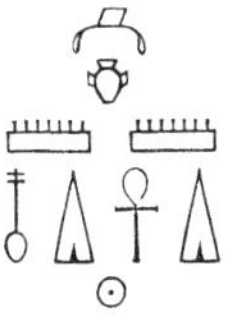 Budge, *Catalogue Meux Collection*, No. 376.

Rā-àu-àb and *Usertsen III.*

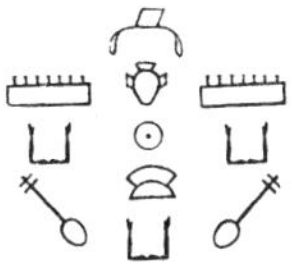 Scarab in the British Museum, No. 37652.

V. 

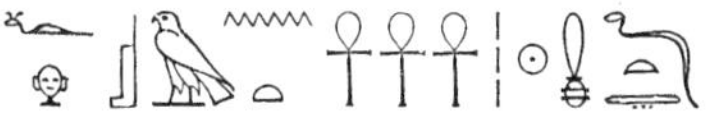 De Morgan, *Dahshûr*, p. 95.

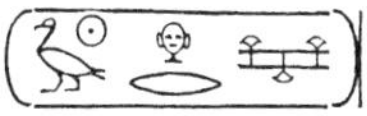 De Morgan, *Dahshûr*, p. 94.

 De Morgan, *Dahshûr*, p. 101.

Ment, a princess.

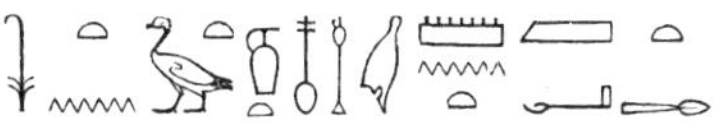 De Morgan, *Dahshûr*, p. 56.

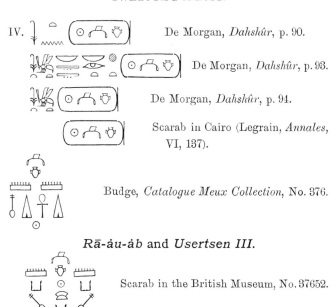

Merit, a princess.

 De Morgan, *Dahshûr*, p. 69.

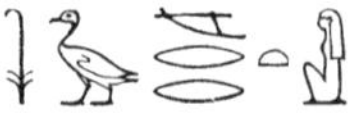 De Morgan, *Dahshûr*, p. 69.

Nub-ḥetep-khart, a princess.

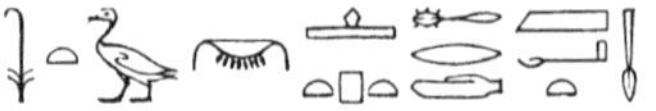 De Morgan, *Dahshûr*, p. 115.

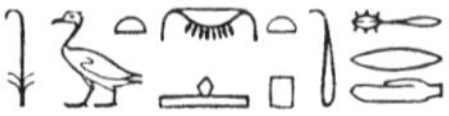 De Morgan, *Dahshûr*, p. 128.

Ḥent, Queen.

 De Morgan, *Dahshûr*, p. 54.

Ḥet-Ḥeru-sat, a princess.

 De Morgan, *Dahshûr*, p. 62.

Sent-Senbet-s, a princess.

 De Morgan, *Dahshûr*, p. 56.

Ȧmen-em-ḥāt IV.

I. Horus name	Kheperȧ Kheper Kheperu.
II. N-U name	...
III. Golden Horus name	...
IV. Suten Bȧt name	Rā-maā-kheru.
V. Son of Rā name	Ȧmen-em-ḥāt.

I.  L. D., II, 140, 152.

IV.  Abydos List, No. 65.

 Second Abydos List, No. 39.

 Tablet of Ṣaḳḳârah.

 Tablet of Karnak.

 Plaque in the British Museum, No. 22879.

V. 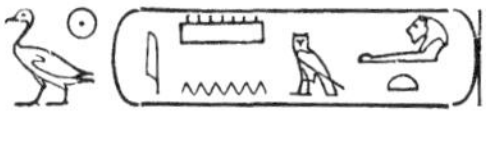 L. D., II, 140.

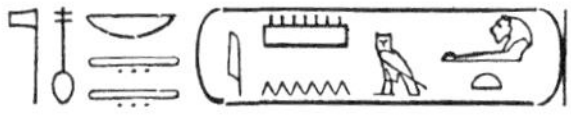 Plaque in the British Museum, No. 22879.

Ȧmeni, a prince.

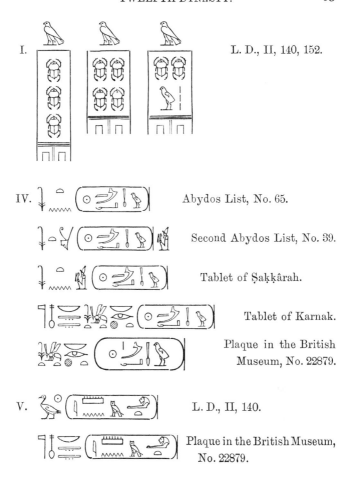

Usertsen [*IV?*].

I. Horus name	...
II. N-U name	SĀNKH-TAUI.
III. Golden Horus name	NEFER-KHĀU.
IV. Suten Bȧt name	RĀ-SENEFER-ȦB.
V. Son of Rā name	USERTSEN.

II.  Legrain, *Annales*, II, 272.

III.  Legrain, *Annales*, II, 272.

IV.  Legrain, *Annales*, II, 272.

V. 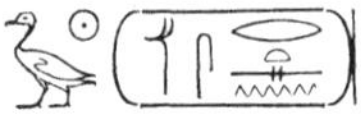 Legrain, *Annales*, II, 272.

Rā-Sebek-Neferu.

I. Horus name	RĀ-MERT.
II. N-U name	SAT-SEKHEM-NEBT-TAUI-ṬEṬT-KHĀ.
III. Golden Horus name	SEBEK-NEFERU (?).
IV. Suten Bȧt name	RĀ-SEBEK-NEFERU.
V. Son of Rā name	...

I.  Seal in the British Museum, No. 16581.

II.  Seal in the British Museum, No. 16581.

III. 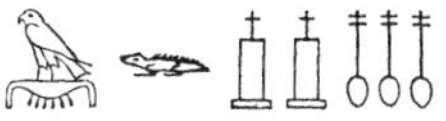 (?) Seal in the British Museum, No. 16581.

IV. 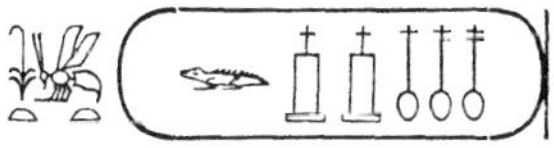 Seal in the British Museum, No. 16581.

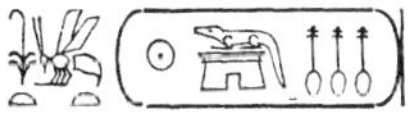 L. D., II, 140.

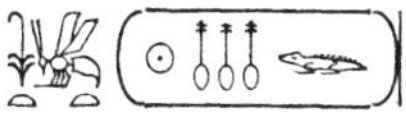 L. D., II, 140.

 Tablet of Karnak.

THE THIRTEENTH TO THE SEVENTEENTH DYNASTIES.

1. Rā-khu-taui Ḥeru-nest-àtebui (?).

I. Horus name	...
II. N-U name	KHĀ-BAIU.
III. Golden Horus name	MERI-...
IV. Suten Bȧt name	RĀ-KHU-TAUI.
V. Son of Rā name	ḤERU-NEST-ȦṬEBUI.

II.  Stele fragment (Legrain, *Annales*, VI, 133).

III.  Legrain, *Annales*, VI, 133.

IV. 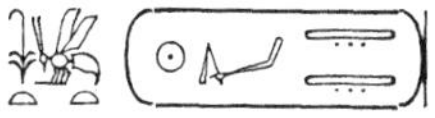 Legrain, *Annales*, VI, 133.

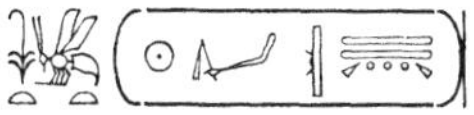 Tablet of Karnak.

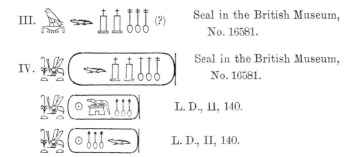

Turin Papyrus.

Statue at Khar-ṭûm.

V. 

Statue at Kharṭûm (Budge, *Egyptian Sûdân*, I, 485).

2. *Sānkh taui Rā-sekhem-ka.*

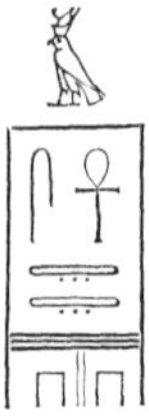

Stele in the B. M., No. 1343.

Stele in the British Museum, No. 1343.

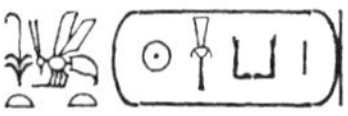

Turin Papyrus.

3. *Ȧmen-em-ḥāt.*

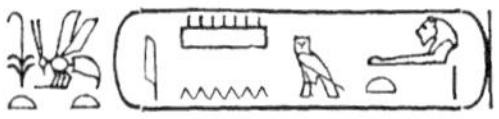

Turin Papyrus.

4. *Rā-seḥetep-ȧb.*

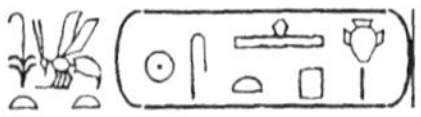

Turin Papyrus.

5. *Ȧufni.*

Turin Papyrus.

6. Ȧmeni Ȧntef Ȧmen-em-ḥāt.

I. Horus name	Seher-taui.
II. N-U name	Sekhem-khāu.
III. Golden Horus name	Ḥeq-Maāt.
IV. Suten Bȧt name	Rā-sānkh-ȧb.
V. Son of Rā name	Ȧmeni Ȧntef Ȧmen-em-ḥāt.

I. 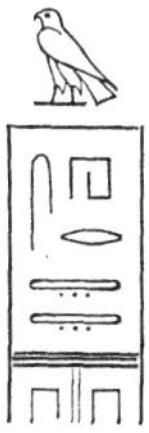 Table of offerings at Cairo (Mariette, *Karnak*, plates 9, 10).

II.  Table of offerings at Cairo.

III.  Table of offerings at Cairo.

 Table of offerings at Cairo.

 Table of offerings at Cairo.

IV.  Table of offerings at Cairo.

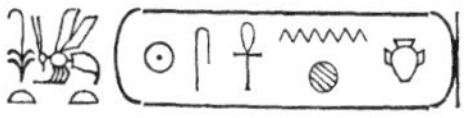 Turin Papyrus.

 Tablet of Karnak.

V.  Table of offerings at Cairo.

7. *Rā-smen-ka.*

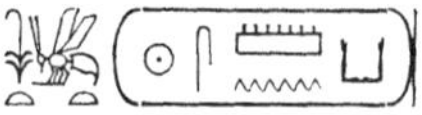

Turin Papyrus.

8. *Rā-seḥetep-ȧb.*

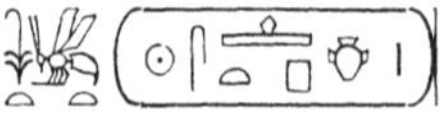

Turin Papyrus.

9. ... - ... - *ka.*

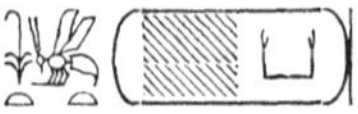

Turin Papyrus.

Here comes a break in the Turin Papyrus.

10. *Rā-netchem-ȧb.*

Turin Papyrus.

11. *Rā-Sebek-ḥetep.*

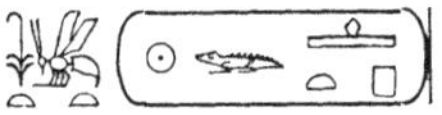

Turin Papyrus.

12. *Ren-*[*Senb?*].

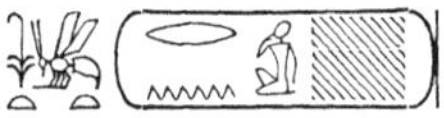

Turin Papyrus.

13. *Rā-ḥ* ... - ...

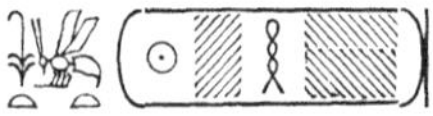

Turin Papyrus.

14. *Rā-setchef-* ...

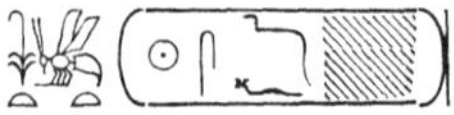

Turin Papyrus.

15. Rā-sekhem-khu-taui Sebek-ḥetep [*I*].

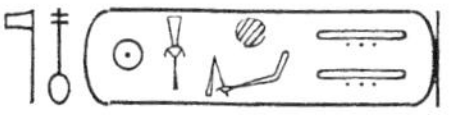

Tablet of Karnak.

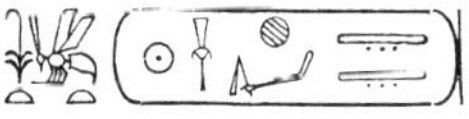

Block at Bubastis (Naville, *Bubastis*, plate XXXIII. H).

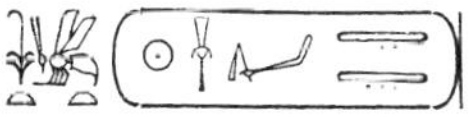

Rock at Semnah, L. D., 152 *a*—*d*.

Rock at Semnah, L. D., 152 *a*—*d*.

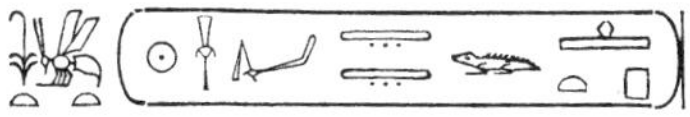

Turin Papyrus.

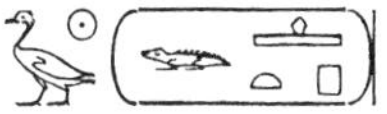

Scarab in the British Museum, No. 15701.

16. Rā-user- ...

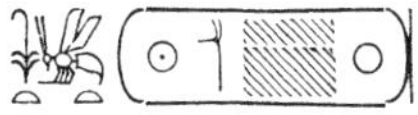

Turin Papyrus.

17. Rā-semenkh-ka Mer-mashāu.

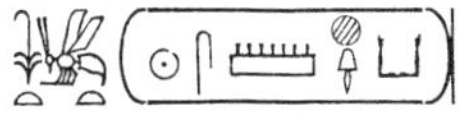

Granite statues in Cairo.

Granite statues in Cairo. See Turin Papyrus, Fragment No. 78.

18. Rā- ... -ka.

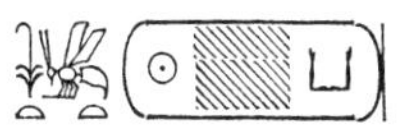

Turin Papyrus.

19. [*Rā*]*-User-Set* (*?*).

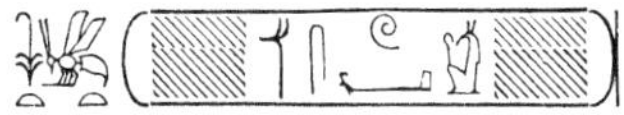

Turin Papyrus.

20. *Khu taui Rā-sekhem-suatch-taui Sebek-ḥetep (II).*

I. Horus name	KHU-TAUI.
II. N-U name	...
III. Golden Horus name	...
IV. Suten Bȧt name	RĀ-SEKHEM-SUATCH-TAUI.
V. Son of Rā name	SEBEK-ḤETEP.

I. 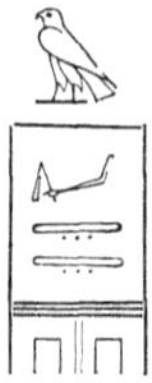 Stele in the Louvre (Mariette, *Monuments*, plate 8).

IV. 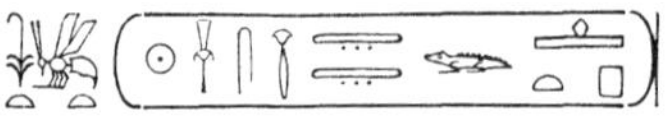 Turin Papyrus.

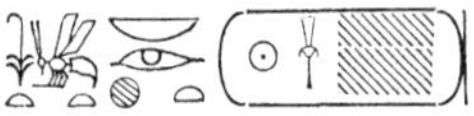 Tablet of Karnak.

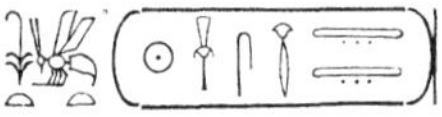 Stele in Paris (Prisse, *Monuments*, pl. VIII).

V. 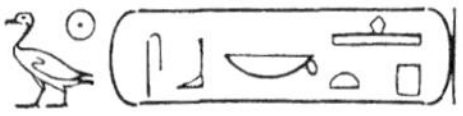 Stele in Paris. (*Ibid.*) Scarab in the British Museum, No. 30506.

Senb, a brother of *Sebek-ḥetep II.*

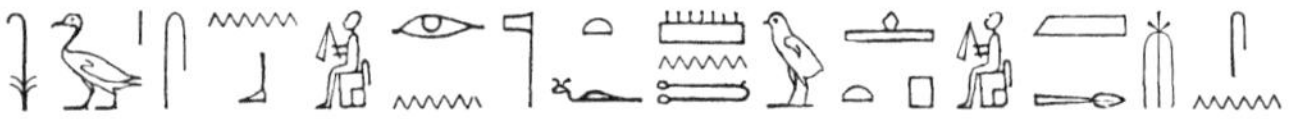

 (*Recueil*, VII, p. 188, No. 10).

Menthu-ḥetep, father of *Sebek-ḥetep II.*

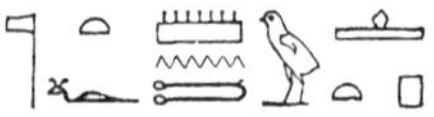 Stele in Vienna (Bergmann, *Recueil*, VII, p. 188, No. 10).

Åu-ḥet-åbu, mother of *Sebek-ḥetep II.*

Stele in Vienna (Bergmann, *Recueil*, VII, p. 188, No. 10).

Ånnå, wife of *Sebek-ḥetep II.*

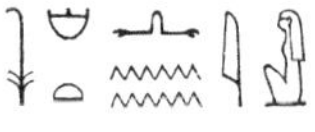

Stelae in Paris (Mariette, *Monuments*, plate 8; Bergmann, *Recueil*, VII, p. 188, No. 10).

Ānqet-ṭāṭāt, a princess, daughter of *Ånnå*.

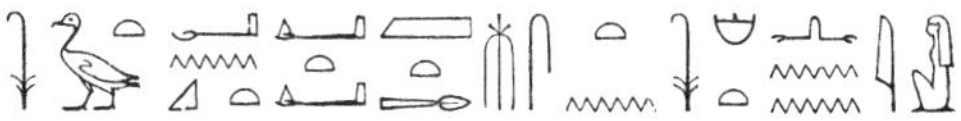

Åuḥet-åbu, surnamed *Fenṭ*, a princess.

Stele in the Louvre (Prisse, *Monuments*, plate 8).

Sebek-ḥetep, a prince, son of *Senb*.

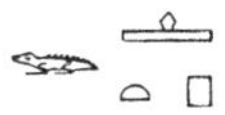

Stele in Vienna (*Recueil*, VII, p. 188).

Åu-ḥet-åbu, daughter of prince *Senb*.

Stele in Vienna (*Recueil*, VII, p. 188, No. 10).

Ḥent, daughter of prince *Senb*.

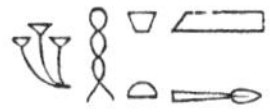

Stele in Vienna (*Recueil*, VII, p. 188, No. 10).

Menthu-ḥetep, son of prince *Senb*.

Stele in Vienna (*Recueil*, VII, p. 188, No. 10).

20 A. [Position doubtful.]
Rā - sekhem - uatch - taui.

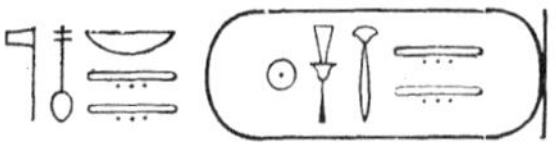

Granite statue in the British Museum, No. 871.

21. Nefer-ḥetep [I].

I. Horus name	Ḥetep-taui(?), and Ḳer-taui.
II. N-U name	Ȧp-Maāt.
III. Golden Horus name	Men-Mertu.
IV. Suten Bât name	Rā-khā-seshesh.
V. Son of Rā name	Nefer-ḥetep.

I. 

Mariette, *Abydos*, II, 28; L.D., II, 151 *e*; Lepsius, *Königsbuch*, 201 *A*; Legrain, *Catalogue*, Cairo, 1906, p. 13.

II. 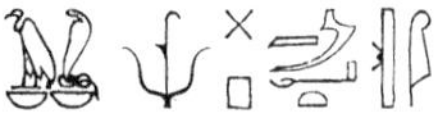

Mariette, *Abydos*, II, 28.

III. 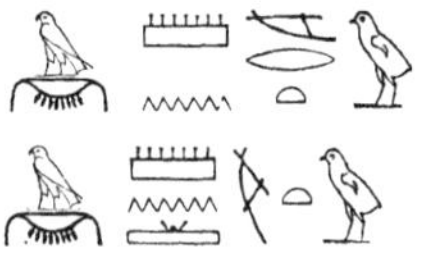

Mariette, *Abydos*, II, 28.

IV. 

L. D., II, 151*f*; Turin Papyrus.

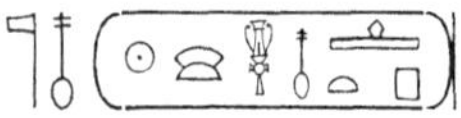

L. D., II, 151*f*.

Mariette, *Karnak*, plate 8.

Mariette, *Abydos*, II, 28.

Tablet of Karnak.

Statue at Bologna (Naville, *Recueil*, I, 109).

V. 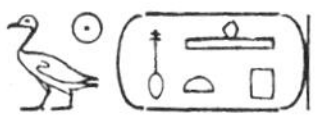
Mariette, *Karnak*, plate 8 ; Mariette, *Abydos*, II, 28.

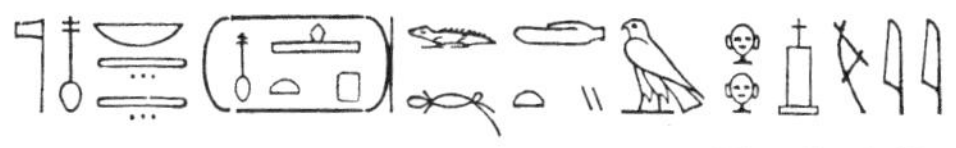
Statue at Bologna (Naville, *Recueil*, I, 109).

Kemā, mother of *Nefer-ḥetep*.

Mariette, *Mon. Div.*, plate 70, No. 3.

Senseneb, wife of *Nefer-ḥetep*.

Mariette, *Mon. Div.*, plate 70, No. 3.

Ḥa-ānkh-f, father of *Nefer-ḥetep*.

Mariette, *Mon. Div.*, plate 70, No. 3.

Ḥet-Ḥeru-sa, a prince, son of *Nefer-ḥetep*.

Mariette, *Mon. Div.*, plate 70, No. 3.

Sebek-ḥetep, a prince, son of *Nefer-ḥetep.*

 Mariette, *Mon. Div.*, plate 70, No. 3.

Ḥa-ānkh-f, a prince, son of *Nefer-ḥetep.*

 Mariette, *Mon. Div.*, plate 70, No. 3.

Kemā, a princess, daughter of *Nefer-ḥetep.*

 Mariette, *Mon. Div.*, plate 70, No. 3.

22. *Rā-Ḥet-Ḥert-sa.*

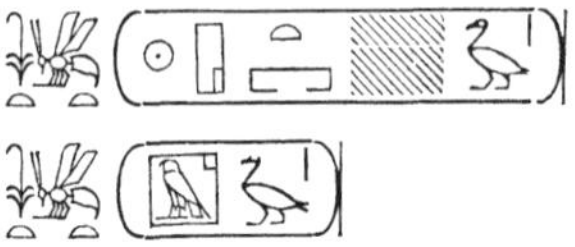 Turin Papyrus.

22 *A.* [Position doubtful.]

Rā-mer-sekhem Nefer-ḥetep.

IV. 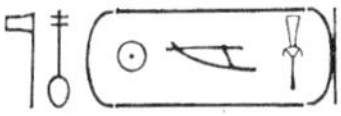 Legrain, *Catalogue*, p. 14.

V. 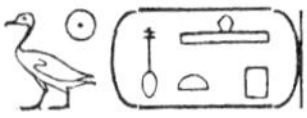 Legrain, *Catalogue*, p. 14.

23. *Sebek-ḥetep* (*III*).

I. Horus name	Ānkh-àb-taui.
II. N-U name	Uatch-khāu.
III. Golden Horus name	...
IV. Suten Bȧt name	Rā-khā-nefer.
V. Son of Rā name	Sebek-ḥetep.

I. 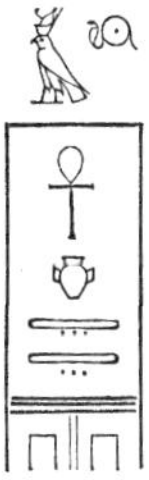 Statue of Usertsen III (Legrain, *Annales*, IV, 26).

II.  Statue on the Island of Arḳô. L. D., II, 120.

IV. 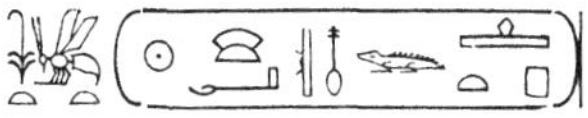 Turin Papyrus.

 Statue on the Island of Arḳô, L. D., II, 120, 151.

 Mariette, *Karnak*, plate 8.

 Statue of Usertsen III (Legrain, *Annales*, IV, 26).

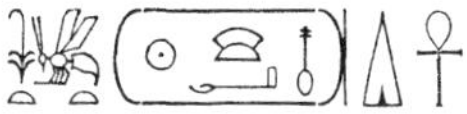 Legrain, *Annales*, VII, 34.

V.  Statue on the Island of Arḳô (L. D., II, 120, 151). Scarab in the British Museum, No. 32434.

Here comes a break in the Turin Papyrus.

24. Rā-khā-ka.

 Tablet of Karnak (Brugsch, *Egypt*, I, p. 188).

25. Rā-khā-ḥetep Sebek-ḥetep (IV).

IV. 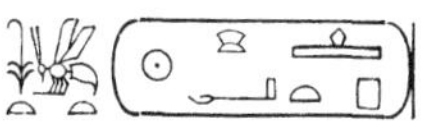 Turin Papyrus.

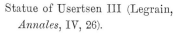

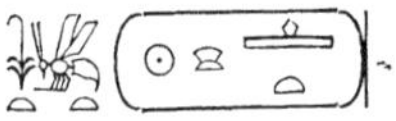 Lepsius, *Königsbuch*, 211 *a*.

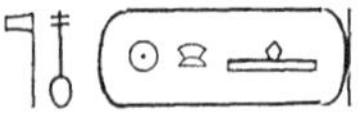 Lepsius, *Königsbuch*, 211 *b*.

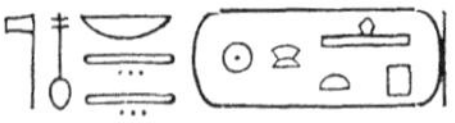 Tablet of Karnak.

V.  Lepsius, *Königsbuch*, 211 *E*.

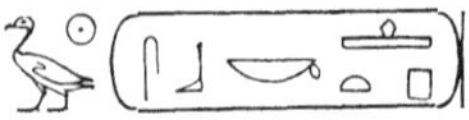 Lepsius, *Königsbuch*, 211 *c*.

 Lepsius, *Königsbuch*, 211 *d*.

26. Sebek-ḥetep [V].

I. Horus name	SMA-TAUI.
II. N-U name	ṬEṬṬEṬ-KHĀU.
III. Golden Horus name	KAU-NETERU.
IV. Suten Bât name	RĀ-KHĀ-ĀNKH.
V. Son of Rā name	SEBEK-ḤETEP.

I. 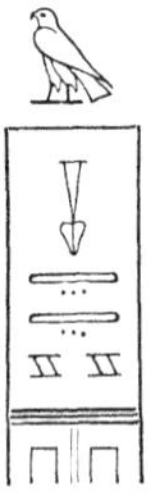 Altar at Leyden (Leemans, *Mon.*, I, plate 37).

II. 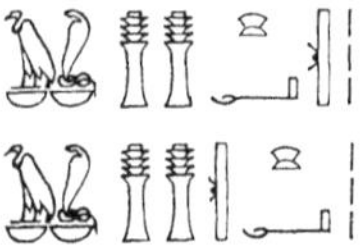 Altar at Leyden (Leemans, *Mon.*, I, plate 37).

III. 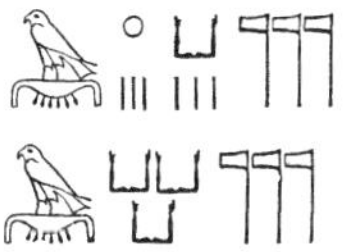 Altar at Leyden (Leemans, *Mon.*, I, plate 37).

IV.  Tablet of Karnak.

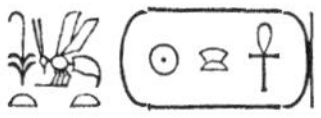 Altar at Leyden (Leemans, *Mon.*, I, plate 37).

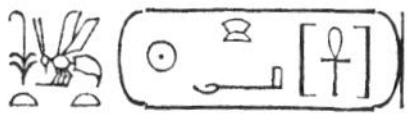 Turin Papyrus.

V.  Altar at Leyden (Leemans, *Mon.*, I, plate 37).

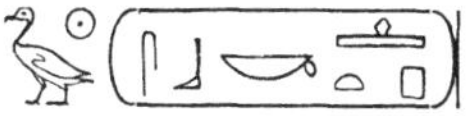

[Position doubtful.]

Rā-mer-ḥetep Sebek-ḥetep.

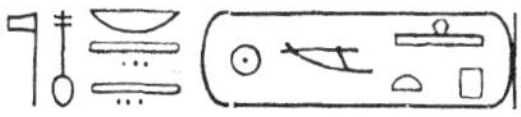  Legrain, *Catalogue*, p. 16.

Rā-mer-kau Sebek-ḥetep.

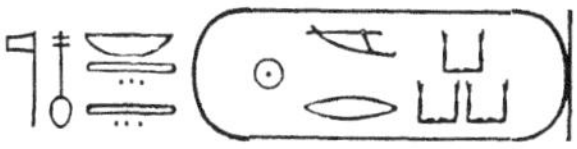 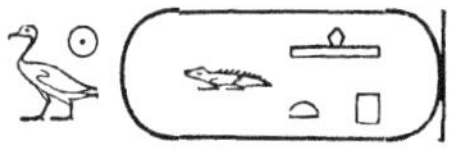

Mariette, *Karnak*, p. 8.

Nub-em-ḥāt, a queen.

 Stele from Coptos (Petrie, XII, No. 2).

Sebek-em-ḥeb, a princess.

Stele from Coptos (Petrie, XII, No. 2).

27. Rā-uaḥ-ȧb-Ȧā-ȧb.

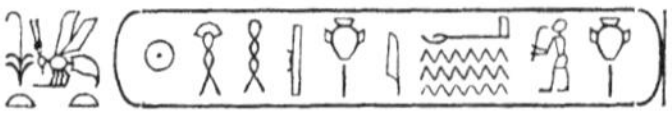

Turin Papyrus.

28. Rā-mer-nefer Ai.

Turin Papyrus; Scarabs.

29. Rā-mer-ḥetep Ȧnȧ.

Turin Papyrus; Scarabs.

30. Rā-[mer]-ka.

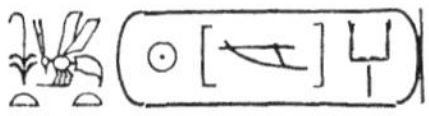

Turin Papyrus.

31. Rā-[neb?]-Maāt Ȧbȧ.

Turin Papyrus.

32. Rā- ... - ...

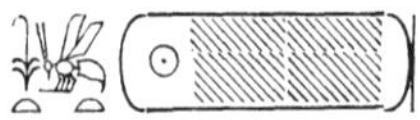

Turin Papyrus.

33. ... ...

Turin Papyrus.

34. [*Rā*]-*Neḥsi.*

Turin Papyrus.

Recueil de Travaux, XV, 99; *Ahnas*, plate 4, B 1 and B 2.

35. *Rā-khā-kheru.*

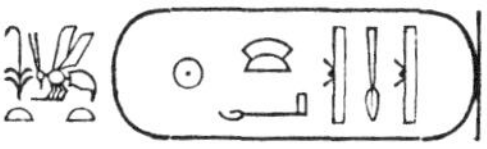

Turin Papyrus.

36. *Rā-neb-f Āa-nekht-meri.*

Turin Papyrus.

37. *Rā-nefer-ȧb.*

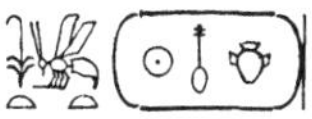

Turin Papyrus.

38. *Rā-ȧ ... - ...*

Turin Papyrus.

Nub-khā-[*s*], a queen.

Abbott Papyrus.

Khensu, a prince.

39. *Rā-nefer-ka.*

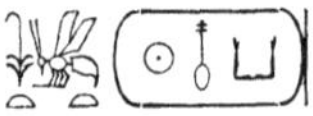

Turin Papyrus.

40. *Rā-smen-...*

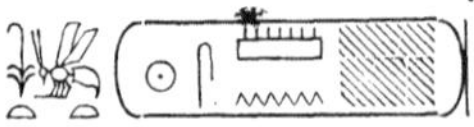

Turin Papyrus.

41. *Rā-mer-sekhem.*

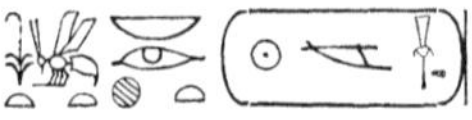

Tablet of Karnak.

42. *... ...*

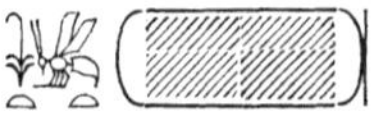

Turin Papyrus.

43. *... ...*

Turin Papyrus.

44. *Rā-senefer- ...*

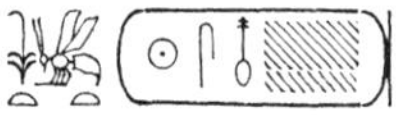

Turin Papyrus.

45. *Ān-àb.*

I.	Horus name	SUATCH-TAUI.
II.	N-U name	...
III.	Golden Horus name	...
IV.	Suten Bȧt name	RĀ-MEN-KHĀU.
V.	Son of Rā name	ĀN-ȦB.

I. 

Stele in Cairo (Mariette, *Abydos*, II, 27).

IV. 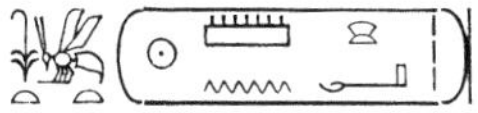 Stele in Cairo (Mariette, *Abydos*, II, 27).

 Stele in Cairo (Mariette, *Abydos*, II, 27).

V.  Stele in Cairo (Mariette, *Abydos*, II, 27).

46. ... ...

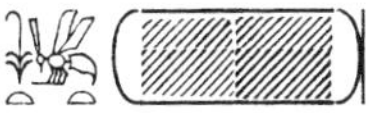 Turin Papyrus.

47. ... ...

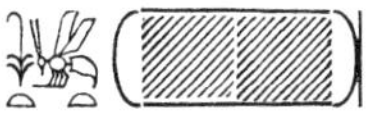 Turin Papyrus.

48. *Sebek-em-sa-f.*

I. Horus name	Ḥetep-neteru.
II. N-U name	Āsh-kheperu.
III. Golden Horus name	Ȧnq-taui.
IV. Suten Bȧt name	Rā-sekhem-uatch-khāu.
V. Son of Rā name	Sebek-em-sa-f.

I. 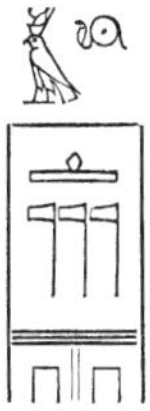 Obelisk, Legrain, *Annales*, VI, 284.

II. 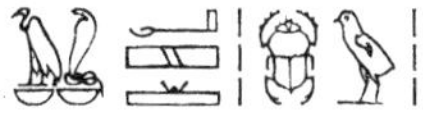 Obelisk, Legrain, *Annales*, VI, 284.

III.  Obelisk, Legrain, *Annales*, VI, 284.

IV. Statue in Cairo.

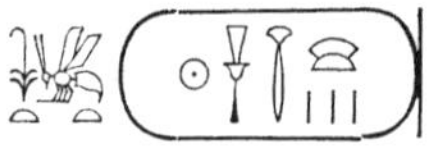

Obelisk, Legrain,
Annales, VI, 284.

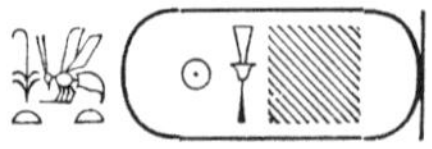

Turin Papyrus.

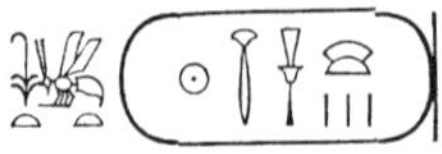

Tablet of Karnak.

V. Statue in Cairo.

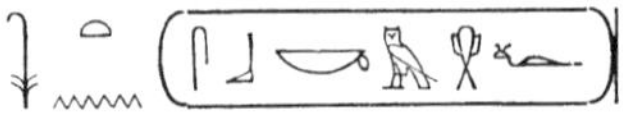

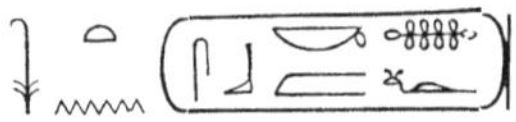

Sebek-em-sa-f, a prince.

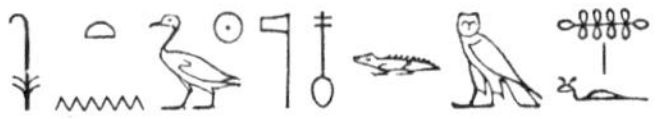

 Statue in Cairo.

[Position doubtful.]
Rā-en-maāt-en-khā Khentcher.

IV. Lepsius, *Königsbuch*, 186.

V. Lepsius, *Königsbuch*, 186.

Rā-sekhem-nefer-khāu Áp-uat-em-sa-f.

IV.

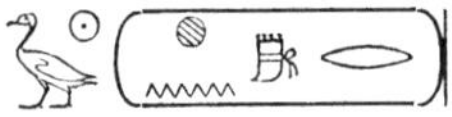

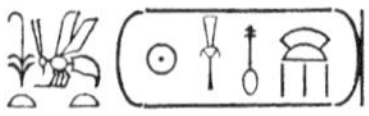

V.

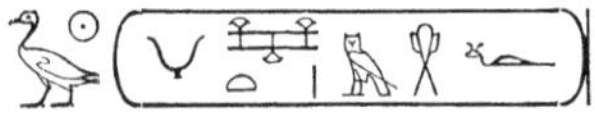

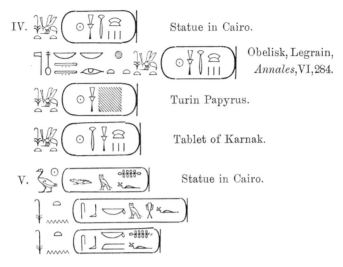

Rā-ṭeṭ-ānkh Mentu-em-sa-f.

IV. 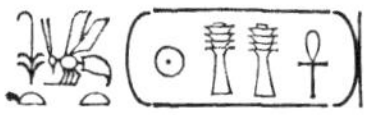 Scarab in the British Museum, No. 40687.

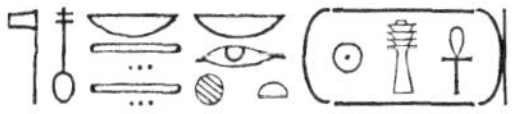 Daressy, *Recueil*, XX, p. 72.

V.  Daressy, *Recueil*, XX, p. 72.

49. *Rā-Sekhem-sesheṭ-taui Sebek-em-sau-f.*

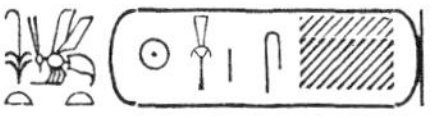 Turin Papyrus.

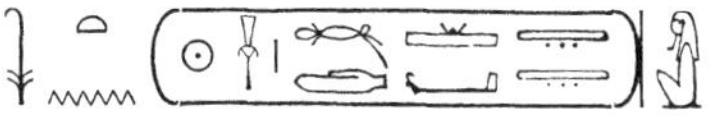 Abbott Papyrus.

 Abbott Papyrus.

50. *Rā-sekhem-nefer-khāu Ȧp-uat-em-sa-f.*

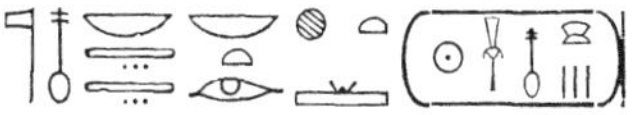 Copy of Devéria (Wiedemann, *Aeg. Zeit.*, 1885, p. 80).

 British Museum Stele, No. 969.

51. *Rā-seshesh-her-ḥer-maāt Ȧntef-āa.*

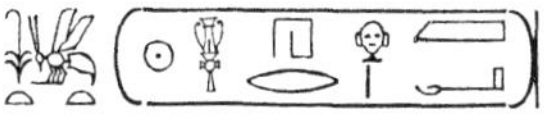 Coffin in the Louvre (Birch, *Aeg. Zeit.*, 1869, p. 52).

 Coffin in the Louvre.

 Coffin in the Louvre.

52. Ȧntef-āa,
brother of *Rā-seshesh-her-ḥer-maāt Ȧntef-āa.*

Coffin in the Louvre (Birch, *Aeg. Zeit.*, 1869, p. 52).

Coffin in the Louvre (Pierret, *Recueil*, I, p. 86).

53. Rā-seshesh-ȧp-maāt Ȧntef-āa.

I. Horus name	Ȧpt-maāt.
II. N-U name	...
III. Golden Horus name	...
IV. Suten Bȧt name	Rā-seshesh-ȧp-maāt.
V. Son of Rā name	Ȧntef-āa.

I. 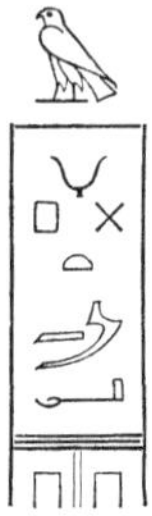

Statue in the B. M., No. 478.

IV. 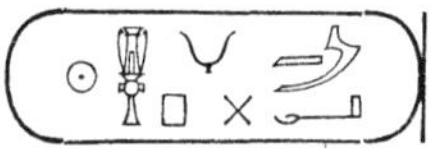

Coffin in the British Museum, No. 6652. Statue in the British Museum, No. 478.

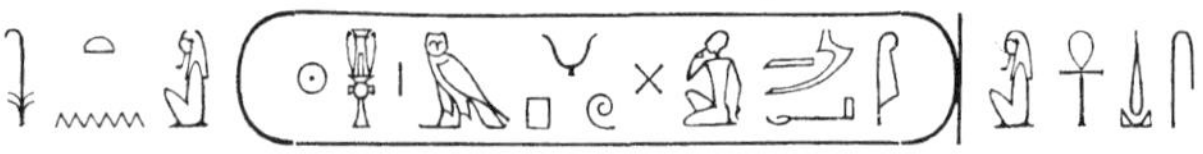

Abbott Papyrus.

V. 

Coffin in the British Museum, No. 6652.

 Statue in the British Museum, No. 478.

 Abbott Papyrus.

54. *Rā-nub-kheper Ȧntef-āa.*

I. Horus name — NEFER-KHEPERU, or KHEPER-[KHEPERU.
II. N-U name — HER-ḤER-NEST-F.
III. Golden Horus name — ...
IV. Suten Bȧt name — RĀ-NUB-KHEPER.
V. Son of Rā name — ȦNTEF, or ȦNTEF-ĀA.

I. 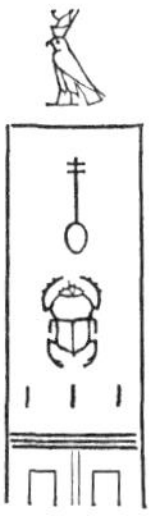 Obelisk in Cairo (Mariette, *Mon. Div.*, plate 50 *a*).

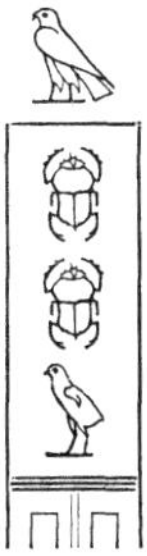 *Annales du Service*, III, 14.

II.  Legrain, *Annales*, III, 114.

 Mariette, *Mon. Div.*, plate 50 *a*.

IV.  Tablet of Karnak.

 Legrain, *Annales*, III, 114; Mariette, *Mon. Div.*, plate 50 *a*.

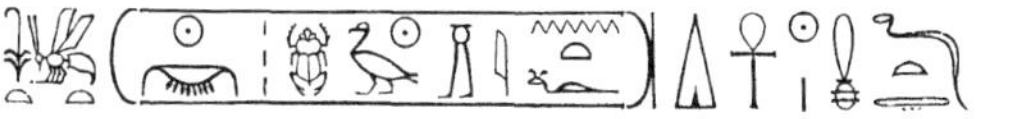 Decree (Petrie, *Koptos*, plate VIII).

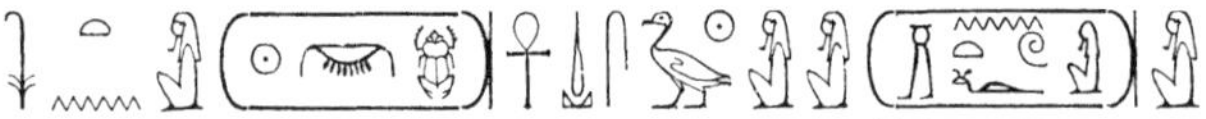

Abbott Papyrus.

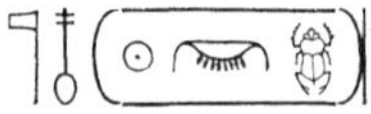

Obelisk (Mariette, *Mon. Div.*, plate 50*a*).
British Museum Stele, No. 631.

V. 

Obelisk (Mariette, *Mon. Div.*, plate 50 *a*).

Obelisk (Mariette, *Mon. Div.*, plate 50 *a*).

55. *Rā-sekhem-ṭā* (?)- ... *Pen-* ... *then.*

Stele of Teḥuti-āa in the British Museum, No. 630.

Teḥuti-āa, a prince, son of *Pen-* ... *then* (?).

Stele in the British Museum, No. 630.

56. *Rā-u-àqer.*

Limestone slab (*Abydos*, II, plate 32).

57. *Ḥeru-netch-tef.*

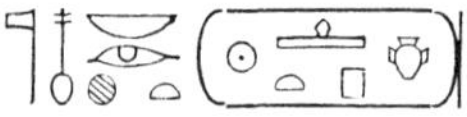

Limestone slab in the Museum at Cairo (Kamal, *Annales*, III, p. 80).

58. *Rā-sesuser-taui.*

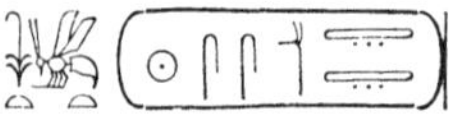

Turin Papyrus.

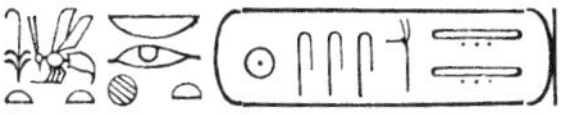

Tablet of Karnak.

59. *Rā-neb-ȧti- ...*

Turin Papyrus.

60. *Rā-neb-ȧten.*

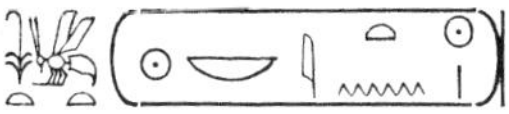

Turin Papyrus.

61. *Rā-smen-[taui].*

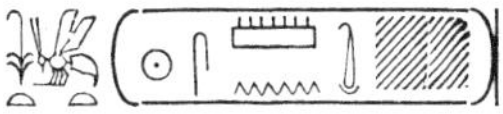

Turin Papyrus.

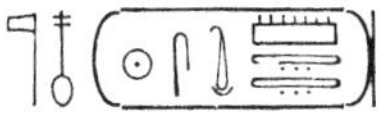

Tablet of Karnak.

62. *Rā-suser-ȧt[en].*

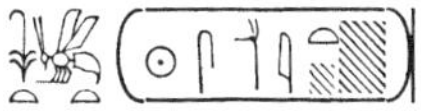

Turin Papyrus.

63. *Rā-sekhem-Uast.*

Turin Papyrus.

64. *Rā-sekhem-uaḥ-khāu Rā-ḥetep.*

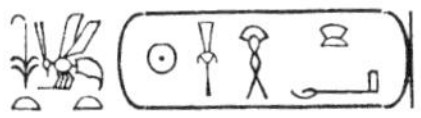

Tablet of Karnak.

65. Rā-sānkh-en-seḥtu.

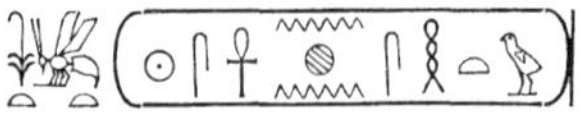
Turin Papyrus.

Khensu-ānkhthȧ, a queen.

Monument in the Louvre.

66. Rā-mer-sekhem Ȧn-ren.

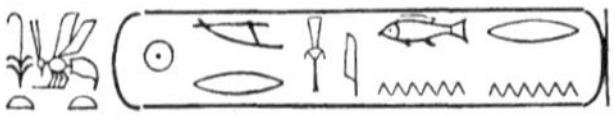
Turin Papyrus.

67. Rā-s[ānkh]-ka Ḥeru-ȧ.

Turin Papyrus.

68. Rā-suatch-en.

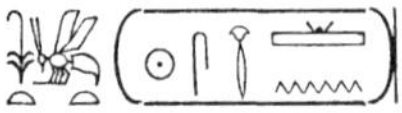
Tablet of Karnak.

69. ... ...

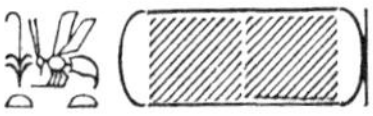
Turin Papyrus.

70. ... ...

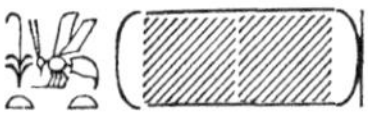
Turin Papyrus.

71. ... ...

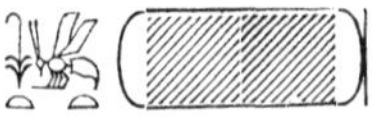
Turin Papyrus.

72. ... ...

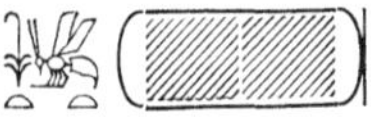
Turin Papyrus.

73. ... ...

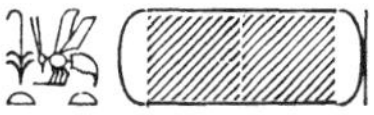

Turin Papyrus.

74. ... ...

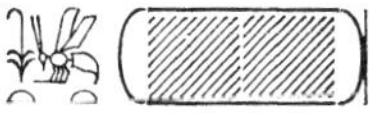

Turin Papyrus.

75. *Rā-khā-ka.*

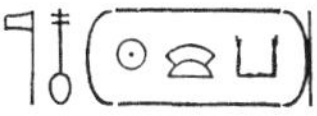

76. ... - ... - *Rā.*

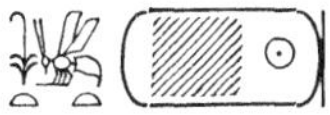

Turin Papyrus.

77. *Rā-mer-kheper.*

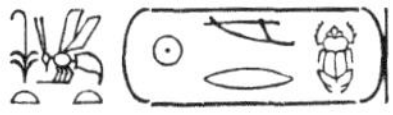

Turin Papyrus.

78. *Rā-mer-kau Sebek-ḥetep.*

Turin Papyrus.

Mariette, *Karnak*, plate 8.

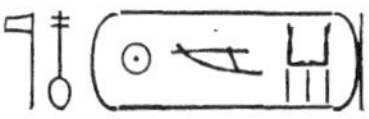

Tablet of Karnak.

Mariette, *Karnak*, plate 8.

79. ... ...

Turin Papyrus.

80. ... ...

Turin Papyrus.

81. ... ...

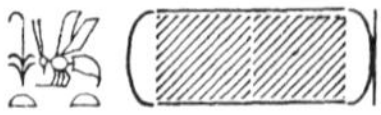

Turin Papyrus.

82. ... - ... mesu.

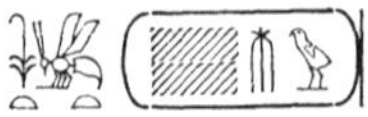

Turin Papyrus.

83. Rā- ... - maāt.

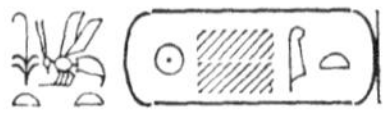

Turin Papyrus.

84, Rā - ... - uben.

Turin Papyrus.

85. Rā-seḥeb.

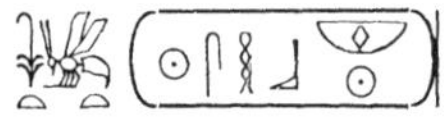

Turin Papyrus.

86. Rā-mer-tchefa.

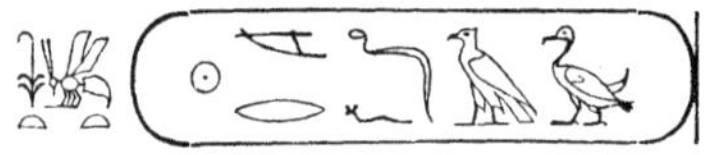

Turin Papyrus.

87. Rā-sta-ka.

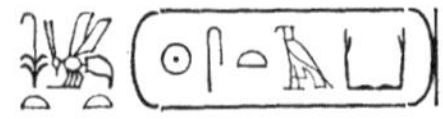

Turin Papyrus.

88. Rā-neb-tchefa-Rā (?).

Turin Papyrus.

89. Rā-senefer- ...

Tablet of Karnak.

90. ... ...

Turin Papyrus.

91. Rā - ... - tchefa.

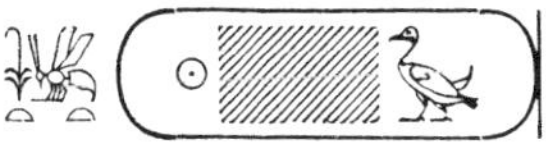

Turin Papyrus.

92. [Rā] - ... - uben.

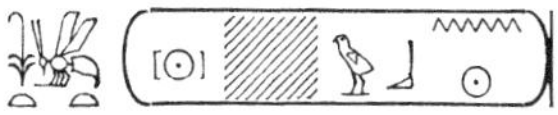

Turin Papyrus.

93. Rā - ... - ȧb.

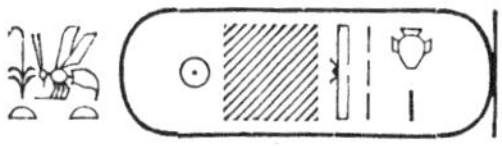

Turin Papyrus.

94. Rā-her-ȧb.

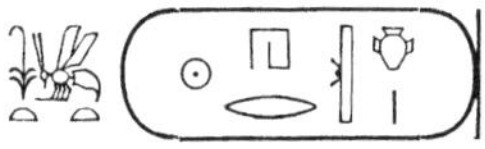

Turin Papyrus.

95. Rā-neb-sen.

Turin Papyrus.

96. ... ...

Turin Papyrus.

97. Rā-suaḥ-en.

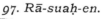

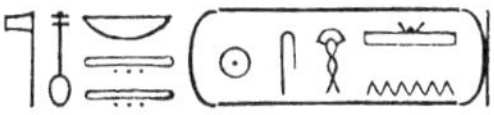

Tablet of Karnak.

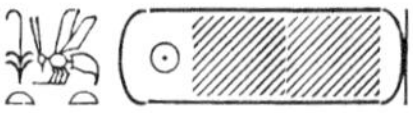

Turin Papyrus.

98. Rā-sekheper-en.

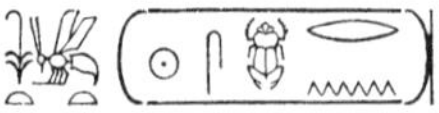

Turin Papyrus.

99. Rā-ṭeṭ-kheru.

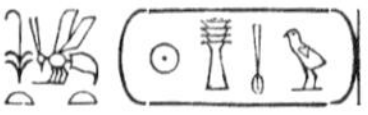

Turin Papyrus.

100. Rā-sānkh-...

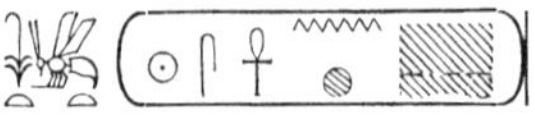

Turin Papyrus.

101. Rā-nefer-sati.

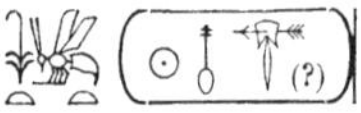

Turin Papyrus.

102. Rā-sekhem- ...

Turin Papyrus.

103. Rā-ka- ...

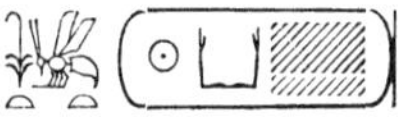

Turin Papyrus.

104. ... ...

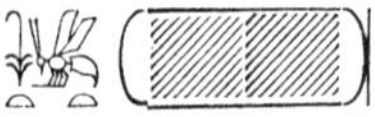

Turin Papyrus.

105. ... ...

Turin Papyrus.

106. ... ...

Turin Papyrus.

107. Rā-user- ...

Turin Papyrus.

108. Rā-user- ...

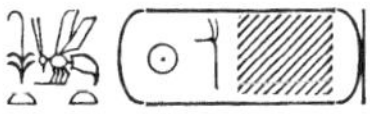

Turin Papyrus.

FIFTEENTH AND SIXTEENTH DYNASTIES. (HYKSOS.)

1. ... bȧnān.

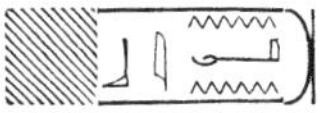

First Sallier Papyrus, p. 1, l. 7.

2. Ȧbeḥ-en-khepesh.

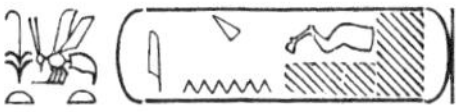

Turin Papyrus.

3. Rā-āa-user Ȧpepa.

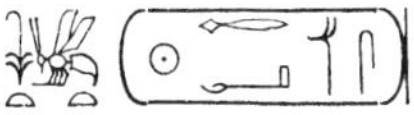

Rhind Papyrus, London, 1898, plate 1; tablet in the Berlin Museum.

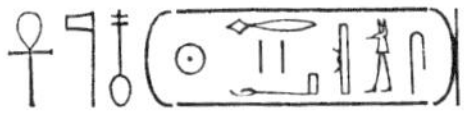

Part of a door in the Cairo Museum, No. 29238 (Daressy, *Recueil*, XIV, 27, No. XXX).

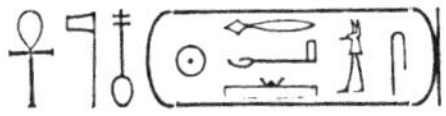

Naville, *Bubastis*, plates 22 and 35.

Turin Papyrus.

Naville, *Bubastis*, plates 22 and 25 ; tablet in the Berlin Museum (Eisenlohr, *P. S. B. A.*, 1881, p. 97).

4. *Rā-āa-qenen Ȧpepȧ.*

I. Horus name	SEḤETEP-TAUI.
II. N-U name	...
III. Golden Horus name	...
IV. Suten Bȧt name	RĀ-ĀA-QENEN.
V. Son of Rā name	ȦPEPȦ.

I. 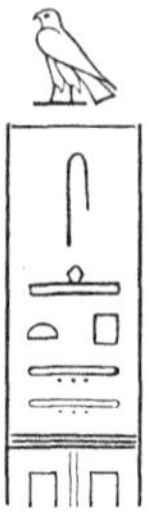

Mariette, *Mon. Div.*, plate 38.

IV. 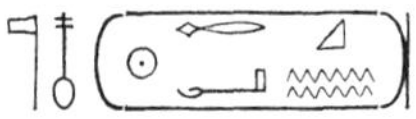

Mariette, *Mon. Div.*, plate 38.

V. 

Mariette, *Mon. Div.*, plate 38.

Ȧ ... ...

Turin Papyrus.

Rā-āa-seḥ.

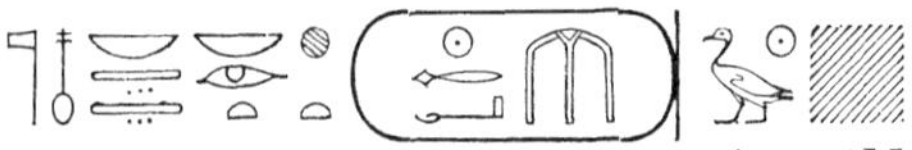

Obelisk found at Ṣân by Mariette (*Mon. Div.*, plate 103).

Per..., mother of *Rā-āa-seḥ.*

Obelisk found at Ṣân by Mariette (*Mon. Div.*, plate 103).

Set-āa-peḥti Nubti.

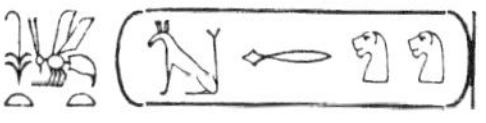

Stele of 400 years (E. de Rougé, *Rev. Arch.*, tome IX, 1864).

Stele of 400 years.

6. Khian.

I.	Horus name	ÅNQ ÅṬEBIU.
II.	N-U name	...
III.	Golden Horus name	...
IV.	Suten Båt name	RĀ-SEUSER-EN.
V.	Son of Rā name	KHIAN.

I. 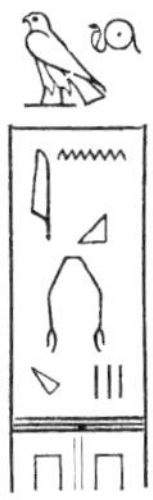

IV. 

Basalt lion, British Museum, No. 987; statue in Cairo (Naville, *Bubastis*, plate XII).

V. 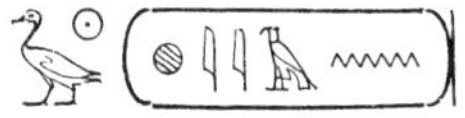

Basalt lion, British Museum, No. 987; statue in Cairo (Naville, *Bubastis*, plate XII).

7. *Rā-Ȧpepi.*

First Sallier Papyrus in the British Museum, No. 10185.

Rā-sebeq-ka.

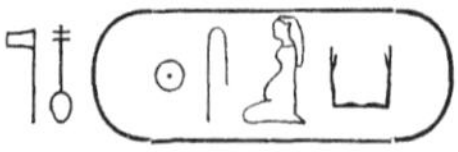

Petrie, *Illahun*, plate VIII, No. 36.

Sekhenen Rā-ka-Set.

Paste bead (Legrain, *Annales*, VI, 135).

Paste bead, Legrain, *Annales*, VI, 135.

Uḳḥuf (?).

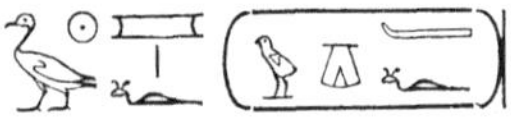

Seat of a statue (Legrain, *Annales*, VI, 130).

Rā-Uatch-ka.

Scarab in the British Museum, No. 40276.

Rā-en-ka.

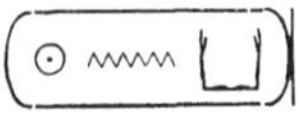

Scarab in the British Museum.

Uatcheṭ

 Scarab in the British Museum.

Ḥeru-Ipeq.

 Scarab in the British Museum.

Senbmȧiu.

 Fragment in the British Museum, No. 24898.

Rā-neb-uārt Ȧpep.

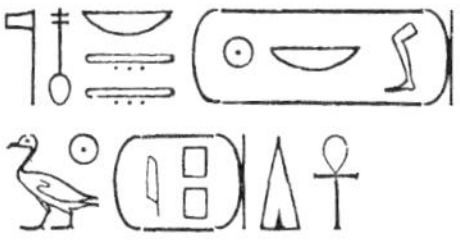 Dagger of Neḥemen , found in a coffin in the funerary temple of queen Ȧpuit at Ṣaḳḳârah by Loret in 1898. Daressy, *Annales du Service*, 1906, p. 115.

Sheshȧ, a prince.

 Scarabs in the British Museum, Nos. 41862, 41868.

Neb-neteru, a prince.

 Scarab in the British Museum, No. 42546.

Rā-āa-neter.

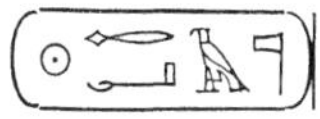 Scarabs in the British Museum, Nos. 38774, 40739.

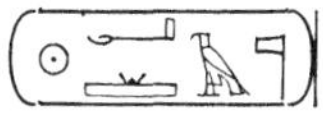 No. 40740.

 No. 38772.

Ȧpeq, a prince.

Scarab in the British Museum, No. 37669.

Seket-i, a prince.

Scarab in the British Museum, No. 37668.

Khen-tcher-āa-khā.

(*sic*) Scarab in the British Museum, No. 42716.

Nub-meri, a princess.

Scarab, 42710.

Rā-neb-ṭeṭ, a king (?).

Scarab in the British Museum, No. 37730.

The following names are taken from scarabs which appear to belong to the Hyksos period (see Newberry, *Scarabs,* plate XXI ff.); no chronological arrangement of them is at present possible.

Rā-Maā-ȧb, a king.

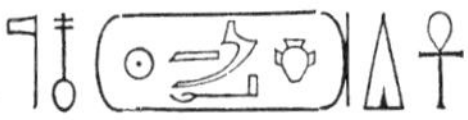

Rā-s-khā-en, a king.

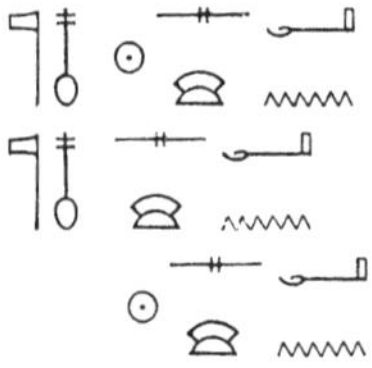

Qar, a prince.

Rā-Khā-user, a king.

Rā-Khā-mu, a king.

Rā-Āa-ḥetep, a king.

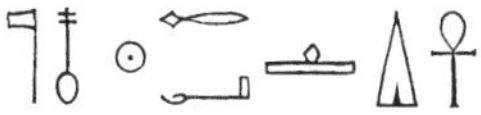

Iā-mu (?), a prince.

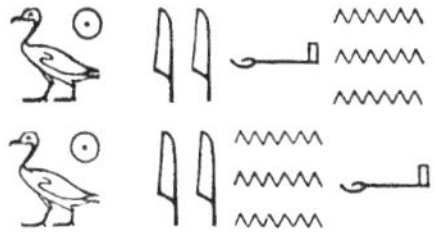

Ikeb, a prince.

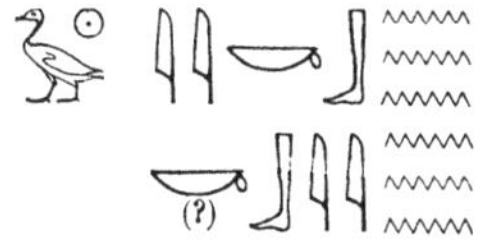

Āa-mu (?), a prince.

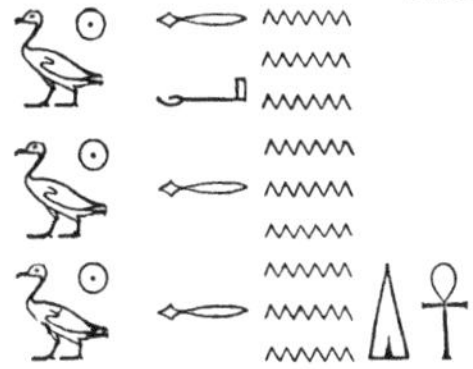

Rā-Nub-taui (?), a king.

Scarab in the British Museum, No. 30512.

Rā-User-en Khian, a king.

Rā-user-mer I-qeb-her (?), a king.

Neḥsi, a prince.

Ānt-her, a governor of countries.

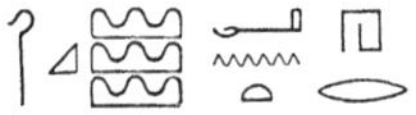

Semqen, a governor of countries.

Qupepen (?), a prince.

Tau-thȧ, a queen.

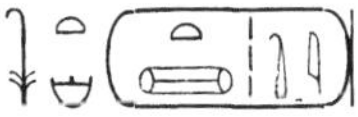

Uatchet, a queen.

Saket (?), a prince.

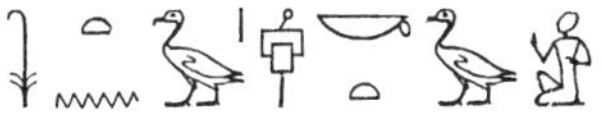

Ȧpepȧ, a prince.

Rā-āa-user (*Ȧpepȧ I*), a king.

Rā-nub-ka.

SEVENTEENTH DYNASTY. FROM THEBES.

1. Rā-seqenen (I) Tau-āa.

Abbott Papyrus.

Palette in the Louvre.

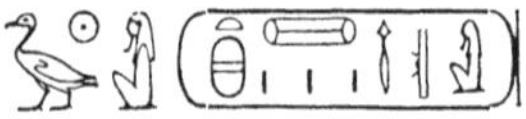

Abbott Papyrus.

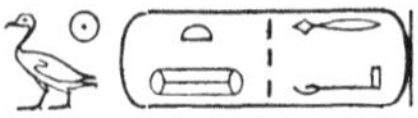

Boomerang in Cairo (Mariette, *Mon. Div.*, plate 51).

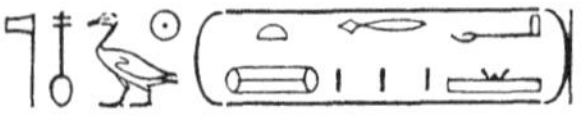

Bouriant, *Recueil*, XI, p. 159.

Āāḥ-ḥetep, wife of *Tau-āa.*

Bouriant, *Recueil*, XI, p. 159.

Thuȧu, son of *Tau-āa.*

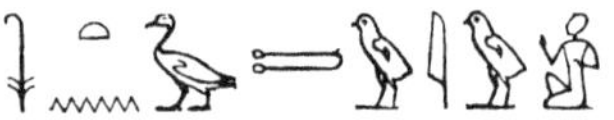

Boomerang in Cairo.

Āāḥ-mes, son of *Tau-āa.*

Bouriant, *Recueil*, XI, p. 159.

Āāḥ-mes, daughter of *Tau-āa.*

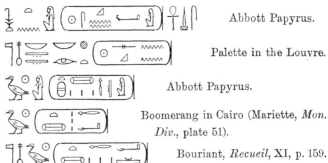

Bouriant, *Recueil*, XI, p. 159.

2. *Rā-seqenen (II) Tau-āa-āa.*

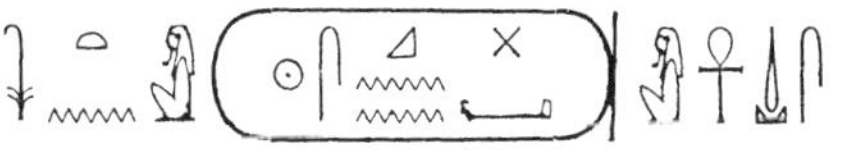

Abbott Papyrus.

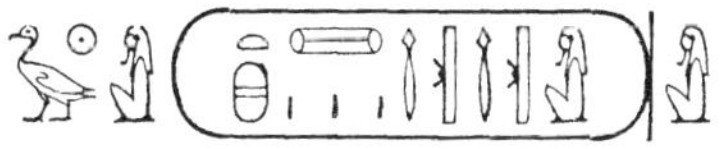

3. *Rā-seqenen (III) Tau-āa-qen.*

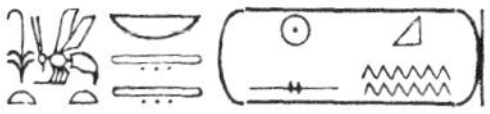

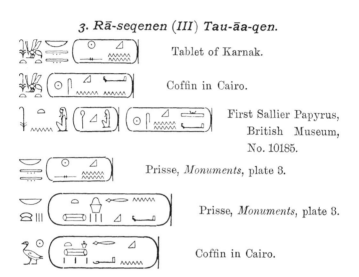

Tablet of Karnak.

Coffin in Cairo.

First Sallier Papyrus, British Museum, No. 10185.

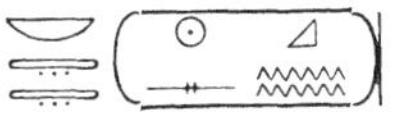

Prisse, *Monuments*, plate 3.

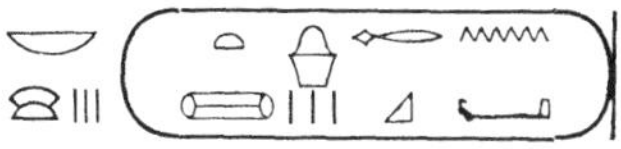

Prisse, *Monuments*, plate 3.

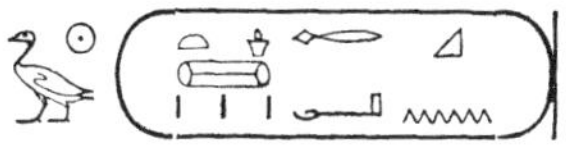

Coffin in Cairo.

Ȧāḥ-ḥetep, wife of *Tau-āa-qen.*

Prisse, *Monuments*, plate 3.

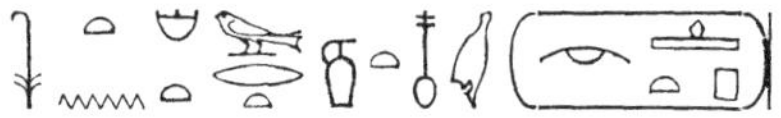

Coffin in Cairo.

Jewellery in Cairo.

4. *Rā-uatch-kheper Ka-mes,*
son of *Ȧāḥ-ḥetep* by first husband.

Abbott Papyrus.

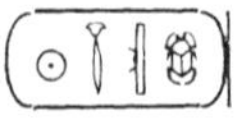
Boat of Ȧāḥ-ḥetep in Cairo.

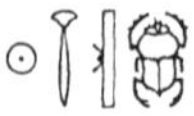
Spear in the Evans Collection.

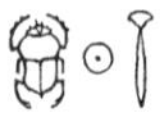
Scarabs in the British Museum, Nos. 42876, 42929.

Abbott Papyrus.

Spear in the Evans Collection.

Boat of Ȧāḥ-ḥetep.

Axe-head in the British Museum, No. 5241 *a*.

Rā-sekhent-neb, son of *Ȧāḥ-ḥetep.*

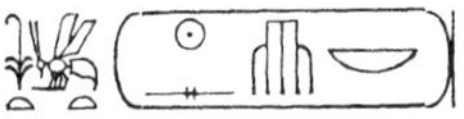
Altar at Marseilles (Maspero, *Catalogue*, 1889, p. 3).

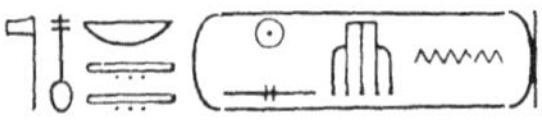
Prisse, *Monuments*, plate 3.

Tablet of Karnak.

Altar at Marseilles.

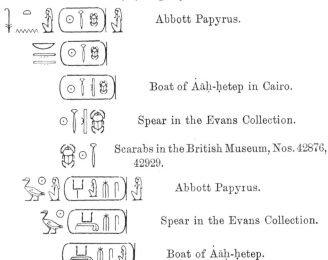

Ȧāḥmes-sa-pa-ȧri.

 Abbott Papyrus.

Binpu, a prince.

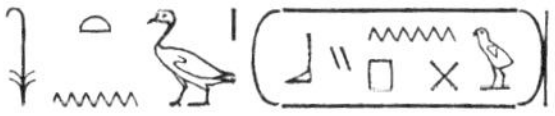 Prisse, *Monuments*, plate 3.

 Statuette in Cairo.

Uatch-mes, a prince.

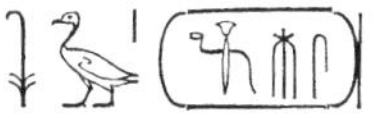 *Annales*, I, 101.

 Prisse, *Monuments*, plate 3.

Ȧmen-mes, a prince.

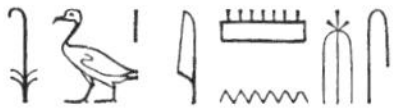 Prisse, *Monuments*, plate 3.

Rā-mes, a prince.

 Prisse, *Monuments*, plate 3.

Nebenḳal, a prince.

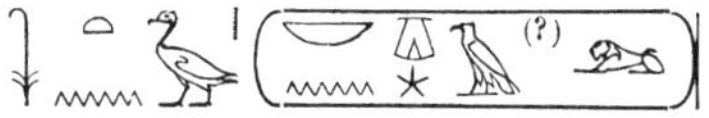 Prisse, *Monuments*, plate 3.

Ȧāḥmes, a prince.

 Prisse, *Monuments*, plate 3.

Kames, a prince.

 Prisse, *Monuments*, plate 3.

Ta-àri-baiu, **a queen.**

 Prisse, *Monuments*, plate 3.

Ta-khart̤-qa, **a queen.**

 Prisse, *Monuments*, plate 3.

EIGHTEENTH DYNASTY. FROM THEBES.

1. Àāḥmes I.

I. Horus name	UATCH-KHEPERU.
II. N-U name	TUT-MESTU.
III. Golden Horus name	THES-TAUI.
IV. Suten Båt name	RĀ-NEB PEḤTI.
V. Son of Rā name	ÀĀḤMES.

I. 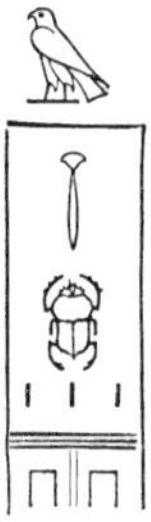 Axe in the Museum at Cairo.

II.  Axe in the Museum at Cairo.

III. 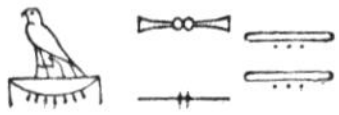 Axe in the Museum at Cairo.

IV.  L. D., III, 3 *a*.

 Jewellery in Cairo; ushabti in the British Museum, No. 32191.

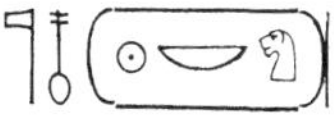 L. D., III, 39 *e*.

 Coffin in Cairo.

 Prisse, *Monuments*, plate 3.

 Abydos List, No. 66.

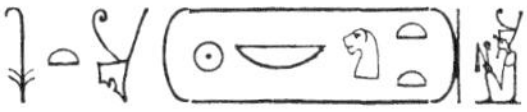 Second Abydos List, No. 40.

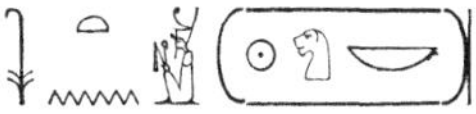 Tablet of Ṣaḳḳârah.

V.  Jewellery in Cairo; ushabti in the British Museum, No. 32191.

 Jewellery in Cairo.

 Coffin in Cairo.

 Prisse, *Monuments*, plate 3.

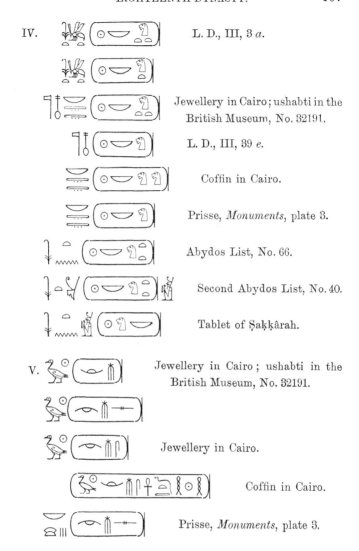

Ȧāḥmes Nefert-ȧri,
daughter of *Tau-āa-qen* and *Ȧāḥ-ḥetep,* and wife of *Ȧāḥmes I.*

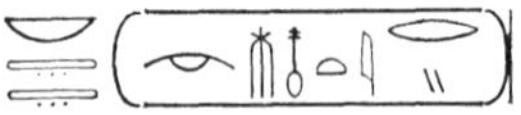
L. D., III, 1.

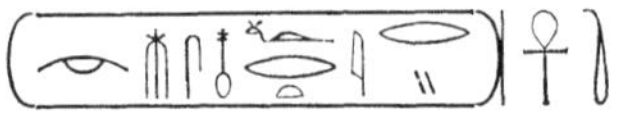
Coffin in Cairo.

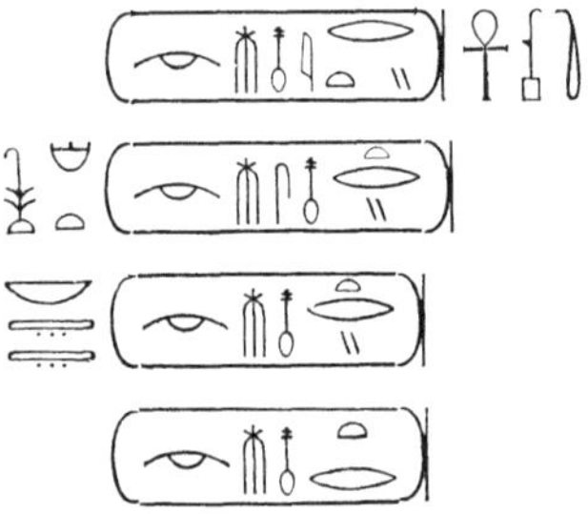

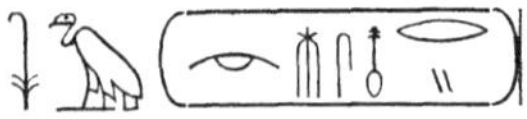
Coffin in Cairo.

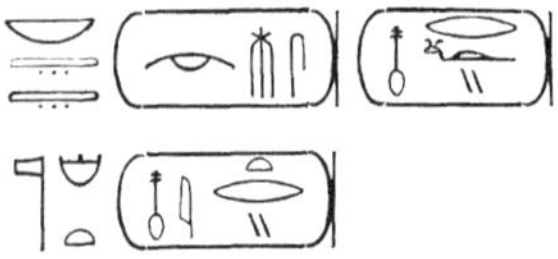

Àāḥ-ḥetep, daughter of *Nefert-àri.*

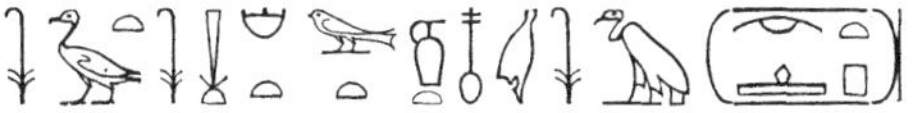

Coffin in Cairo.

Maspero, *Momies Royales*, p. 545.

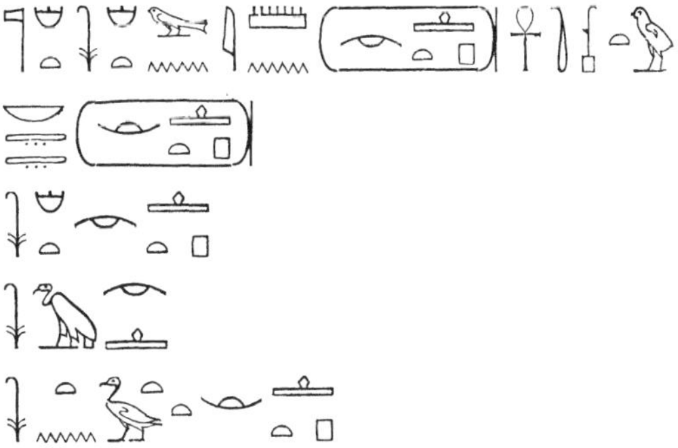

Àmen-mert, or *Àmen-merit,* daughter of *Nefert-àri.*

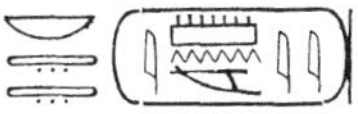

Coffin in Cairo.

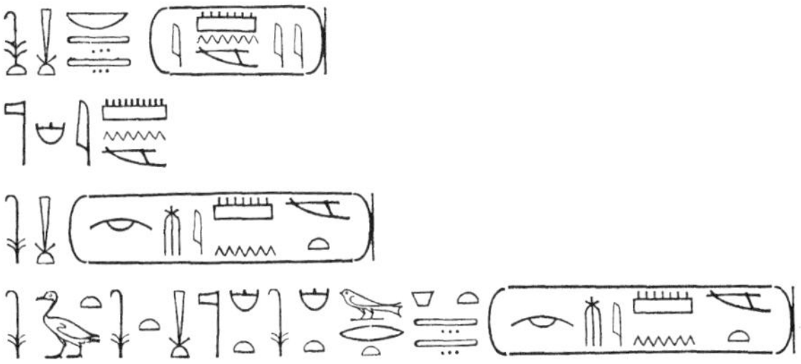

Àmen-sat, daughter of *Nefert-àri.*

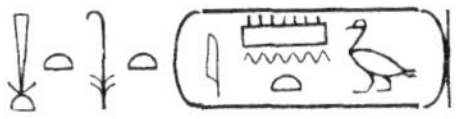

Prisse, *Monuments*, plate 3.

Coffin in Cairo.

Sat-ka-mes, daughter of *Nefert-ȧri.*

Maspero, *Momies Royales*, p. 541.

Sa-pa-ȧri, or *Ȧāḥmes-sa-pa-ȧri,* son of *Nefert-ȧri.*

Maspero, *Momies Royales*, p. 641.

Ȧmen-ḥetep,
son of *Nefert-ȧri* (became *Ȧmen-ḥetep I*).

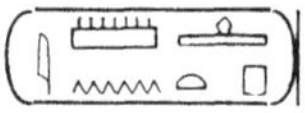

Thent-Ḥep, a wife of *Ȧāḥmes I.*

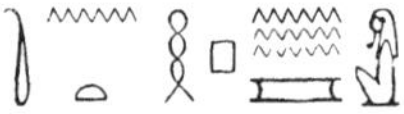

Maspero, *Momies Royales*, p. 544.

Ḥent-Themeḥu, daughter of *Thent-Ḥep.*

Maspero, *Momies Royales*, pp. 543, 544.

Ȧn-Ḥep, a wife of *Ȧāḥmes I.*

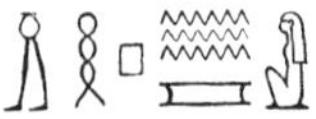

Ḥent-ta-meḥ, daughter of *Ȧn-Ḥep.*

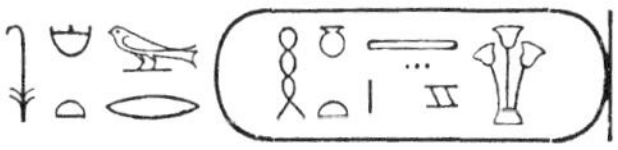

Prisse, *Monuments*, plate 3.

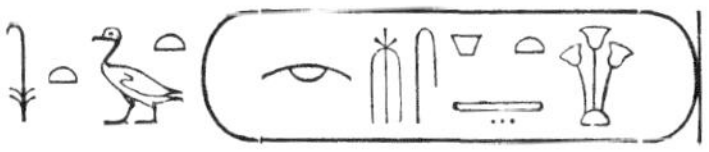

Maspero, *Momies Royales*, p. 622.

Kasmut, a wife of *Ȧāḥmes I.*

Prisse, *Monuments*, plate 3.

Ta-ȧrn, daughter of *Kasmut.*

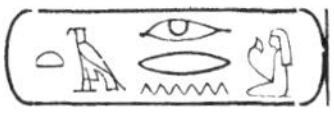

L. D., III, 2.

Ȧmen-sa, a prince, son of *Ȧāḥmes I.*

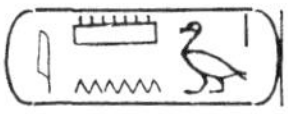

Coffin in Cairo.

Tures, daughter of *Ȧāḥmes I.*

Prisse, *Monuments*, plate 3.

Ȧāḥmes, a princess, daughter of *Ȧāḥmes I.*

Prisse, *Monuments*, plate 3.

Ȧāḥmes-nebt-ta, a princess.

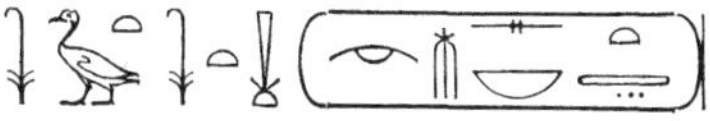

Ȧmen-ḥetep I.

I. Horus name — KA-UĀF.
II. N-U name — ...
III. Golden Horus name — ...
IV. Suten Bȧt name — RĀ-TCHESER-KA.
V. Son of Rā name — ȦMEN-ḤETEP.

I.  Limestone statue in the British Museum, No. 683.

IV. 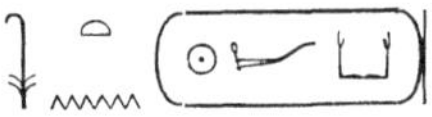 Abydos List, No. 67.

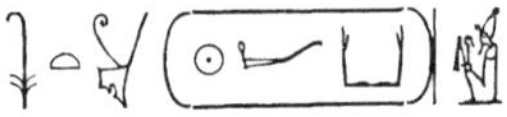 Second Abydos List, No. 41.

 Tablet of Ṣaḳḳârah.

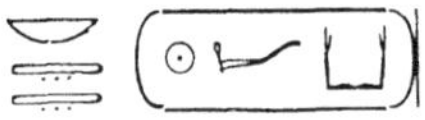 Prisse, *Monuments*, plate 3.

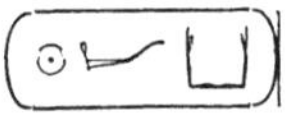 Brick, L. D., III, 4 *b*.

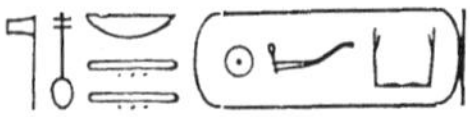 Stele, L. D., III, 4 *e*.

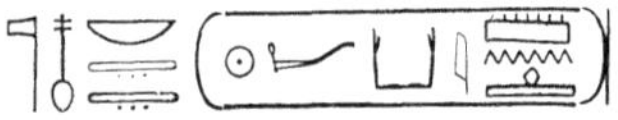 L. D., III, 4 *e*.

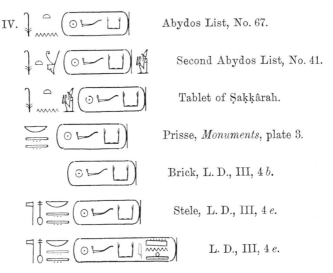

L. D., III, 4 *e*.

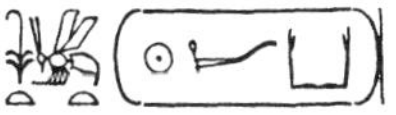
Temple at Karnak.

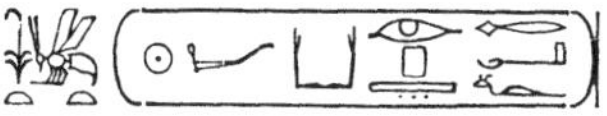

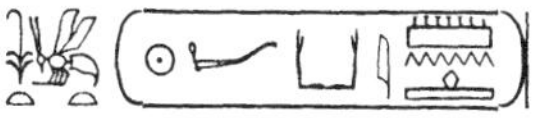
L. D., III, 4.

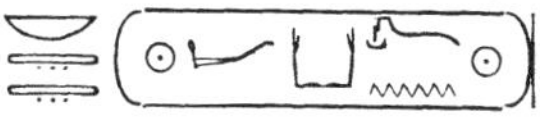

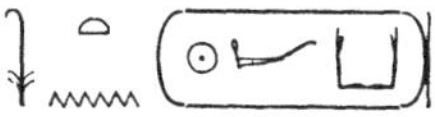
Coffin in Cairo.

V. 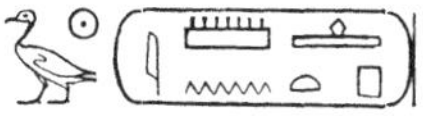
L. D., III, 4.

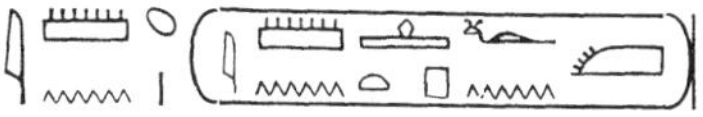
Coffin in Cairo.

Abbott Papyrus.

Thothmes I.

I. Horus names

1. KA-NEKHT-MERI MAĀT.
2. KA-NEKHT-EN-RĀ.
3. KA-NEKHT-RĀ-EN-QEMT.
4. KA-NEKHT-ĀNKH-EM-MAĀT.
5. KA-NEKHT-PEḤTI-MȦ-ȦMEN.

6. KA-NEKHT-UR-BAIU.
7. RĀ-MERI-KHĀ-EM-ḤETCHET.

II. N-U names
1. KHĀ-EM-NESERT-PEḤTI.
2. KHĀ-EM-NESERT-ĀA-PEḤTI.
3. THET-TAIU-NEB.
4. TEM-ṬUA-KHĀ-KHĀU.

III. Golden Horus names
1. NEFER-RENPUT-SĀNKH-ȦBU.
2. ḤU-PEṬI.
3. ĀA - PEḤTI - USR - KHEPESH-UATCH - RENPUT - EM - ḤET - ĀA-MAĀT.

IV. Suten Bȧt name — RĀ-ĀA-KHEPER-KA; and with the additions: SETEP-EN-RĀ, ȦRI-EN-RĀ, TȦA-ȦMEN, MER-EN-RĀ, etc.

V. Son of Rā name — TEḤUTI-MES; and with the additions: KHĀ-MȦ-RĀ, KHĀ-NEFERU, ȦRI-EN-ȦMEN, SETEP-EN-ȦMEN, MERI-ȦMEN.

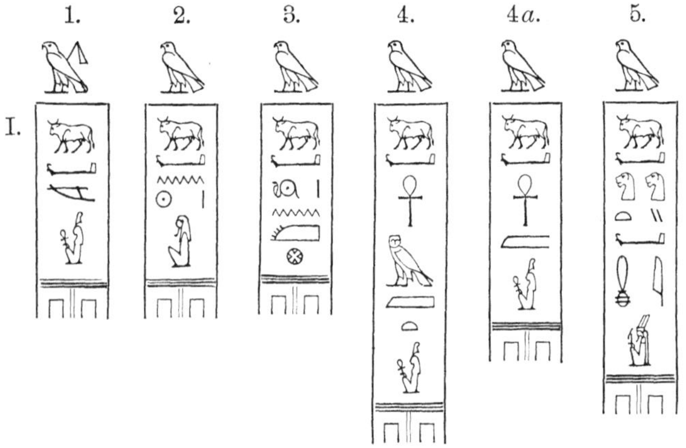

6. 7.

Tombos Inscription, L. D., III, 5; and Obelisk at Thebes, L. D., III, 6.

II. 1. 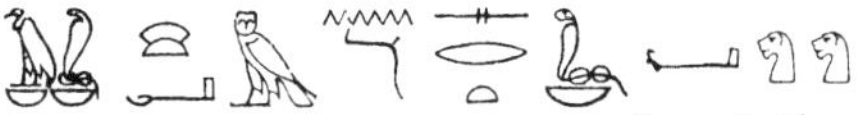 Tombos Inscription, L. D., III, 5.

2.  Obelisk *o*, L. D., III, 6.

3. 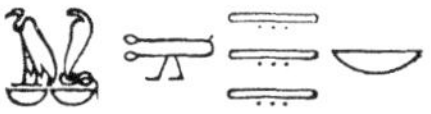 Obelisk *s*, L. D., III, 6.

4.  Obelisk *n*, L. D., III, 6.

III. 1. 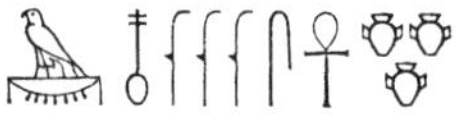 Tombos Inscription, L. D., III, 5.

2.  Obelisk *s*, L. D., III, 6.

3. 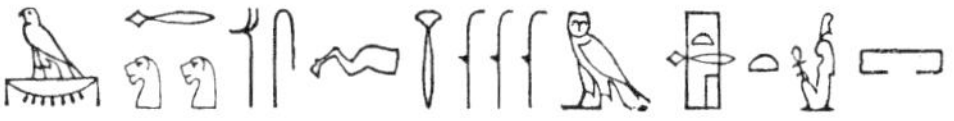 Obelisk *n*, L. D., III, 6.

IV. 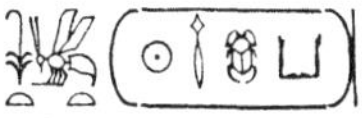 Tombos Inscription, L. D., III, 5; and Obelisk, L. D., III, 6.

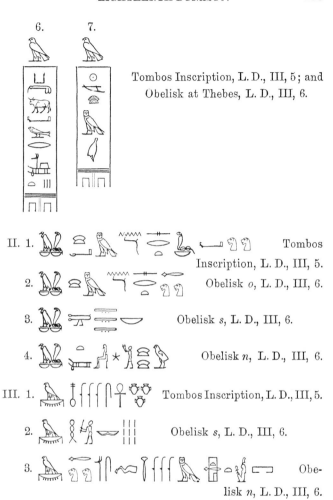

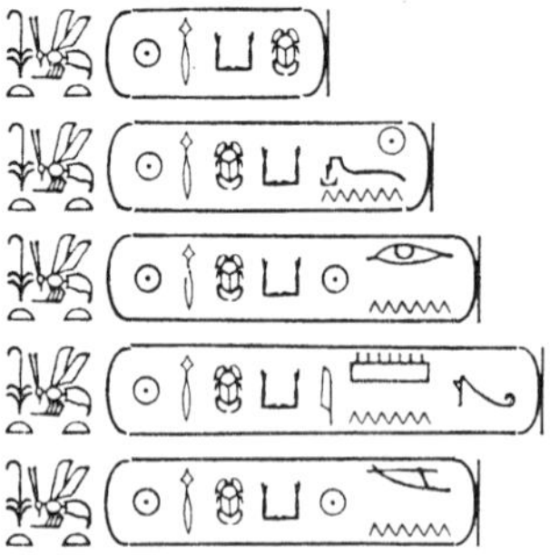

Abydos List, No. 68.

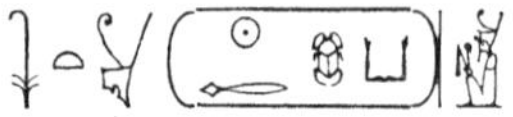

Second Abydos List, No. 47.

V. 

Tombos Inscription, L. D., III, 5; and Obelisk, L. D., III, 6.

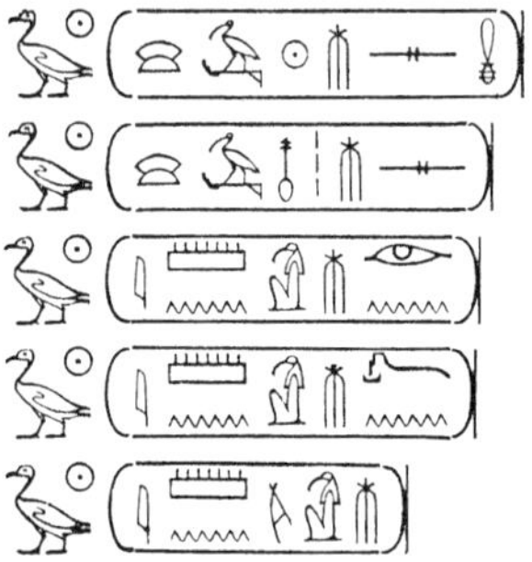

Àāḥmes, a wife of *Thothmes I.*

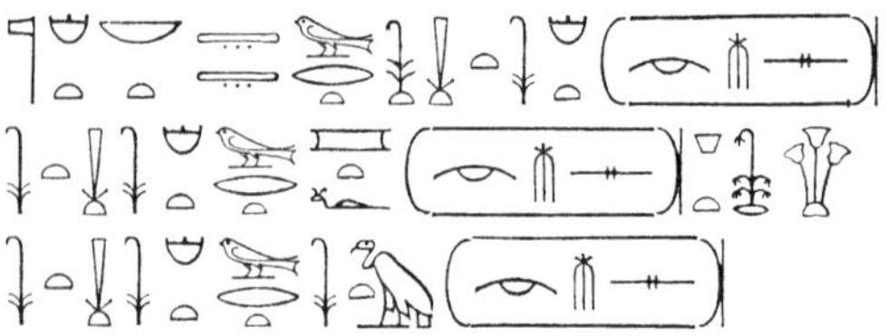

Temple of Dêr al-Baḥarî; and L. D., III, 8.

Ḥāt-shepset,
daughter of *Thothmes I* and queen *Åāḥmes.*

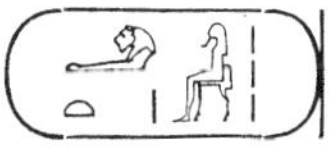

Khebit-neferu, daughter of *Thothmes I* and *Åāḥmes.*

 L. D., III, 8.

Mut-nefert,
wife of *Thothmes I* and mother of *Thothmes II.*

 *Aeg. Zeit.*, 1887, p. 125.

 Mariette, *Karnak*, pl. 38 *b*, 4.

 *Annales du Service*, I, 98.

Åmen-ḥetep, a prince.

 L. D., III, 9 *f.*

Åāḥ-ḥetep, a royal mother and queen.

Thothmes II.

I. Horus name — KA-NEKHT-USR-PEḤTI.
II. N-U name — NETER-SUTENIT.
III. Golden Horus name — SEKHEM-KHEPERU.
IV. Suten Båt name — RĀ-ĀA-KHEPER-EN.
V. Son of Rā name — TEḤUTI-MES.

I.  Pylon at Karnak, L. D., III, 16; Inscription at Aswân, L. D., III, 16 *a*.

II. 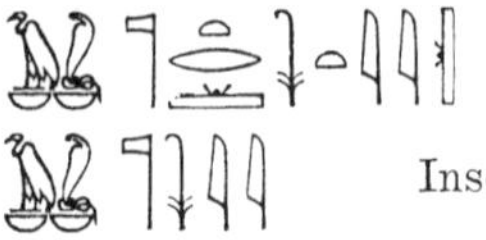 Inscription at Aswân, L. D., III, 16 *a*.

III.  Inscription at Aswân, L. D., III, 16 *a*.

IV. 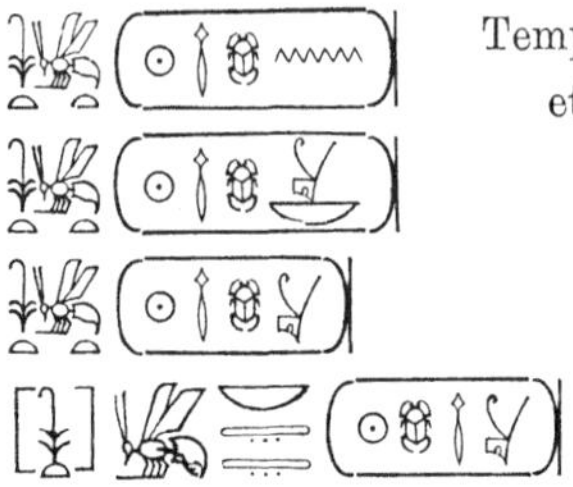 Temples at Dêr al-Baḥarî, Karnak, etc.; see L. D., III, 14—17, 20.

 Abydos List, No. 69.

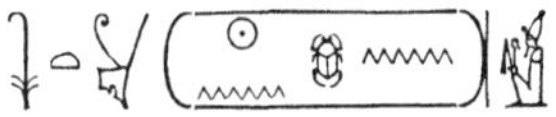 Second Abydos List, No. 43.

V. 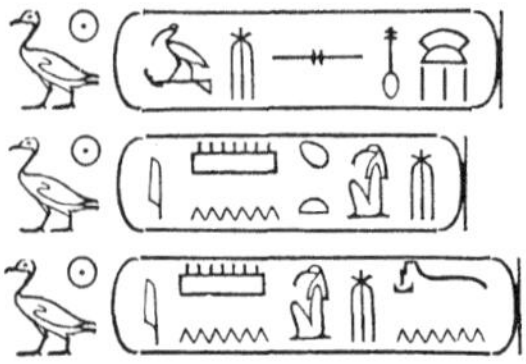 Temples at Madînat Habû, Karnak, Dêr al-Baḥarî, rock inscription at Aswân, etc., L. D., III, 14—16; coffin and mummy at Cairo, etc.

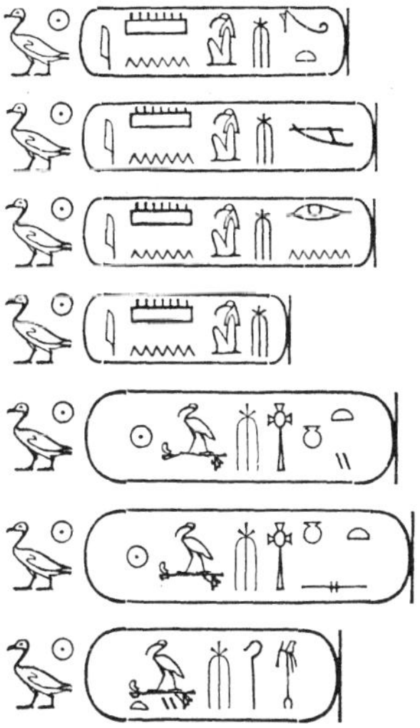

Ḥātshepset, wife of *Thothmes II.*

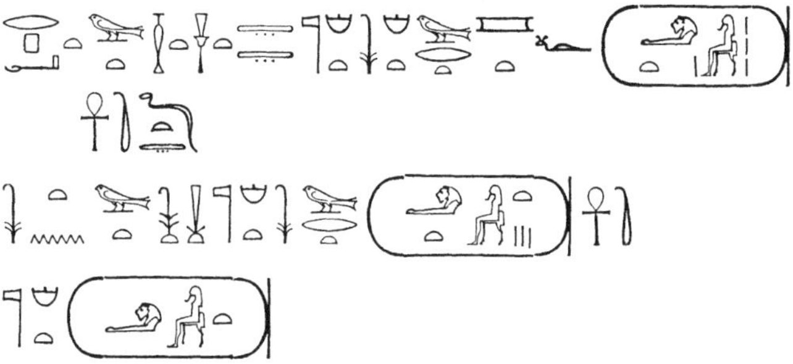

Ȧst,

a wife of *Thothmes II* and mother of *Thothmes III.*

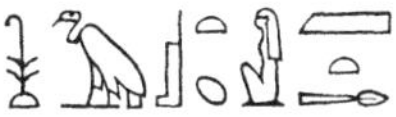

Mummy bandage of Thothmes III (Maspero, *Momies*, p. 548).

Ḥātshepset.

I. Horus name	USERT-KAU. [TAIU-NEBU.
II. N-U name	UATCHET - RENPUT. THET-
III. Golden Horus name	NETERT-KHĀU. SĀNKH-ÀBU.
IV. Suten Bȧt name	RĀ-MAĀT-KA.
V. Daughter of Rā name (?)	ḤĀT-SHEPSET.

I. 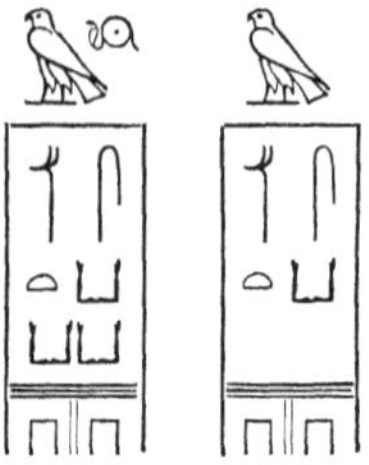

Obelisks at Karnak, L. D., III, 22, 23, 24.

II. 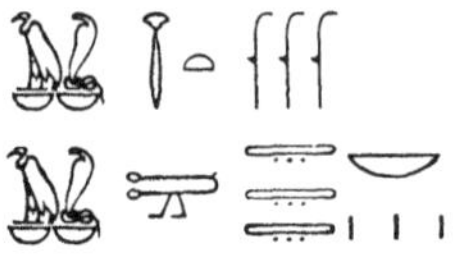

Obelisks at Karnak, L. D., III, 24; and see the texts in Naville, *Deir el-Bahari*, vols. 1—5.

III. 

IV. 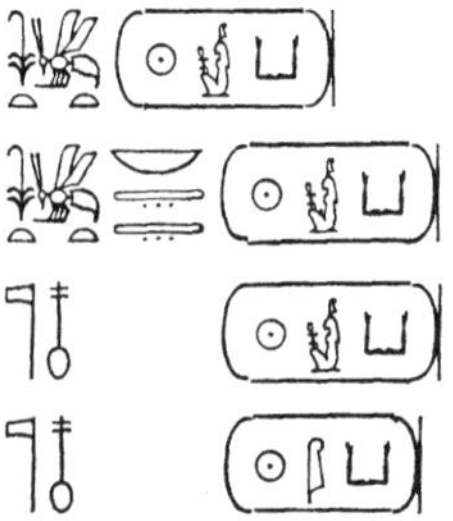

Obelisks at Karnak, L. D., III, 22—24; alabaster vases from Abydos in Cairo; temple at Dêr al-Baḥarî (ed. Naville); statue at Ḳûrna, etc.

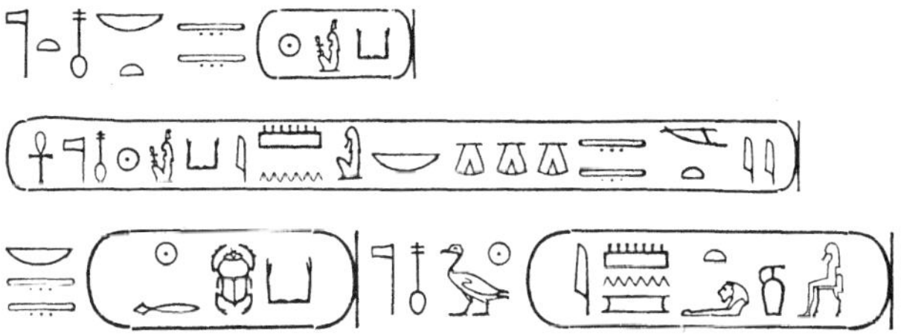

Lepsius, *Königsbuch*, No. 347.

L. D., III, 25 bis, *i*.

V. 

Rā-neferu, a queen.

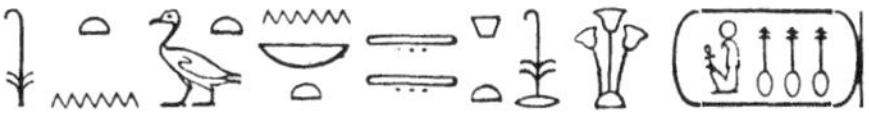

L. D., III, 20.

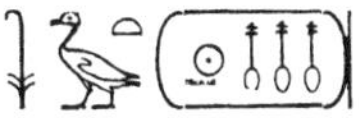

L. D., III, 25 bis, *n*.

Ȧnebni, a prince.

Sen, a prince, governor of Nubia.

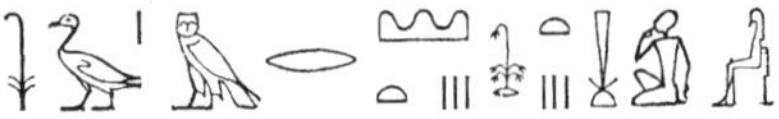

Thothmes III.[1]

I. Horus names 1—3. Ka-nekht-khā-em-Uast.

4, 5. Ka-nekht-khā-em-Maāt.

6. Ka-nekht-khā-em-Maāt-neb-ȧri-khet-Rā-men-kheper.

7. Ka-nekht-ḥā-em-Maāt.

8, 9. Ka-nekht-Rā-meri.

10—14. Ḥetch-qa-Rā-meri.

II. N-U names 1—6. Uaḥ-sutenit, or Uaḥ-sutenit-mȧ-Rā-em-pet.

7. Sekhā-Maāt-meri-taui.

8. Āa-shefit-em-taiu-neb.

III. Golden Horus names

1—4. Tcheser-khāu-sekhem-peḥti.

5, 6. Āa-khepesh-ḥu-peṭ-paut.

7. Her-ḥer-nekht-ḥu-ḥequ-semti.

IV. Suten Bȧt name Rā-men-kheper.[2] With additions: Ȧri-en-Rā, Setep-en-Rā, Mer-en-Rā, Ḥeq-Maāt, Ḥeq-Maāt-tȧa-Rā, Tȧa-Ȧmen, Rā-sāa-en, Nekht-

1. See L. D., III, 29 ff.; Mariette, *Karnak*; Naville, *Deir el-Bahari*, etc.

2. In cuneiform,

Ma-na-akh-bi-ya ,

and Ma-na-akh-bi-ir-ya .

KHEPESH, NEB-NEKHT, KA, ḤEQ-UAST, NETER-NEFER-KA.

V. Son of Rā name TEḤUTI-MES. With additions: NEFER-KHEPER, NEFER-KHEPERU, SMA-KHEPER, NEFER-KHĀU, ḤEQ-MAĀT, ḤEQ-UAST, ḤEQ-ÀNNU, NETER-ḤEQ, SEKHĀ-NEFER.

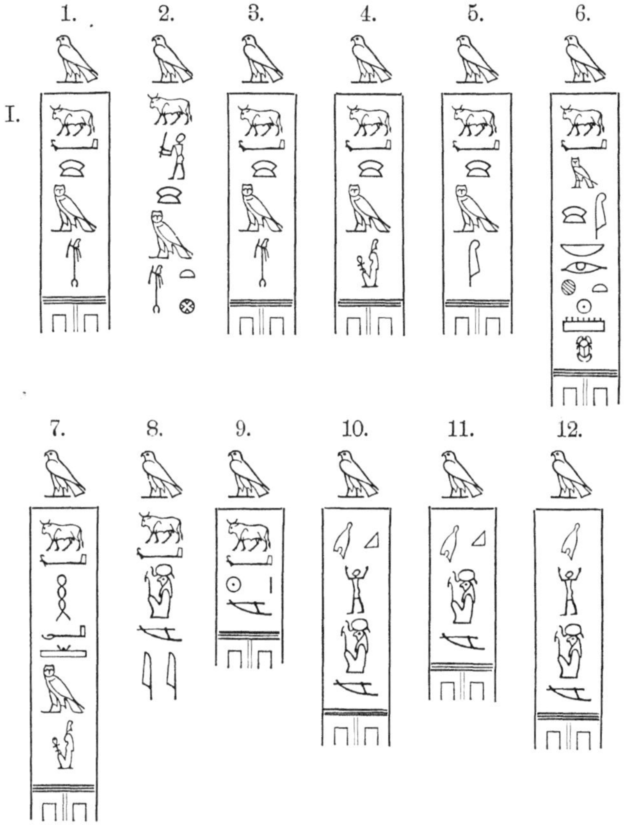

13. 14.

Temple at Karnak, Temple at Kummah, Temple at Ṣaḳḳârah, Obelisks at Rome, Constantinople, London, New York, etc. See L. D., III, 29, 37, 38, 60, 65; Gorringe, *Obelisks*; Mariette, *Karnak*, 38; etc.

II. 1.–8.

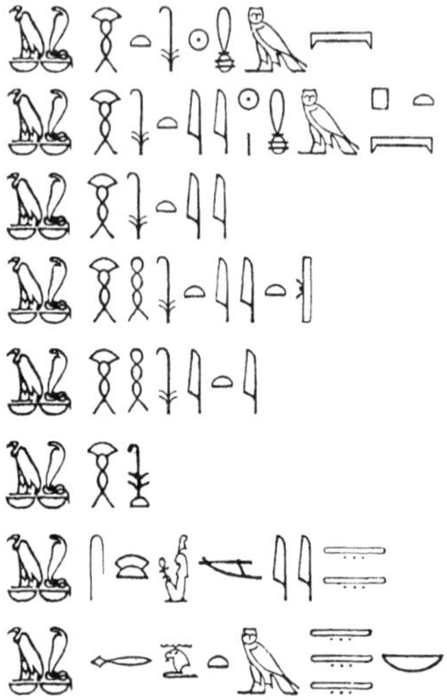

[See above mentioned authorities.]

III. 1.–2.

[See above mentioned authorities.]

3.
4.
5.
6.
7.

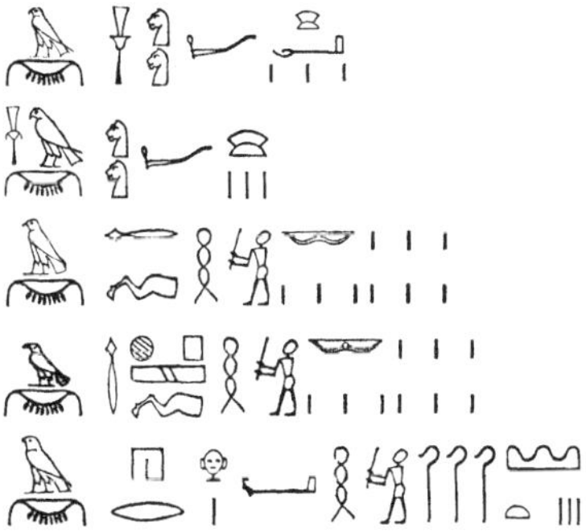

IV. [See above mentioned authorities.]

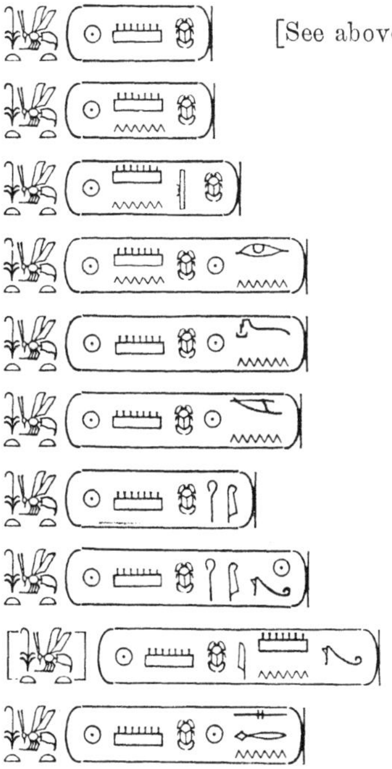

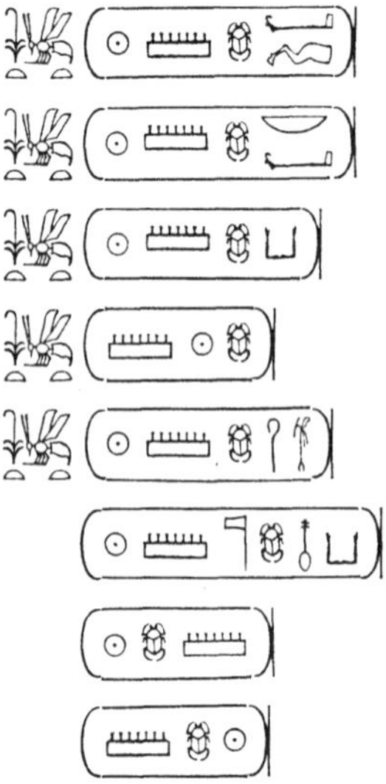

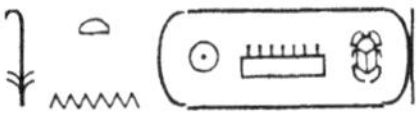 Abydos List, No. 70.

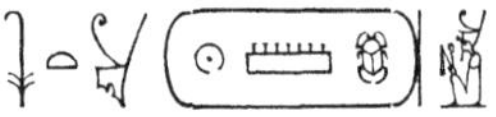 Second Abydos List, No. 44.

V.  [See above mentioned authorities.]

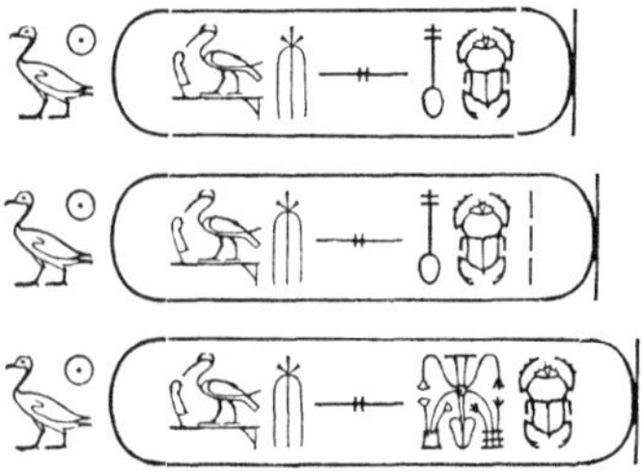

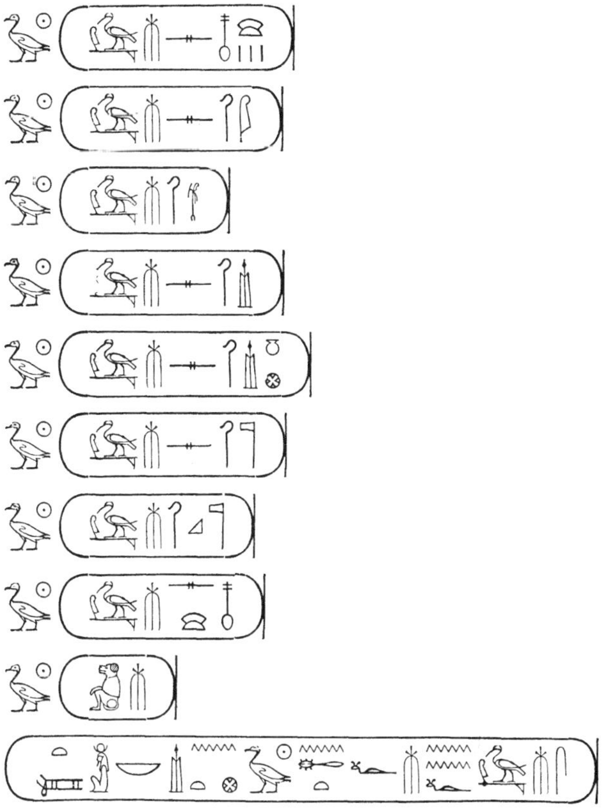

Mert-Rā Ḥātshepset,

daughter of *Ḥātshepset,* and wife of *Thothmes III.*

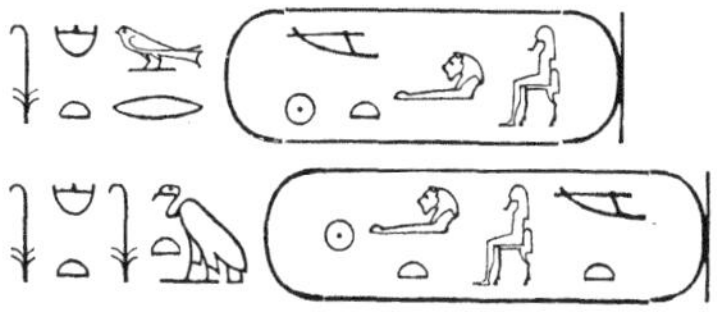

L. D., III, 38 *a* and *b*, and 62—64.

Åst, mother of *Thothmes III.*

 Maspero, *Momies,* p. 548.

Åāḥ-sat, a wife of *Thothmes III.*

 *Annales,* III, 108.

Nebtu, a wife of *Thothmes III.*

 Tomb of Neb-Åmen (Bouriant, *Recueil,* IX, p. 97).

Mersekẹr, a wife of *Thothmes III.*

 Temple at Semnah, L. D., III, 55 *a,* line 12.

Nebåu, daughter of princess *Sa-Tem.*

Birch, *Two Papyri,* XII, 1.

Taui, a princess.

 Birch, *Two Papyri,* XII, 2.

Thå-kheta (?), a princess.

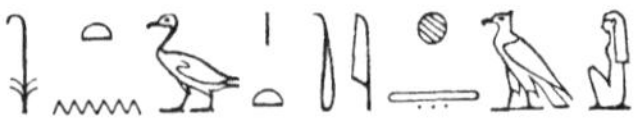 (?) Birch, *Two Papyri,* XII, 3.

Pet-ka-åa, a princess.

 Birch, *Two Papyri,* XII, 4.

Petpui, surnamed *Ta- ... àui,* a princess.

Birch, *Two Papyri,* XII, 6.

Ptaḥ-merit, a princess.

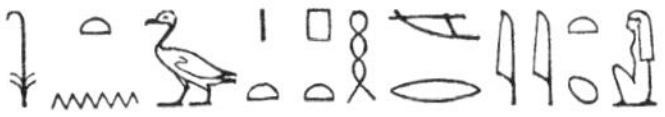

Birch, *Two Papyri,* XII, 9.

Sat-Ḥeruà, a princess.

Birch, *Two Papyri,* XII, 10.

Nefer-Àmen, a princess.

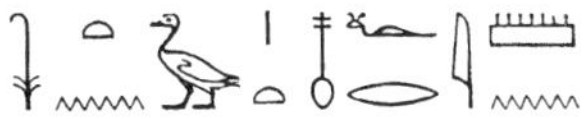

Birch, *Two Papyri,* XII, 11.

Uàai, a princess.

Birch, *Two Papyri,* XII, 12.

Ḥenut-Ànnu, a princess.

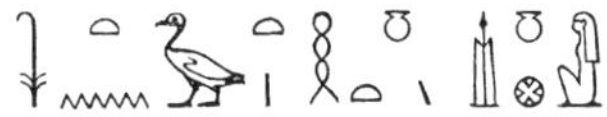

Birch, *Two Papyri,* XII, 14.

Neḥi, a prince, governor of Nubia.

L. D., III, 47 *a.*

Àmen-ḥetep II.

I. Horus name	KA-NEKHT-UR-PEḤTI.
II. N-U name	USR-F-ÀU-SEKHĀ-EM-UAST.
III. Golden Horus name	THET-SEKHEM-F-EM-TAIU-NEBU.
IV. Suten Bàt name	RĀ-ĀA-KHEPERU.
V. Son of Rā name	ÀMEN-ḤETEP. With additions: ḤEQ-ÀNNU, ḤEQ-UAST.

9

I.

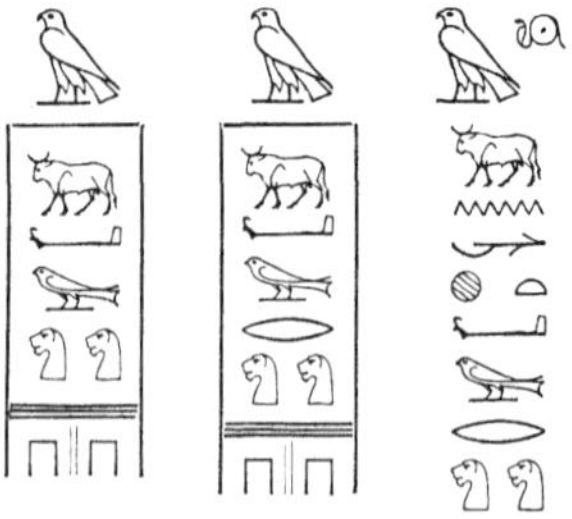

Pylon at Thebes, L. D., III, 61; Stele at Amâda, L. D., III, 65; Temple at Kummah, L. D., III, 66 ff.

II.

Stele at Amâda, L. D., III, 65; Temple at Kummah, L. D., III, 66 ff.

III.

Stele at Amâda, L. D., III, 65; Temple at Kummah, L. D., III, 66 ff.

IV.

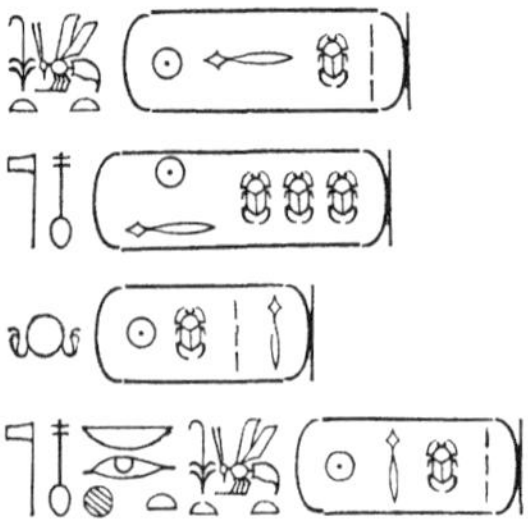

Pylon at Thebes, L. D., III, 61; Stele at Amâda, L. D., III, 65; Temple at Kummah, L. D., III, 66 ff.; Bouriant, *Recueil*, VII, 29.

Statue in Berlin, L. D., III, 70.

Abydos List, No. 71.

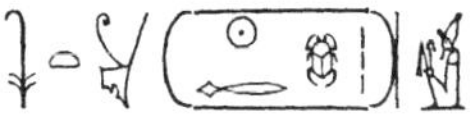
Second Abydos List, No. 45.

V. 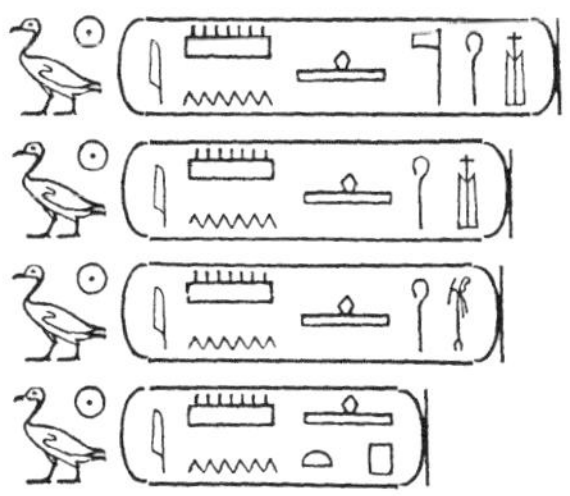
Bricks, L. D., III, 62; Pylon at Thebes, L. D., III, 61; Bouriant, *Recueil*, VII, 29.

User-Satet, a prince, governor of Nubia.

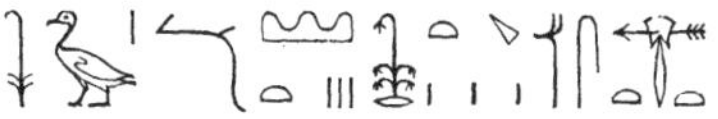

Khā-em-Uast, a prince.

Khā-em-Uast, a prince, high-priest of Nekhebit.

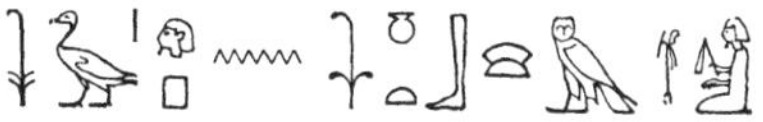

Ȧmen-ḥetep, a prince, high-priest of Nekhebit.

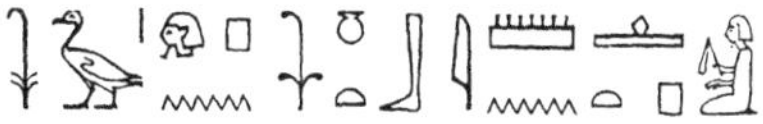

Teḥuti-mes, a prince, high-priest of Nekhebit.

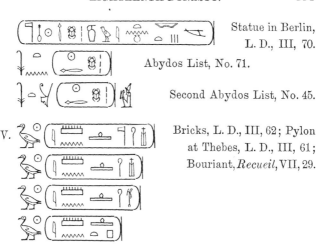

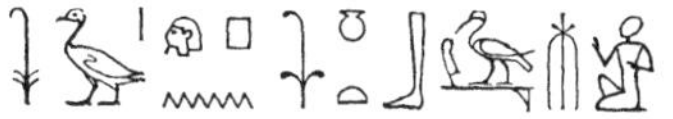

Ȧāḥmes,

surnamed *Pen-Nekhebit,* high-priest of Nekhebit.

Both his brother and his son held the same title; their names are unknown.

Ȧmen-ḥetep,

surnamed *Ḥāpu,* high-priest of Nekhebit.

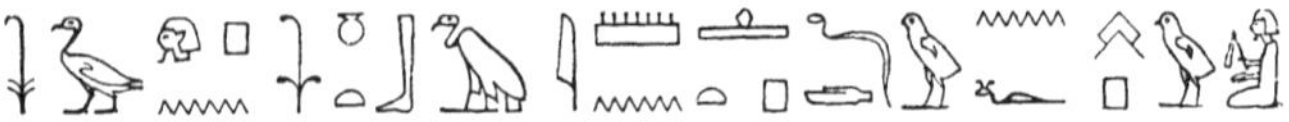

Thothmes IV.

I. Horus name	KA-NEKHT-TUT-KHĀU.
II. N-U name	ṬEṬṬEṬ SUTENIT-MȦ-TEM.
III. Golden Horus name	USER-KHEPESH-ṬER-PEṬ-PAUT.
IV. Suten Bȧt name	RĀ-MEN-KHEPERU. With additions: ḤEQ-MAĀT, KA, MER-EN-RĀ, ȦRI-EN-RĀ, SETEP-EN-RĀ.
V. Son of Rā name	TEḤUTI-MES.

I.

Tablet of the Sphinx, L. D., III, 68; Tablet at Konosso, L. D., III, 69.

II. 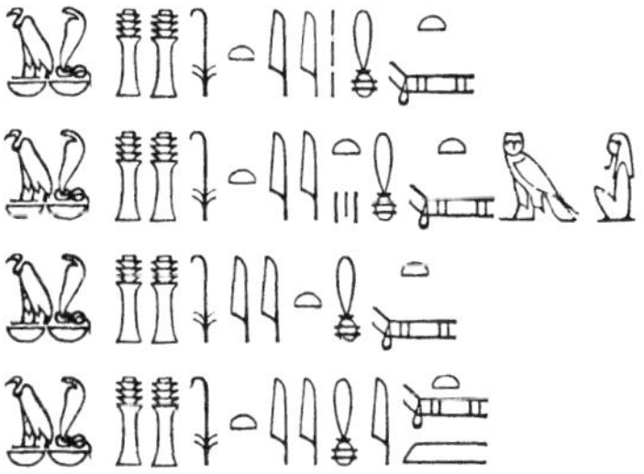

Tablet of the Sphinx, L. D., III, 68; Tablet at Konosso, L. D., III, 69.

III. 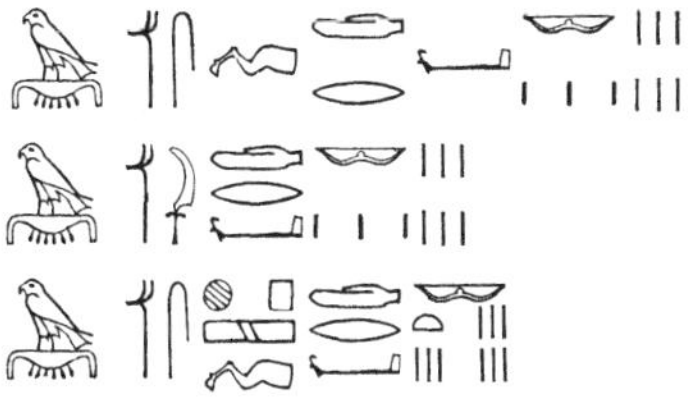

Tablet of the Sphinx, L. D., III, 68; Tablet at Konosso, L. D., III, 69.

IV. 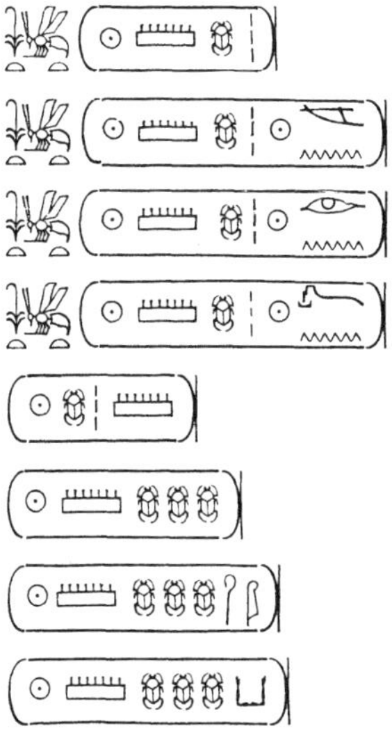

Tablet of the Sphinx, L. D., III, 68; Tablet at Konosso, Bricks, etc., L. D., III, 69.

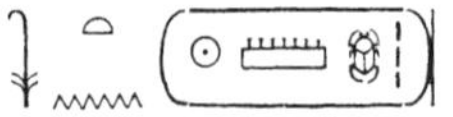

Abydos List, No. 72.

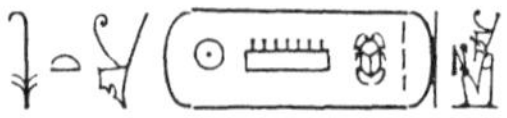

Second Abydos List, No. 46.

V. 

Tablet of the Sphinx, L. D., III, 68; Tablet at Konosso, L. D., III, 69.

Mut-em-uȧa, a royal wife.

L. D., III, 70 bis.

Mut-em-uȧa, a queen.

Boat in the British Museum, No. 43.

Ārat (?), a royal daughter, royal sister, and royal wife.

L. D., III, 69 *e*.

Teḥuti-mes, a prince.

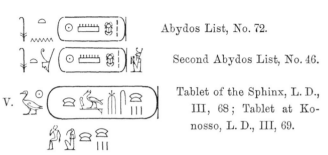

Stele of the Sphinx, L. D., III, 68.

Ȧmen-ḥetep, a prince (*Ȧmen-ḥetep III*).

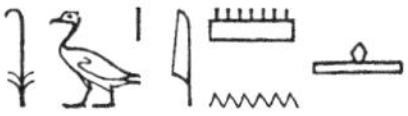

Rā-āa-kheperu, a prince.

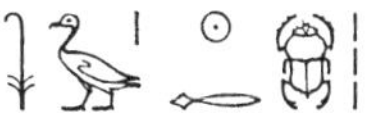

Lepsius, *Königsbuch*, No. 370.

Thāa, a queen.

Lepsius, *Königsbuch*, No. 371.

Ȧmen-ḥetep III.

I. Horus names
1. KA-NEKHT-KHĀ-EM-MAĀT.
2. SMA-ḤETCHET-MER-ȦNNU.
3. UAḤ-RENPUT-ĀSHT-ḤEBU.
4. KA-NEKHT-SEKHEM-F-ȦU.
5. KA-NEKHT-ḤEQ-ḤEQU.
6. KA-NEKHT-ṬUT-KHĀU.
7. KHENTI-KAU-ĀNKHIU-NEBU.

II. N-U names
1, 2. SMEN-HEPU-SEKERḤ-TAUI.
3. SMEN-HEPU-THES-TAUI.
4. UR-MEN-ER-TCHAT-PEḤTI-F-SHEN-EM-ȦNNU-MEḤT-ER-ȦNNU-RESU.
5. KHENTI-KAU-ĀNKHIU-NEBU.

III. Golden Horus names
1, 2. ĀA-KHEPESH-ḤU-SATIU.
3. ḤU-MENTIU-ṬER-THEḤENNU.
4. PETPET ȦNTIU-THET-TA-SEN.
5. KA-NEKHT-SUTEN-SUTENIU-ṬER-PEṬ-PAUT.
6, 7. THEḤEN-KHEPERU-UR-BAIT.

8. Ḥefenu-nebu-mȧti-Rā.
9. Netch-neteru-mes-ḥenu-sen.
10. Khenti-kau-ānkhiu.

IV. Suten Bȧt name — Rā-neb-Maāt.[1] With additions: Mer-en-Rā, Ȧri-en-Rā, Tȧat-Rā, Setep-en-Rā, Ȧsu-Ra, Theḥen-Rā, Mer-Ȧmen, Tȧat-Ȧmen, Setep-en-Ȧmen, Setep-en-Tem, etc.

V. Son of Rā name — Ȧmen-ḥetep. With additions: Ḥeq-Uast, Sa-Rā and Neter-ḥeq-Uast.

1. 2. 3. 4. 5.

I.

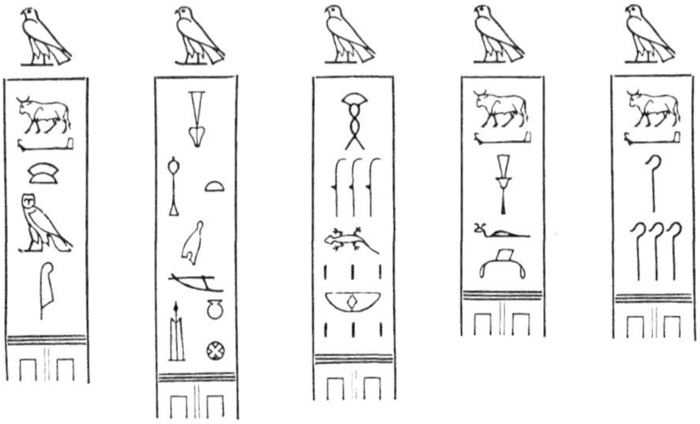

1. The principal forms of the prenomen Neb-Maāt-Rā found in the Tell al-ʿAmarna Tablets are:—

Ni-ib-mu-a-ri-ya 

Ni-mu-wa-ri-ya 

Nam-mur-ya 

Mi-im-mu-ri-ya 

6.

7.

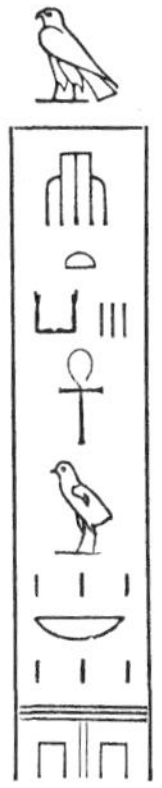

Temple of Ṣulb, L. D., 83.

II. 1. 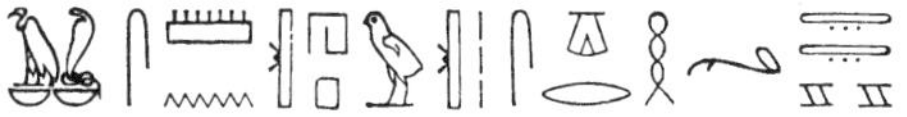

2. 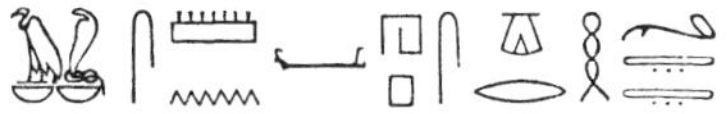

3. 

4. 

5. 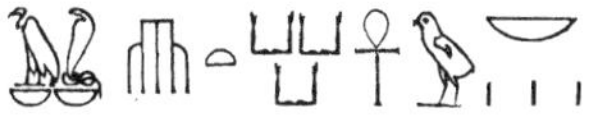

L. D., III, 72; Temple of Luxor, L. D., III, 74; Al-Kâb, L. D., III, 80; Rock inscriptions, L. D., III, 81; Temple of Ṣulb, L. D., III, 83.

III. 1. 

2. 

3. 

4. 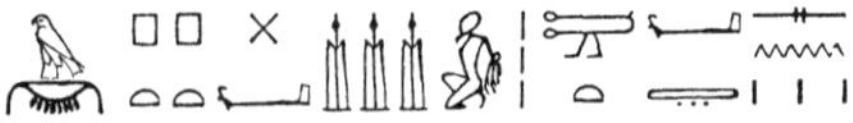

5. 

6. 

7. 

8. 

9. 

10. 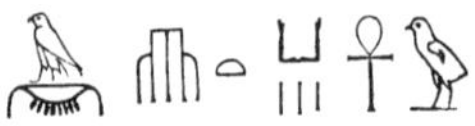

L. D., III, 72 ; Temple of Luxor, L. D., III, 74 ; Al-Kâb, L. D., III, 80 ; Rock inscriptions, L. D., III, 81 ; Temple of Ṣulb, L. D., III, 83 ; etc.

IV.  Abydos List, No. 73.

 Second Abydos List, No. 47.

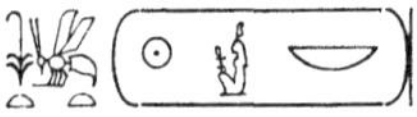

L. D., III, 72 ; Bricks, L. D., III, 78 ; Al-Kâb, L. D., III, 80 ; Rock inscriptions at Silsilah, Philae, Aswân, etc., L. D., III, 81; Temple of Ṣulb, L. D., III, 83.

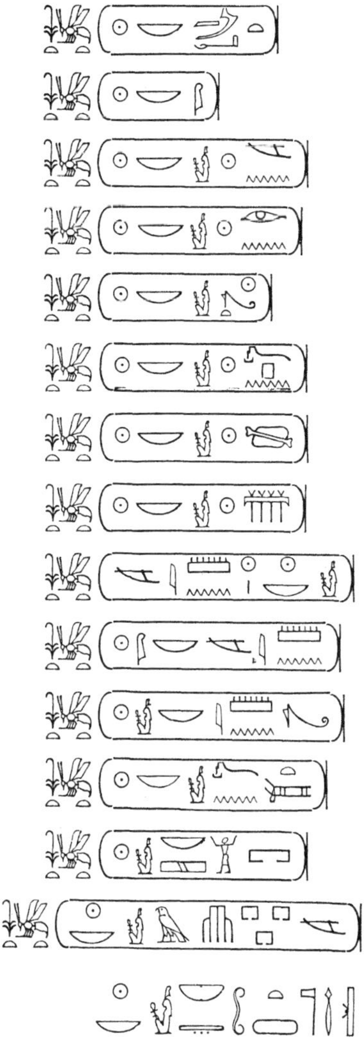

Granite column in the British Museum, No. 64.

V. 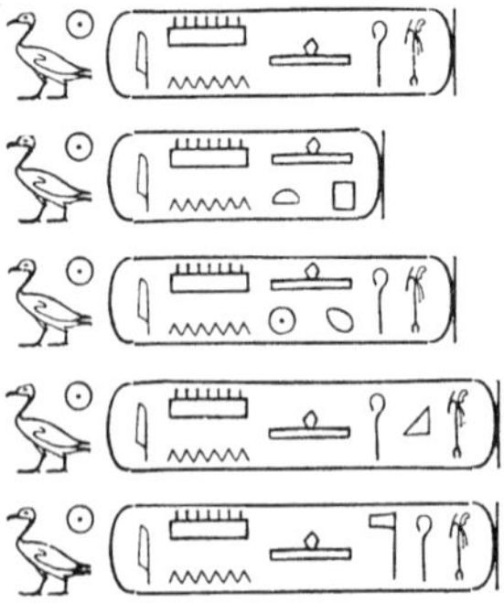

L. D., III, 72; Bricks, L. D., III, 78; Al-Kâb, L. D., III, 80; Rock inscriptions at Silsilah, Philae, Aswân, etc., L. D., III, 81; Temple of Ṣulb, L. D., III, 83.

Thi,*[1] daughter of *Thuȧu,* and queen of *Ȧmen-ḥetep III.

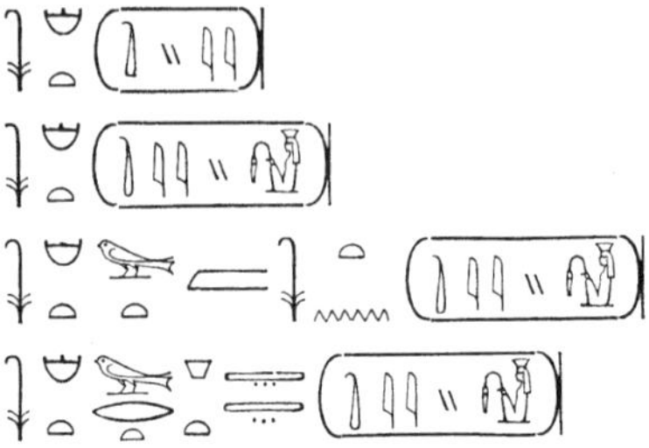

Scarabs in the British Museum; tombs at Tell al-ʿAmarna, L. D., III, 100 *c*; *koḥl* tubes in the British Museum, etc.

Sat-Ȧmen,* daughter of *Ȧmen-ḥetep III* by *Thi.

Davis, *Tomb of Iouiya*, p. 38.

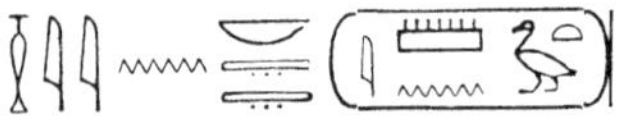

Davis, *op. cit.*, p. 43.

Iuȧa,* father-in-law of *Ȧmen-ḥetep III.

Scarab published by Brugsch, *Aeg. Zeit.*, 1880, p. 82.

1. In cuneiform TE-I-I .

 (variants  ) Tomb furniture in Cairo.

	Sarcophagus	of IUÀA	in Cairo.	Davis, *Tomb of Iouiya and Iouiyou*, London, 1907.
	"	"	"	
	"	"	"	
	Mask	"	"	
	Canopic Jar box	"	"	
	" "	"	"	
	" "	"	"	
	Papyrus	"	"	
	"	"	"	
	"	"	"	
	"	"	"	

 Ushabtiu of IUÀA in Cairo.

 " " "

 " " "

 " " "

 Cartonnage " "

 Vase " "

His titles were :

 Maspero in Davis, *op. cit.*, p. XIV.

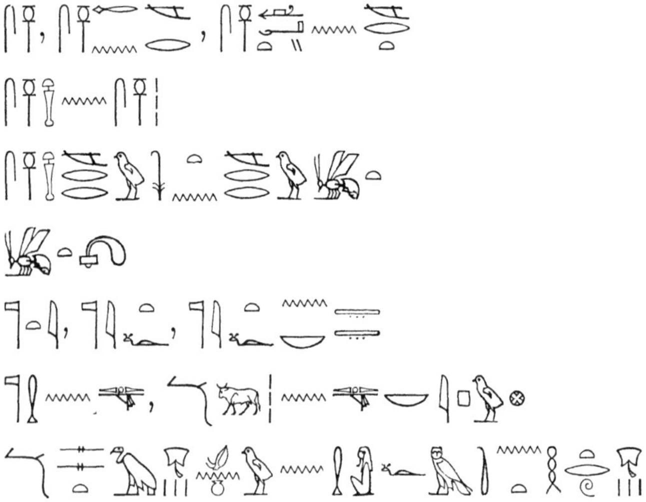

Thuȧu, mother-in-law of *Ȧmen-ḥetep III.*

Scarab published by Brugsch, *Aeg. Zeit.*, 1880, p. 82.

Tomb furniture in Cairo.

Āa-nenu, son of *Thuȧu.*

Davis, *op. cit.*, p. 18.

Kilḳipa, sister of *Tushratta,*
king of *Mitani,* and a wife of *Ȧmen-ḥetep III.*

Scarab published by Brugsch, *Aeg. Zeit.*, 1880, p. 82.

Tatum-khipa, daughter of *Tushratta,*
king of *Mitani,* and a wife of *Ȧmen-ḥetep III.*

'Da-a-du-khi-e-pa 

Da-a-du-khi-e-pa 

Teḥuti-mes, a prince.

Lepsius, *Königsbuch*, No. 377.

Ȧst, a princess.

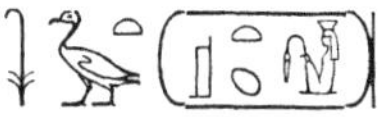

Temple at Ṣulb, L. D., III, 86 *b*.

Ḥent-em-ḥeb, a princess.

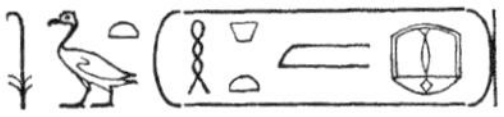

Temple at Ṣulb, L. D., III, 86 *b*.

Ȧmen-sat, a princess.

Stele in Cairo, Mariette, *Abydos*, II, plate 49.

Baket-Ȧten, a princess.

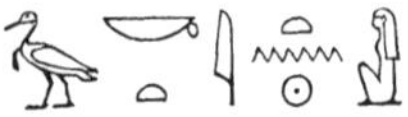

Tomb at Tell al-ʿAmarna, L. D., III, 100.

Meri-mes, a prince, governor of Nubia.

Coffin in the British Museum, No. 1001.

L. D., III, 82 *b*; J. de Morgan, *Catalogue*, vol. I, pp. 91, 96.

Ȧmen-ḥetep, a prince, governor of Nubia.

Ḥui, a prince, governor of Nubia.[1]

1. In cuneiform  (Berlin Tablet, No. 6).

A. *Åmen-ḥetep IV.*

I. Horus name — KA-NEKHT-QA-SHUTI.
II. N-U name — UR-SUTENIT-EM-SEMT-ÅTEN.
III. Golden Horus name — THES-KHĀU-EM-ÅNNU-QEMA.
IV. Suten Båt name[1] — RĀ-NEFER-KHEPERU-UĀ-EN-RĀ "High-priest of Ḥeru-khuti, exalted one in the horizon in his name 'Shu-in-the Disk'".
V. Son of Rā name — ÅMEN-ḤETEP. With addition: NETER-ḤEQ-UAST (or, ÅNNU) ĀA-EM-ĀḤĀ-F.

I.  Stele at Gebel Silsilah, L. D., III, 110*i*.

1. The commonest forms under which this prenomen appears in cuneiform are:—

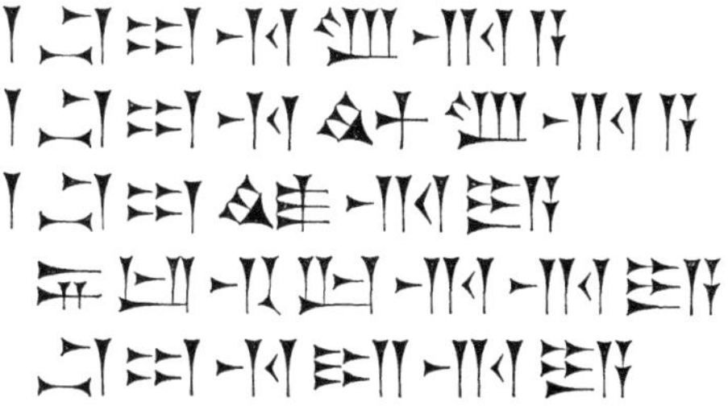

II. 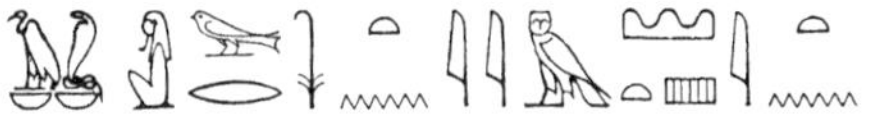 Stele at Gebel Silsilah, L. D., III, 110 *i.*

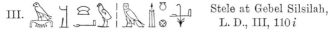

III.  Stele at Gebel Silsilah, L. D., III, 110 *i*

IV. 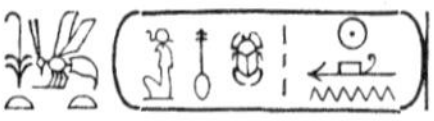

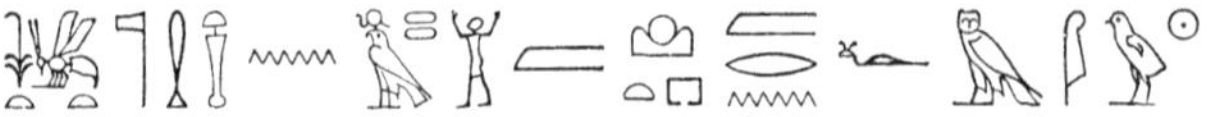

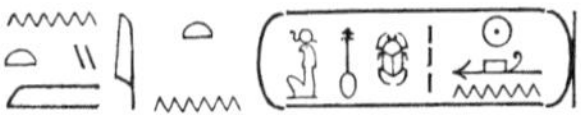

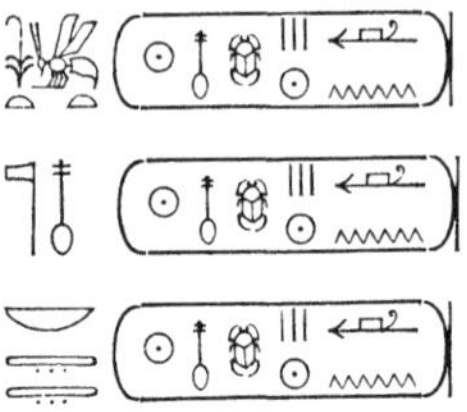

Tombs, etc., at Tell al-'Amarna; see L. D., III, 91 ff.; Petrie, *Tell el-Amarna*; N. de G. Davies, *The Rock Tombs of el-Amarna*, 3 parts; rings in the British Museum, etc. Slab in the British Museum, No. 1000.

L. D., III, 110 *a.*

V. 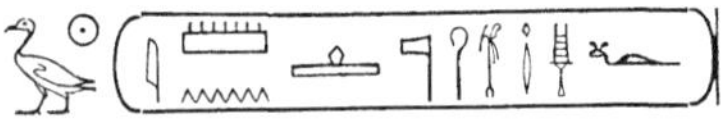 L. D., III, 110 *d.*

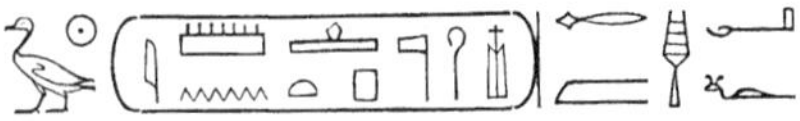 L. D., III, 110 *i.*

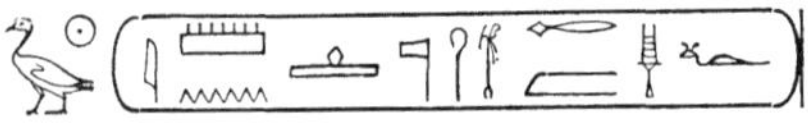

B. *Ȧmen-ḥetep IV* (*Khu-en-Ȧten*).

I.	Horus name	Ka-nekht-Ȧten-meri.
II.	N-U name	Ur-sutenit-em-khut-Ȧten.
III.	Golden Horus name	Thes-ren-f-en-Ȧten.
IV.	Suten Bȧt name	Rā-nefer-kheperu-uā-en-Rā-Ȧten-meri.
V.	Son of Rā name	Ȧten-khu-en. With addition: Āa-em-āḥā-f.

I. 

Stelae at Tell al-ʿAmarna, L. D., III, 93 ff.

II. 

Stelae at Tell al-ʿAmarna, L. D., III, 93 ff.; N. de G. Davies, *Rock Tombs of el-Amarna*, 3 parts.

III. 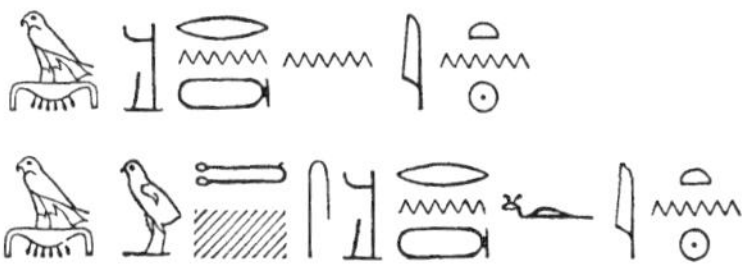

Stelae and tombs at Tell al-ʿAmarna.

IV. 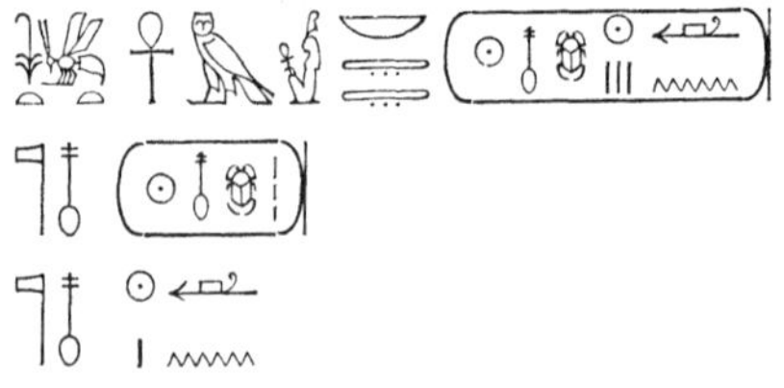

Stelae and tombs at Tell al-ʿAmarna; scarabs, rings, etc.

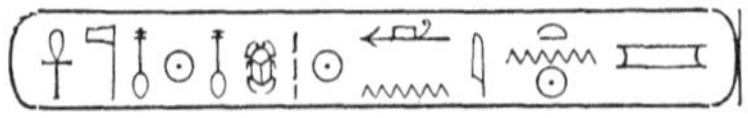

V. 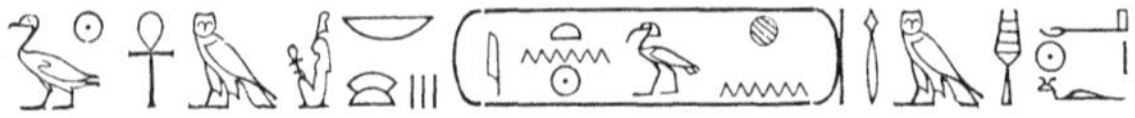

A. *Nefertith*, queen of *Ȧmen-ḥetep IV*.

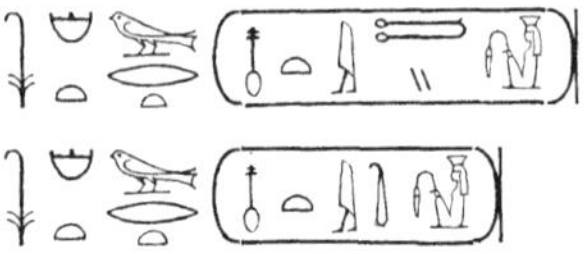

Stelae at Tell al-ʿAmarna.

B. *Nefertith Nefer-neferu-Ȧten*,
queen of *Ȧmen-ḥetep IV*.

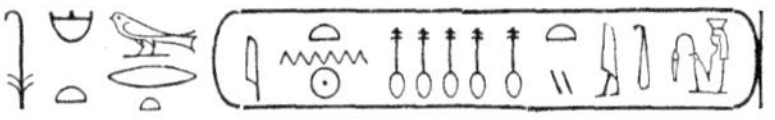

L. D., III, 109.

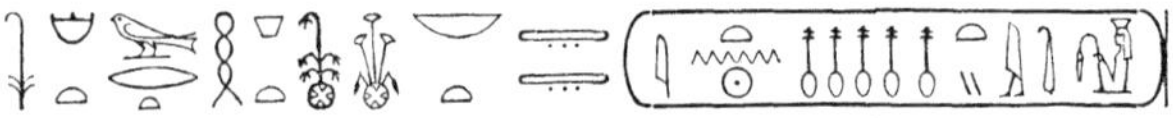

L. D., III, 109, 111.

Netchemet-Mut, sister of *Nefertith*.

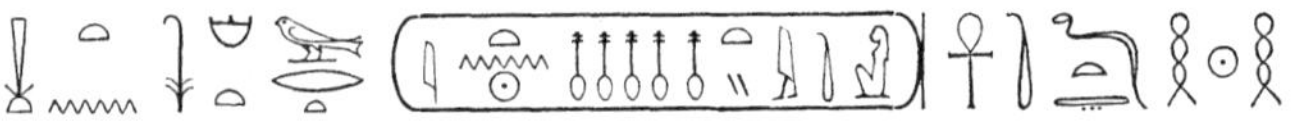

Tomb at Tell al-ʿAmarna.

Aṭen-mert, or *Àten-merit,*
a princess, wife of *Rā-smenkh-ka.*

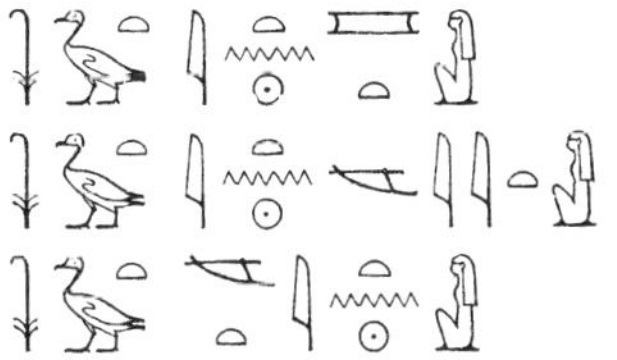

Stelae, etc., at Tell al-ʿAmarna, L. D., III, 99 *a*.

Àten-māket, a princess.

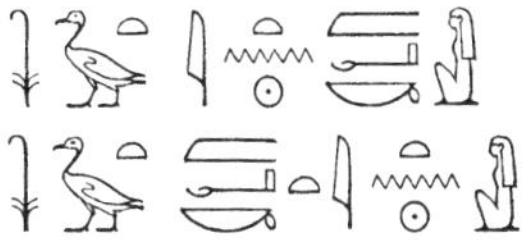

Stelae at Tell al-ʿAmarna.

Ānkh-s-en-pa-Àten,
a princess, married *Tut-ānkh-Àmen.*

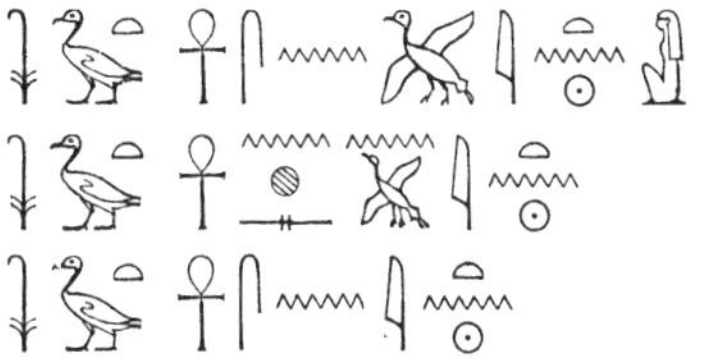

Stelae at Tell al-ʿAmarna.

Àten-nefer-neferu Ta-sherà, a princess.

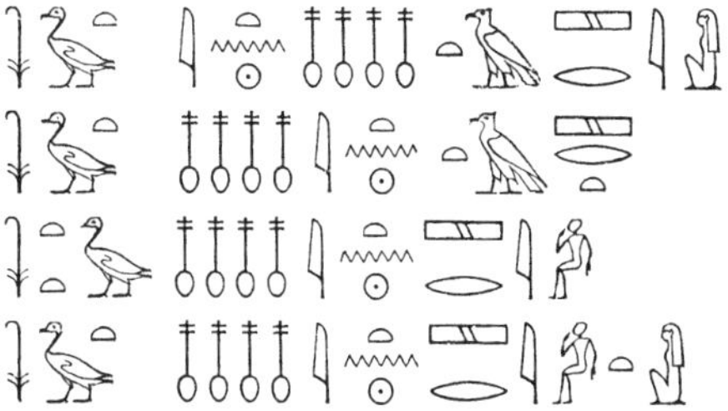

Stelae at Tell al-ʿAmarna, L. D., III, 93.

Rā-nefer-neferu, a princess.

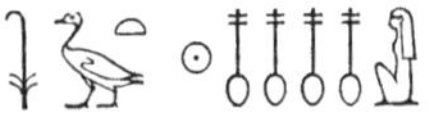 L. D., III, 99.

Setept-en-Rā, a princess.

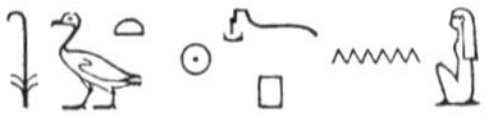 L. D., III, 99.

Àten-Baket, a princess, daughter of *Thi*.

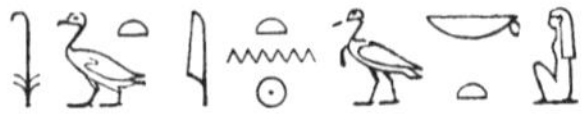

Rā-ānkh-kheperu Rā-sāa-ka-tcheser-kheperu.

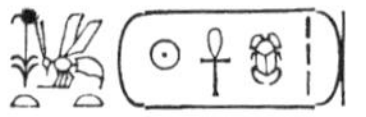 L. D., III, 99 *a*.

 L. D., III, 99 *a*.

Àten-meri, wife of *Rā-ānkh-kheperu*.

 L. D., III, 99 *a*.

Tut-ānkh-Àmen.

I. Horus name — KA-NEKHT-TUT-MES.
II. N-U name — NEFER-...-TAUI.
III. Golden Horus name — RENP-KHĀU-SEHETEP-NETERU.
IV. Suten Bàt name — RĀ-KHEPERU-NEB.
V. Son of Rā name — TUT-ĀNKH-ÀMEN.

I. 

Legrain, *Annales*, VI, 192.

II. 

Legrain, *Annales*, VI, 192; Legrain, *Recueil*, XXIX, 162.

III. 

Legrain, *Annales*, VI, 192; Legrain, *Recueil*, XXIX, 162.

IV. 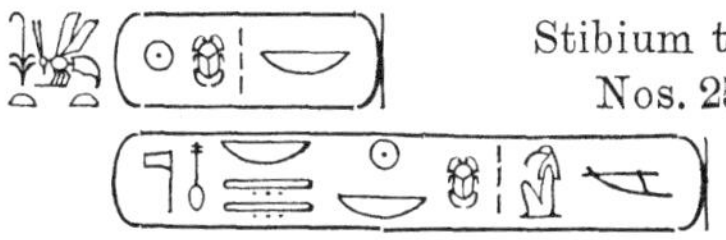

Stibium tubes, British Museum, Nos. 25731 and 27376.

V. 

Prisse, *Monuments*, pl. XI; Granite lion in the British Museum; L. D., III, 115, 118, 119 *b*.

Ȧmen-ānkh-nes, wife of **Tut-ānkh-Ȧmen.**

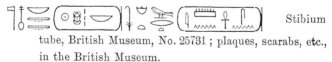

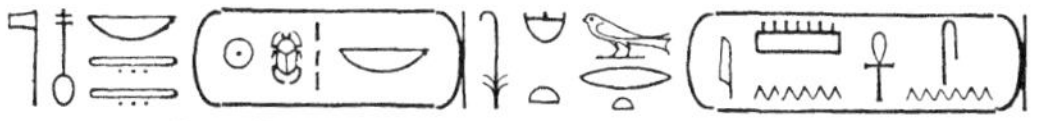

Stibium tube, British Museum, No. 25731; plaques, scarabs, etc., in the British Museum.

Ȧi, divine father of *Ȧmen-ḥetep IV*.

Tomb at Tell al-ʿAmarna.

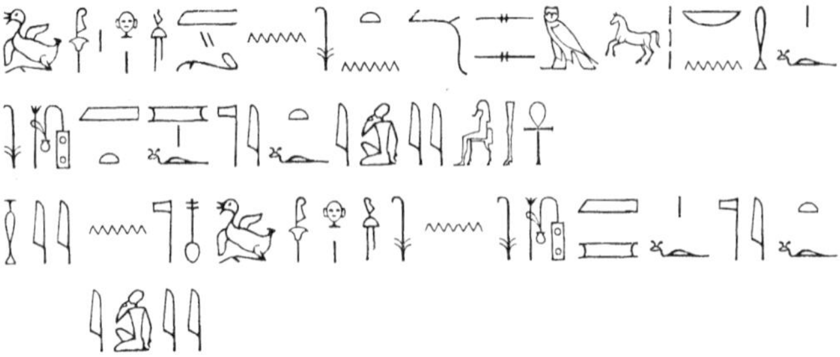

Ȧi.

I. Horus name	KA-NEKHT-THEḤEN-KHĀU (or, KHEPERU).
II. N-U name	SEKHEM-PEḤTI-ṬER-SATET.
III. Golden Horus name	ḤEQ-MAĀT-SEKHEPER-TAUI.
IV. Suten Bȧt name	RĀ-KHEPER-KHEPERU-ȦRI-MAĀT.
V. Son of Rā name	ȦI. With addition: NETER-ḤEQ-UAST.

I.

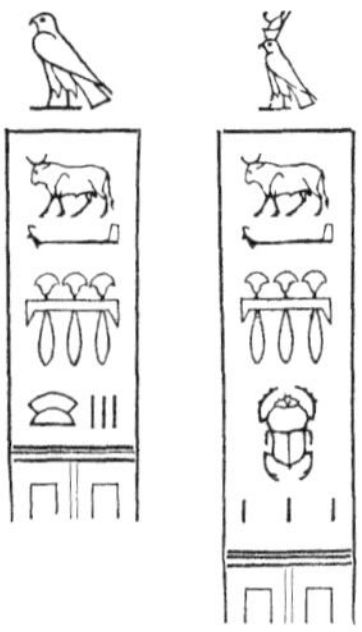

Rock temple at Akhmîm (L. D., III, 114 *b*) and Bibân al-Mulûk, L. D., III, 113 *a*.

II. 

Rock temple at Akhmîm. See L. D., III, 114 ff.

III. 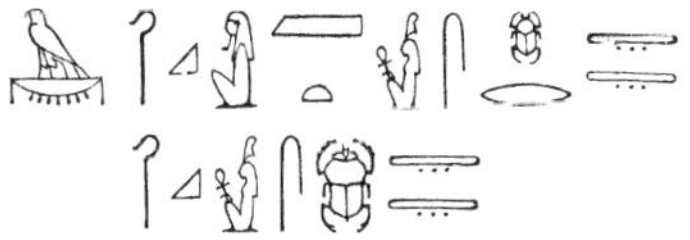

Rock temple at Akhmîm. See L. D., III, 114 ff.

IV. 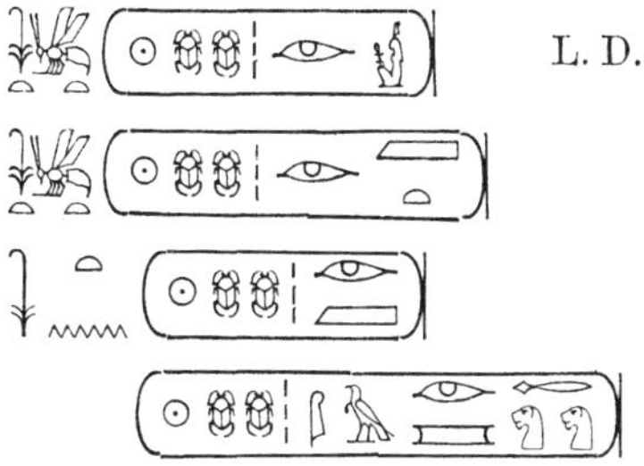

L. D., III, 113; 114 *a*, *b*, *c*.

V. 

L. D., III, 114 *b*.

Thi, chief royal nurse.

Tomb at Tell al-ʿAmarna.

Thi, a queen.

L. D., III, 114 *d*.

Pa-sar, a prince, governor of Nubia.

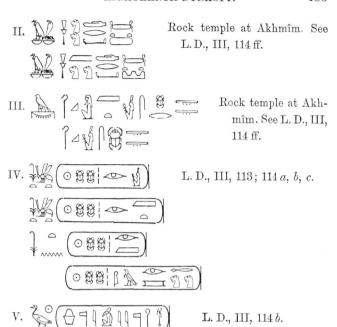

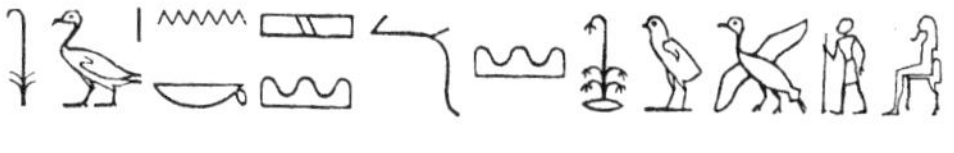

Shrine at Akhmîm.

Ḥeru-em-ḥeb.

I. Horus name — KA-NEKHT-SEPṬ-SEKHERU.

II. N-U name — UR-BAIT-EM-ÅPT.

III. Golden Horus name — HERI-ḤER-MAĀT-SEKHEPER-TAUI. / Ā-KHEPESH.

IV. Suten Båt name — RĀ-TCHESER-KHEPERU. With additions: SETEP-EN-RĀ, ḤEQ-MAĀT-SETEP-EN-RĀ, ḤEQ-UAST-SETEP-EN-RĀ, ḤEQ-ÅNNU-SETEP-EN-RĀ.

V. Son of Rā name — ḤERU-EM-ḤEB. With addition: MER-EN-ÅMEN.

I. 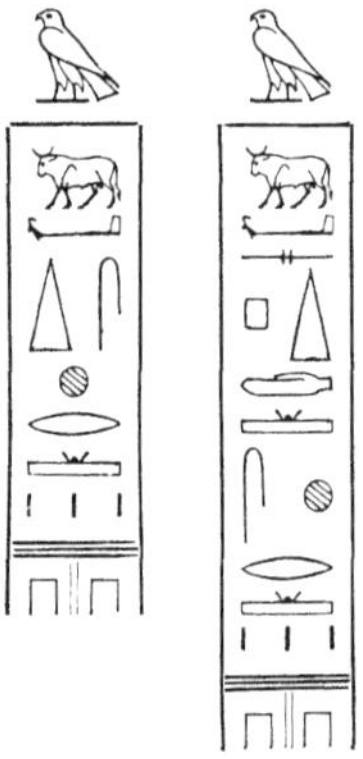

Pylons, etc. at Karnak. L. D., III, 112.

II. 

Pylons, etc. at Karnak.

III. 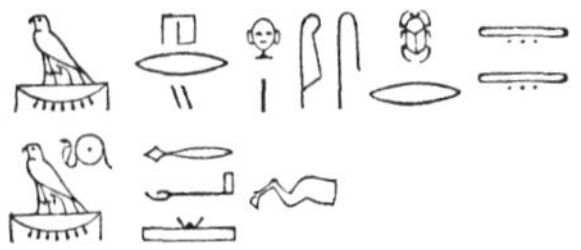

Pylons, etc. at Karnak.

IV. 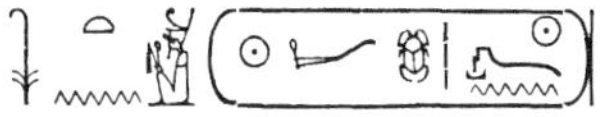 Tablet of Ṣaḳḳârah.

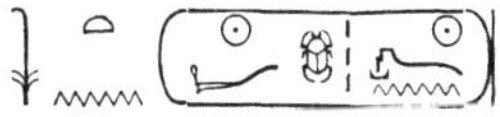 Abydos List, No. 74.

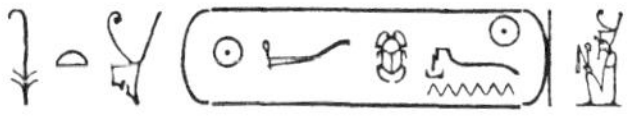 Second Abydos List, No. 48.

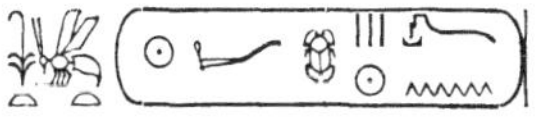
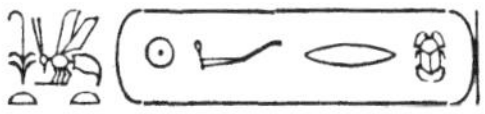
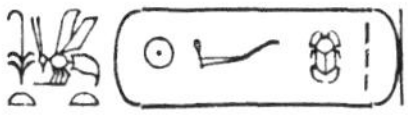

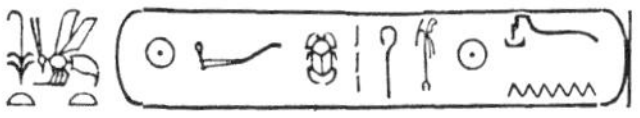
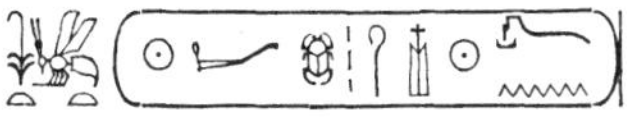

Pylons at Karnak, inscription at Madînat Habû, Rock temple at Silsilah (L. D., III, 112, 119 ff.), and scarabs, etc., in the British Museum.

V. 
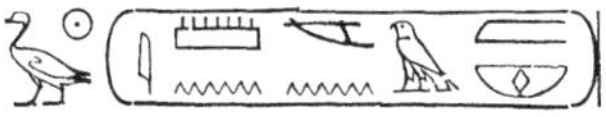
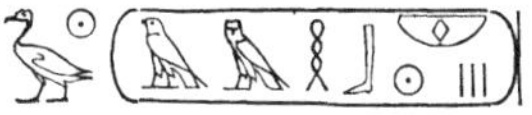

L. D., III, 119, 120, 121.

Mut-Netchemet, a queen.

 Rosellini, *Monumenti Stor.*, XLIV.

Menkh-p-Rā Teḥuti-mes (*Thothmes V*).

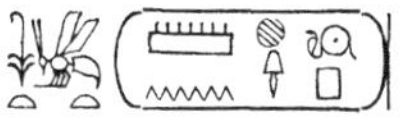 Legrain, *Annales*, VII, 35.

 Do. Do. Do.

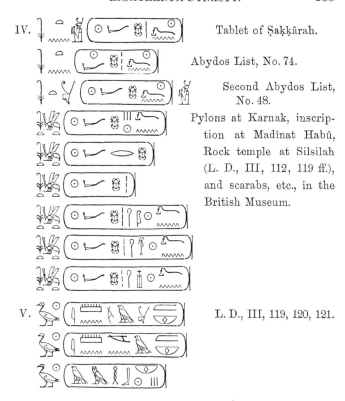

NINETEENTH DYNASTY. FROM THEBES.

Rameses I.

I. Horus name	KA-NEKHT-UATCH-SUTENIU.
II. N-U name	KHĀ-EM-SUTEN-MȦ-...
III. Golden Horus name	...-EM-KHET-TAUI.
IV. Suten Bȧt name	RĀ-MEN-PEḤTI.
V. Son of Rā name	RĀ-MESSU, or, RĀ-MESES.

I. 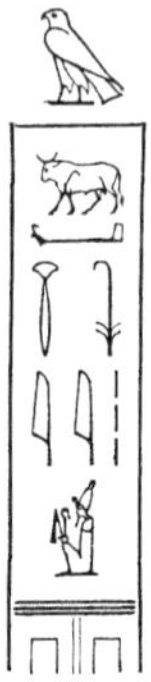 Temple of the Ramesseum.

II. 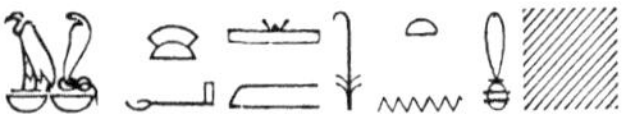 Temple of the Ramesseum.

III.  Temple of the Ramesseum.

IV. 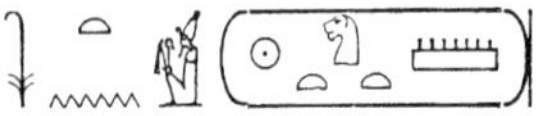 Tablet of Ṣaḳḳârah.

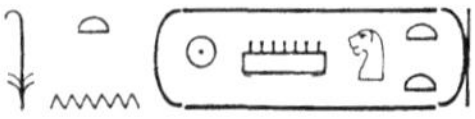 Abydos List, No. 75.

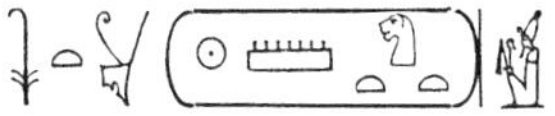

Second Abydos List, No. 49.

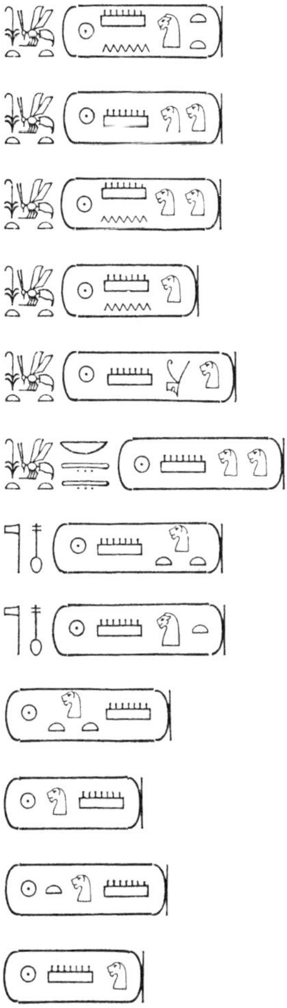

Bibân al-Mulûk, Ramesseum, Temple of Karnak, Coffin cover at Cairo, etc. See L. D., III, 123, 124, 131, etc.

V. 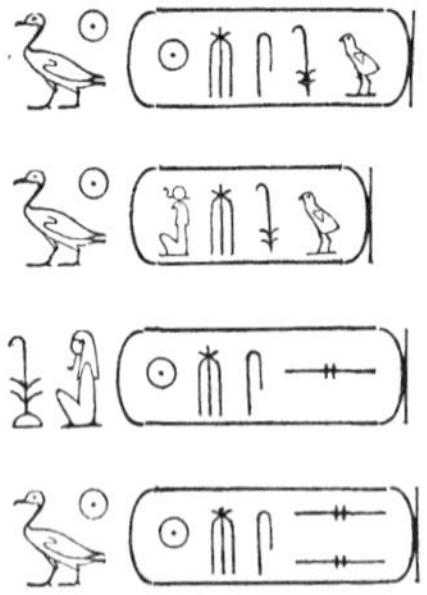

L. D., III, 123, 124; Prisse, *Monuments*, plate XIX.

Sat-Rā, wife of *Rameses I.*

Temple of Seti I (Mariette, *Abydos*, I, pl. 32).

Seti I.

I. Horus names

1—4. KA-NEKHT-KHĀ-EM-UAST-SĀNKH-TAUI.
5, 6. KA-NEKHT-NEM-MESTU.
7—9. KA-NEKHT-SEKHEM-KHEPESH.
10. KA-NEKHT-ṬER-PEṬ-PAUT.
11—13. KA-NEKHT-NEM-KHĀU.
14. KA-NEKHT-MȦTET-MENTH.
15. KA-NEKHT-SA-TEM.
16. KA-EN-RĀ-MERI-MAĀT.
17. KA-NEKHT-ḤETEP-ḤER-MAĀT.
18, 19. KA-NEKHT-USER-PEṬI.
20. KA-NEKHT-PEṬ-PEḤTI.
21. KA-NEKHT-SEKHEM-PEḤTI.
22. KA-NEKHT-ĀA-KHEPESH.
23. KA-NEKHT-KHĀ-KHĀU.

1. 2. 3. 4. 5. 6.

I.

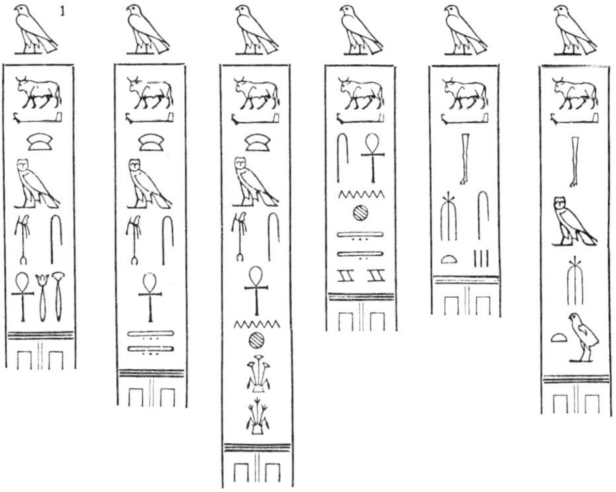

7. 8. 9. 10. 11. 12.

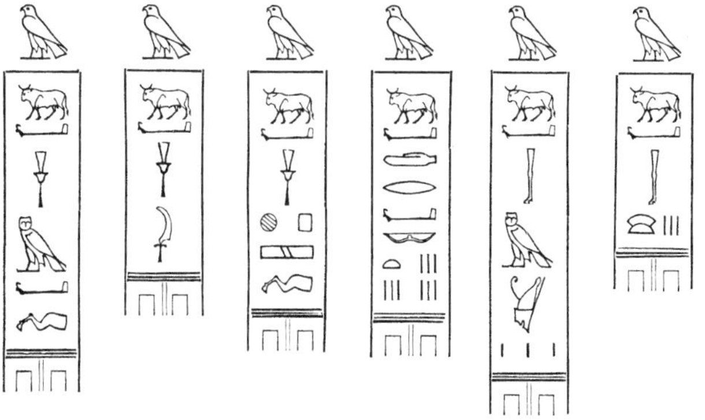

1. For these Horus names see Mariette, *Abydos*, tomes 1 and 2, Paris, 1869.

13. 14. 15. 16. 17. 18.

19. 20. 21. 22. 23.

II. N-U names 1. Sekhem-peḥti-ṭer-peṭ-paut.
2. Uāfu-semti-ṭer-Mentiu.
3. Men-mennu-tchetta-ḥeḥ.
4. Menthu-en-meri-māk-Qemt.
5. Māk-Qemt-uāfu-semti.
6, 7. Nem-mestu-sekhem-khepesh-ṭer-peṭ-paut.

8. Nem-mestu-sekhem-ṭer-peṭ-paut.

9. Nem-mestu-user-peṭi.

II. 1.  Temple of Abydos, the Speos Artemidos, etc.

2. 

3. 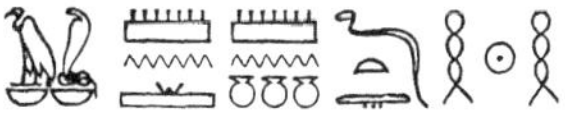

4. 

5. 

6. 

7. 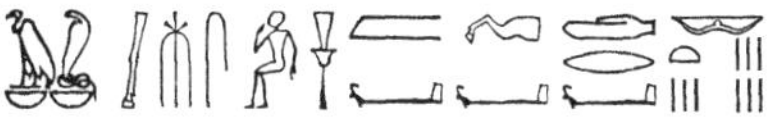

8. 

9. 

III. Golden Horus names 1, 2. Nem-khāu-user-peṭi-em-taiu-nebu.

3. User-peṭi-em-taiu-nebu.

4. Mer-en-Rā-sāa-ka-f.

5. Seḥetep-em-Rā-merrt-f.

6. Sekhem-neter-en-kheperȧ.

III. 1. 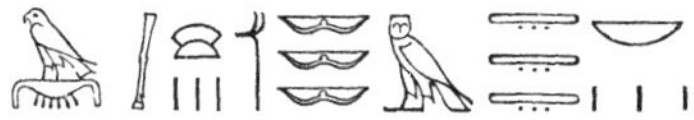 Temple of Abydos.

2. 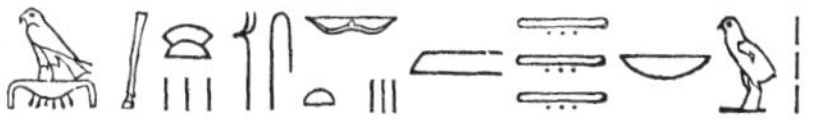

3. 

4. 

5. 

6. 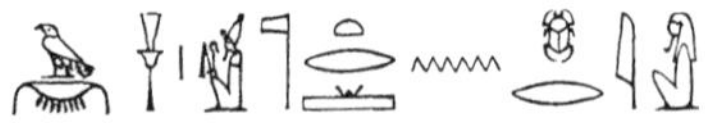

IV. Suten Bȧt name Rā-Maāt-men.

With additions: 12. Ḥeq-taiu, 13. Ȧsu-Rā, 14. Tȧa-Rā, 15. Ptaḥ-meri, 16. Ḥeq-Uast, 17. Setep-[en]-Rā, 18. Ȧri-en-Rā, 19. Ȧri-en-Rā-meri-Ȧmen, 20. Ḥeq-Ȧnnu, 21. Tȧa-Rā-meri-Ȧmen.

1. 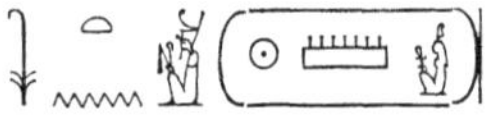 Tablet of Ṣaḳḳârah.

2.  Abydos List, No. 75.

3. 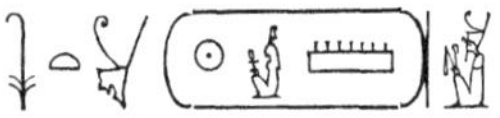 Second Abydos List, No. 50.

4. 

5. 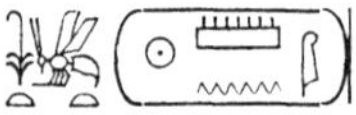

6. 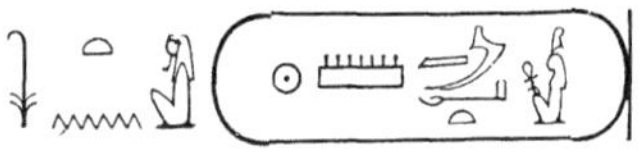

7. 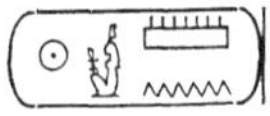

8.  9. 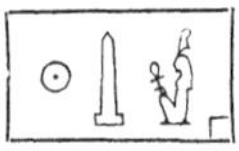

Mummy and Coffin in Cairo; Tomb No. 17 at Thebes; Alabaster sarcophagus in Sir John Soane's Museum; L. D., III, 133–138; temples at Karnak, Ḳûrnah, Abydos, etc., and rock inscriptions at Ḥammâmât, Silsilah, Aswân, etc.

10. 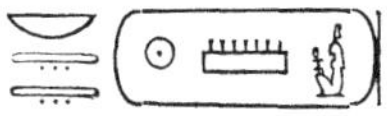

11. 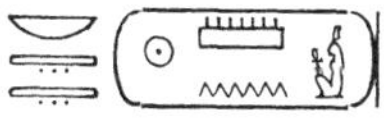

12. 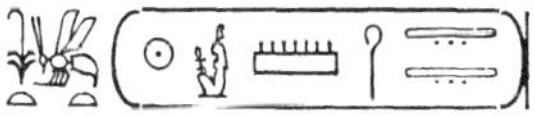

13. 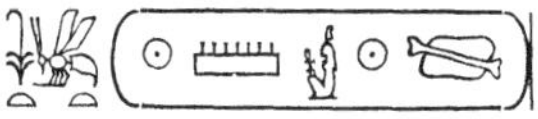

14. 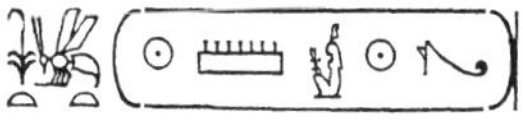

15. 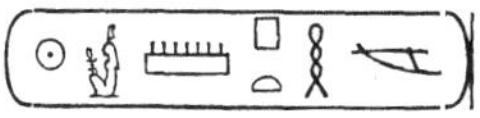

16. 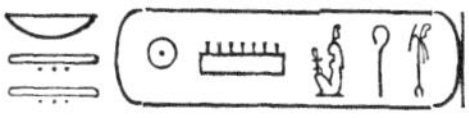

17. 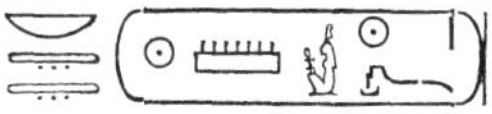

18. 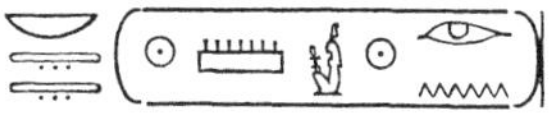

19. 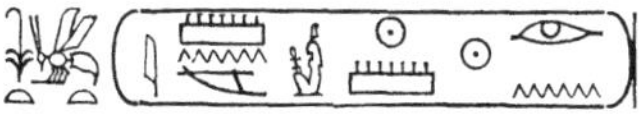

20. 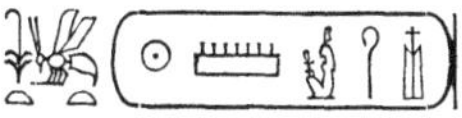

21. 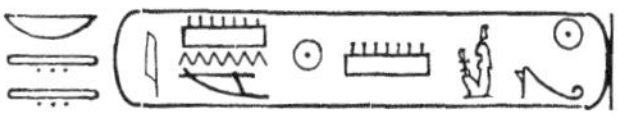

V. Son of Rā name — SETI.

With additions: 1—8. MERI-PTAḤ, or MER-EN-PTAḤ, 9. MER-EN-PTAḤ-MER-ȦMEN, 10. MERI-PTAḤ-RĀ, 11, 12. MERI-EN-ȦMEN.

V. 1. 2. 3. 4. 5. 6. 7. 8. 9. 10. 11. 12.

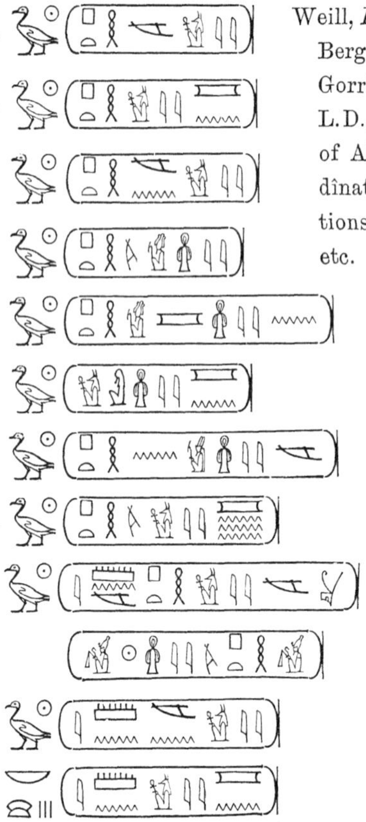

Weill, *Recueil*, Nos. 110, 111; Bergmann, *Recueil*, XII, 4; Gorringe, *Obelisks*, p. 130; L. D., III, 138, 202; temples of Abydos, Karnak, Madînat Habû, etc.; inscriptions at Silsilah, Aswân, etc.

Tui, or Tuȧa,
wife of *Seti I* and mother of *Rameses II.*

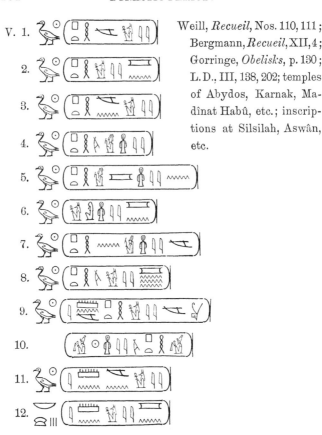

Mariette, *Abydos*, II, 16.

Sons and daughters of *Seti I.*

Ȧmen-nefer-neb-f.

Mariette, *Mon. Div.*, plate 73, No. 68.

Rā-ḥent-mȧ, daughter of *Seti I.*

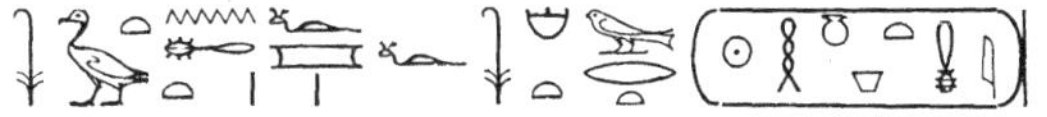

Daninos Pâshâ, *Recueil*, XII, 211.

Ȧni, a prince, governor of Nubia.

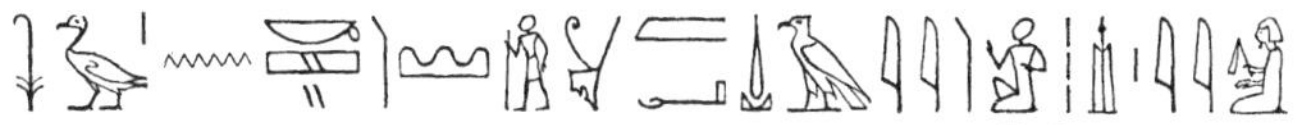

L. D., III, 138.

Ȧmen-em-ȧpt, a prince, governor of Nubia.

L. D., III, 176.

Rameses II Sesetsu.

I. Horus names 1—4. KA-NEKHT-MERI-MAĀT.

5. KA-NEKHT-MĀK-QEMT.

6. KA-NEKHT-KHĀ-EM-MAĀT-SĀNKH-TAUI.

7. Ka-nekht-uāfu-semti.
8. Ka-nekht-Rā-meri.
9. Ka-nekht-sa-Set.
10. Ka-nekht-sa-Seb (?).
11. Ka-nekht-sa-Àsàr.
12. Ka-nekht-sa-Tem.
13. Ka-nekht-sa-Tenen.
14. Ka-nekht-sa-Kheperà.
15. Ka-nekht-sa-Àmen.
16. Ka-nekht-ur-peḥti.
17. Ka-nekht-ur-nekht-ḥer-āḥa-khepesh-f.
18. Ka-nekht-ur-ḥebu-meri-taui.
19. Ka-nekht-āḥa-ḥer-khepesh-f.
20. Ka-nekht-usr-peḥti.
21. Ka-nekht-usr-Maāt.
22. Ka-nekht-usr-khepesh.
23. Ka-nekht-usr-renput.
24. Ka-nekht-usr-renput-ḥefennu.
25. Ka-nekht-renput-ḥefennu.
26. Ka-nekht-thes-Maāt.
27. Ka-nekht-men-àb-sekhem-peḥti.
28. Ka-nekht-en-Rā-seṭ-Sati.
29. Ka-nekht-meriu-Maāt.
30. Ka-nekht-seqa-Uast.
31. Ka-nekht-meri-Maāt-neb-ḥebu-mà-tef-Ptaḥ-tunen.
32. Ka-nekht-meri-Maāt-Menthu-en-suteniu-ka-en-ḥeqiu-ur-peḥti-mà-àtef-Set-em-Nubti.
33. Ka-nekht-meri-Maāt-heb...-ḥer-qen-i-ḥer-nekht.

1. 2. 3. 4. 5. 6.

I.

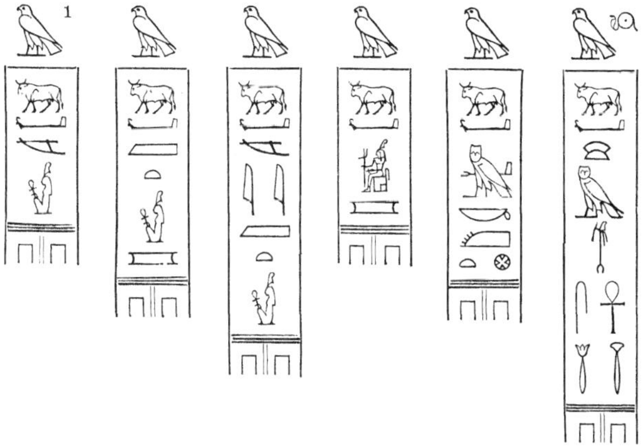

7. 8. 9. 10. 11. 12.

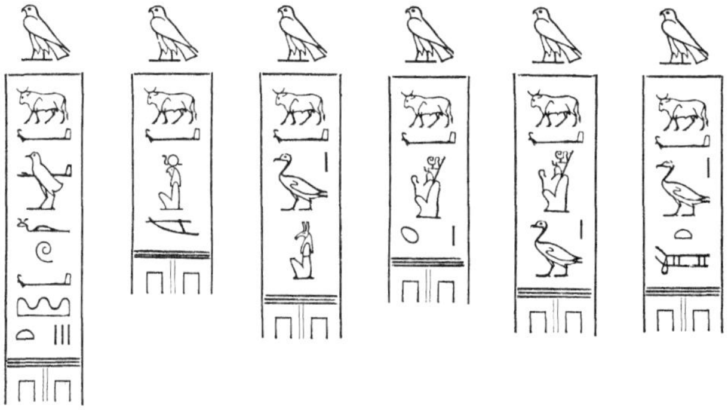

1. For the various names of Rameses II see his Coffin and Mummy in Cairo; Temples at Abydos, Karnak, Luxor, Ramesseum; inscriptions on rocks and stelae, and monuments of every kind from Tanis to Wâdî Ḥalfah.

13.

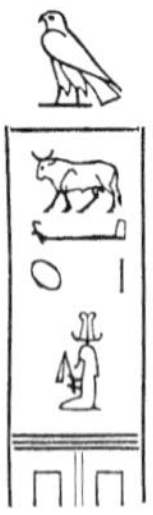

14.

15.

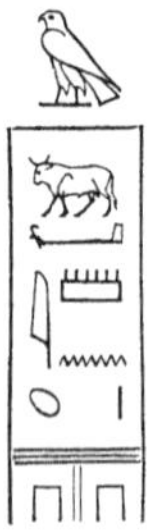

16.

17.

18.

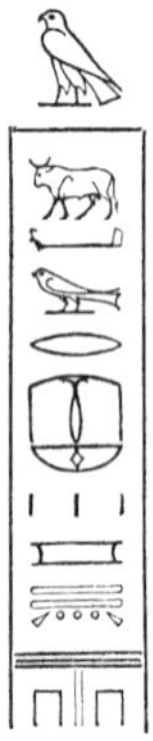

19.

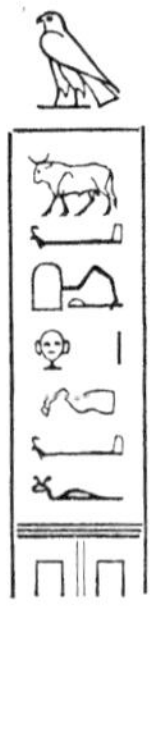

20.

21.

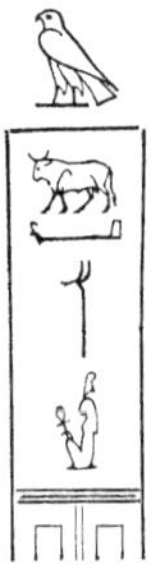

22.

23.

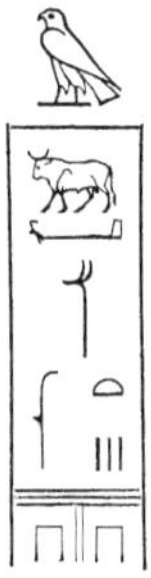

24.

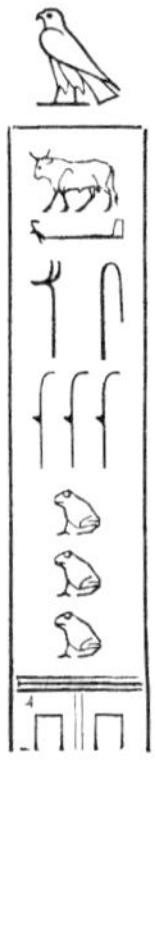

25.

26.

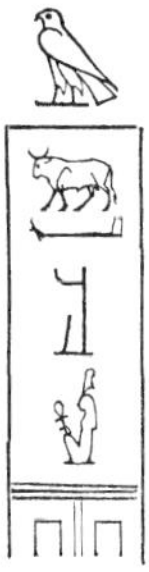

27.

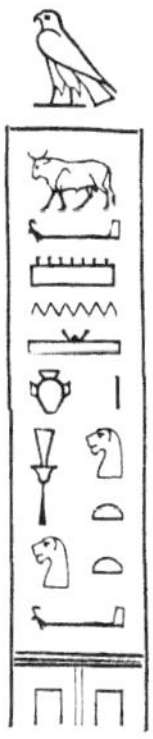

28.

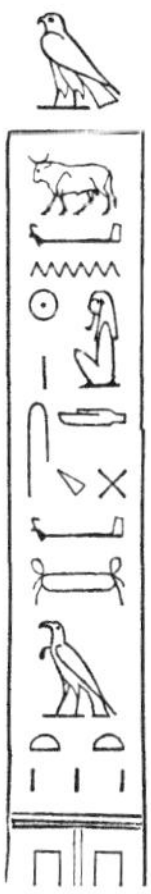

29.

30.

31.

32.

33.

II. N-U names

1—3. MĀK-QEMT-UĀFU-SEMTI.

4, 5. MĀK-QEMT-UĀF-SEMTI-RĀ-MES-NETERU-ḲER-TAUI.

6. MĀK-QEMT-UĀFU-SEMTI-ȦRI-URU-SEN-EM-ȦNTIU-SMA-EM-ȦST-SEN.

7. MĀK-QEMT-UĀFU-SEMTI-ȦN-URU-SEN-EM-...-ER-TA-MERȦ.

8. MĀK-QEMT-UĀFU-SEMTI-NEB-SENṬ-SHEFIT-EM-TAIU-NEBU-ȦRI-TA-EN-KESHI-EM-TEM-UN-ṬĀ-EN-TA-EN-KHETA-ĀB-RE-F.

9. SMENKH-MENNU-EM-ȦPT-REST-EN-TEF-ȦMEN-ṬĀ-SU-ḤER-NEST-F.

10. SMENKH-MENNU-EM-ȦN-RESU-EN-TEF-ȦMEN-ṬĀ-SU-ḤER-NEST-F.

11. ĀḤA-EN-ḤEḤ-EN-RENPUT-MȦU-SEKHEM-ȦB.

12. SESHEP-NEB-NETER-EN-KHEPERȦ.

13. SEKHER-PEḤ-SU-EN-ȦN-PEḤUI-TA.

14. UR-SHEFIT-MĀK-QEMT.

II. 1. 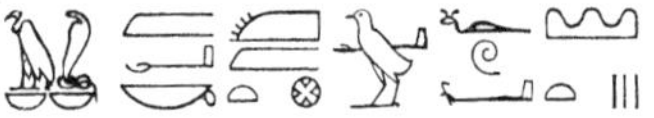

2. 

3. 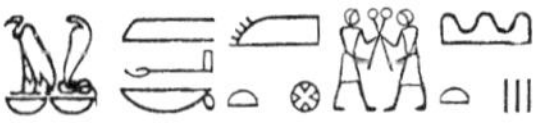

4. 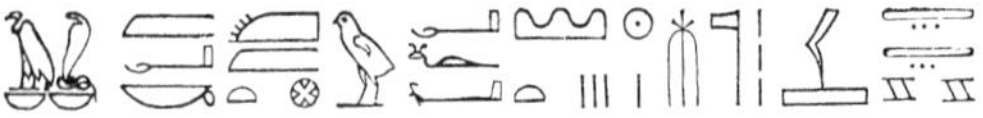

5. 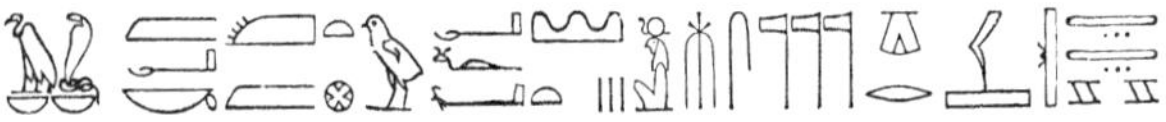

6. 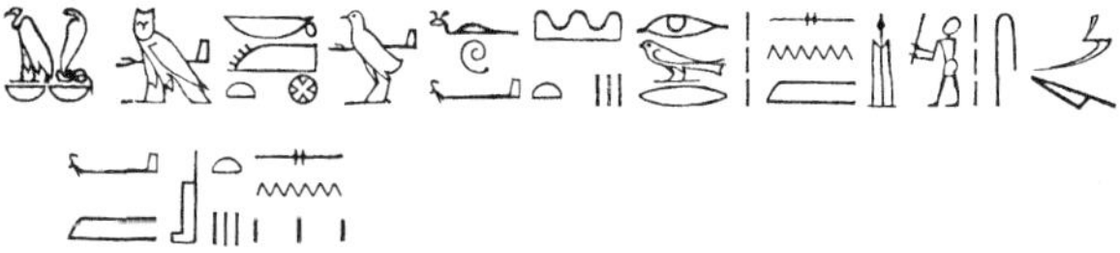

7. 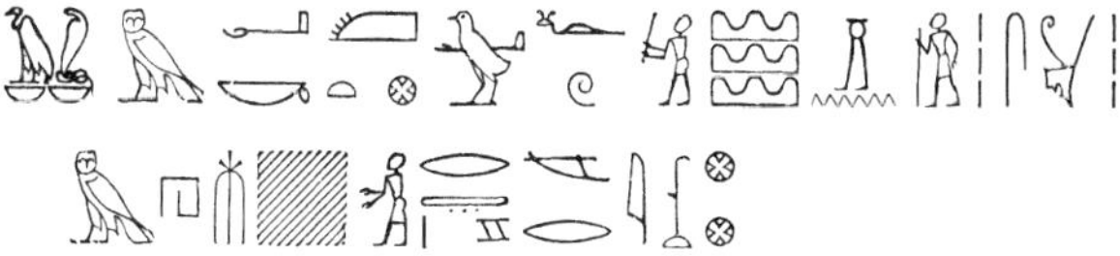

8. 

9. 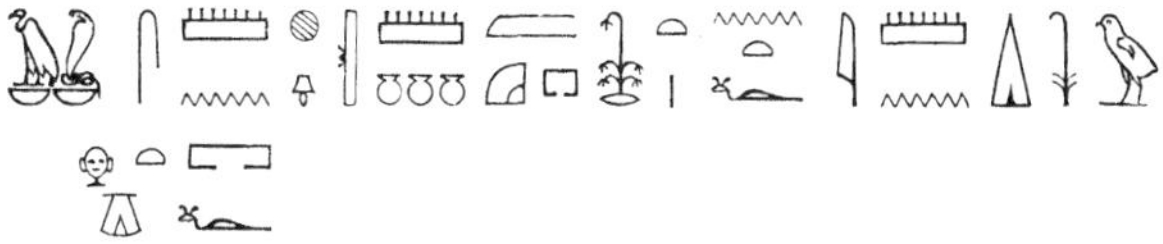

10. 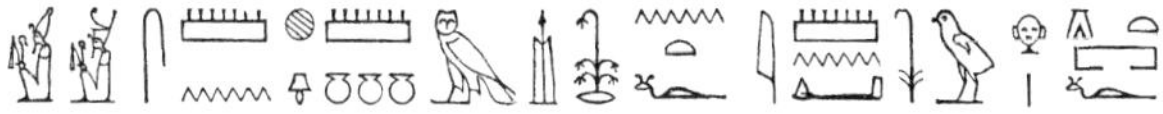

11. 

12. 

13. 

14. 

III. Golden Horus names

1—5. USR-RENPUT-ĀA-NEKHTUT.

6. USR-RENPUT-ĀA-NEKHTUT-RĀ-MES-NETERU-ḲER-TAUI.

7. USR-RENPUT-ĀA-NEKHTUT-ȦN-TCHERU-PE-ḤUUI-TA-ḤER-ḤEḤ-ĀḤA-SEḤENS-NEF-RE-USEKH-EN-...-SEMTI.

8. USR-KHEPESH-MERI-TA.

9. ḤEḤ-KHU-EN-MESES.

10. UĀFU-SEMTI-ER-NEKHT-BETESHU.

11. SHUTI-MȦ-RĀ-ȦM-UAST-SUTEN-BȦT-ĀAT-MERI-EN-ḤERU.

12. UR-F-ȦUTU-SEKHEM-PEḤTI.

13. UR-NEKHTU-ḤER-SEMT-NEBT.

III. 1. 

2. 

3. 

4. 

5. 

6. 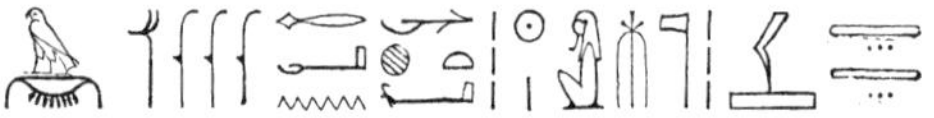

7. 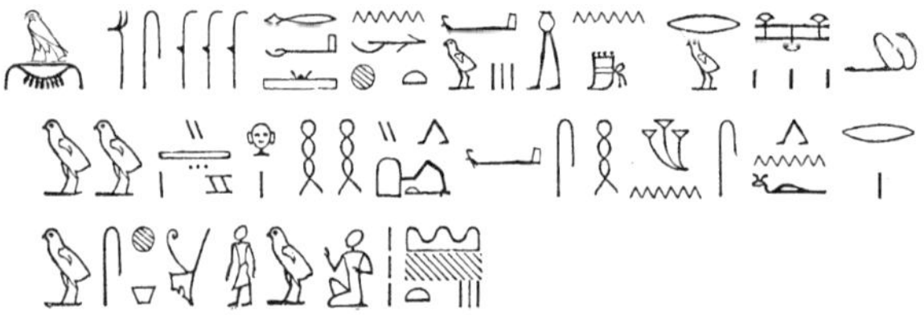

8. 

9. 

10. 

11. 

12. 

13. 

IV. Suten Bȧt names

1—7, 9. Rā-user-Maāt-setep-en-Rā.

8. Rā-user-Maāt-setep-en-Rā-meri-Ȧmen.

10—15. Rā-user-Maāt.

16—19. Rā-user-Maāt-s.

20. Rā-user-Maāt-tȧa-Rā.

21. Rā-user-Maāt-tȧa-en-Rā.

22. Rā-user-Maāt-ḥeq-Uast.

23, 24. Rā-user-Maāt-ȧsu-Rā.

25. Rā user-Maāt-Rā-meri.

26. Rā-user-Maāt-setep-en-Rā? Rā-meses-meri-Ptaḥ-Rā-Ȧmen.

27. Rā-user-Maāt-Rā-messu-meri-Ȧmen.

28. Rā-user-Maāt-setep-en-Rā-meri-Ȧmen.

IV. 1.  Tablet of Ṣaḳḳârâh.

2. 

3. 

4. 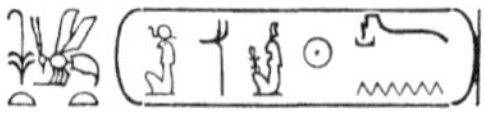

5. 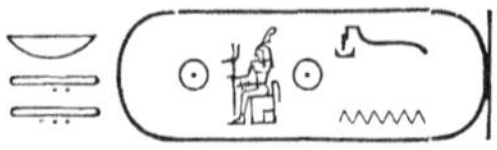

6. 

7. 

8. 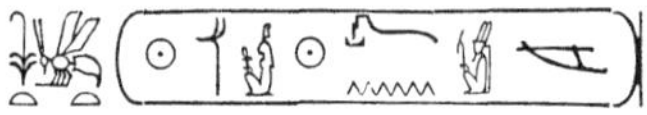

9. 

10. 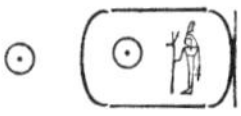

11. 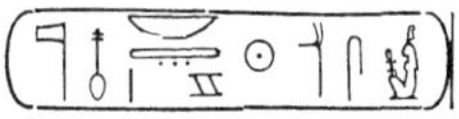

12. 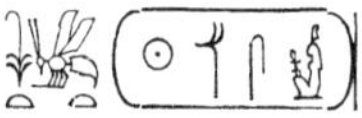

13. 

14. 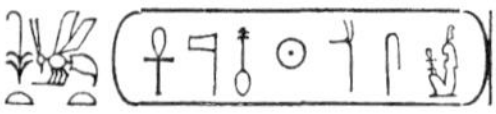

15. 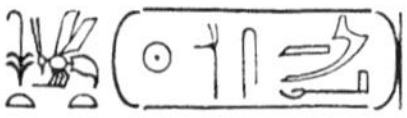

16. 

17. 

18. 

19. 

20. 

21. 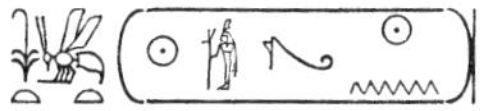

22. 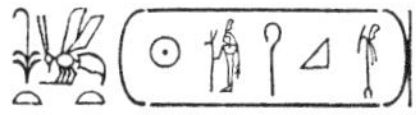

23. 

24. 

25. 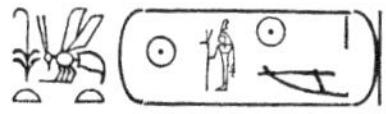

26. 

27. 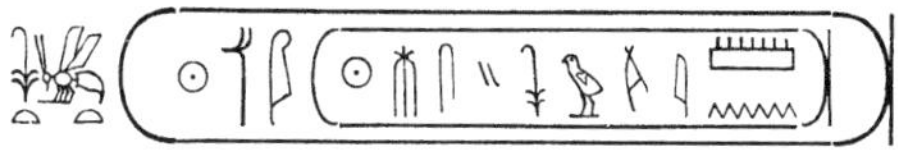

28. 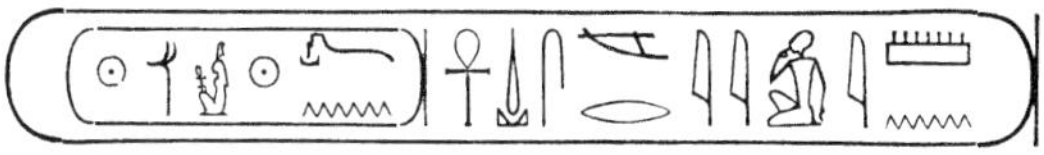

V. Son of Rā names

1. Rā-meses.
2. Rā-messu.
3. Rā-meses-neter-ḥeq-Ȧn-meri-Ȧmen.
4—7. Rā-meses-meri-Ȧmen.
8. Rā-messu-meri-Ȧmen-neter-ḥeq-Ȧnnu.
9, 10. Rā-messu-meri-Ȧmen.
11. Rā-messu-pa-neter-āa.
12. Rā-meses-neter-ḥeq-Ȧn-meri-Set.
13. Rā-messu-meri-Set.
14. Rā-meses-meri-Ȧmen-neter-āa-neb-pet.

V. 1. 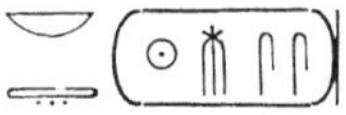

2. 

3. 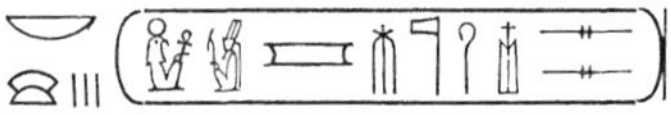

4. 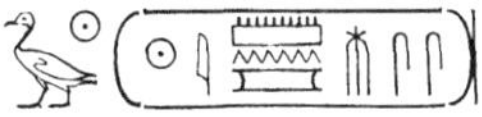

5. 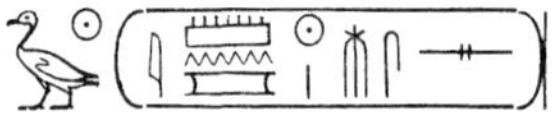

6. 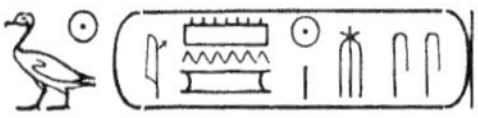

7. 

8. 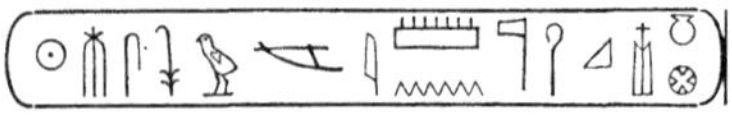

9. 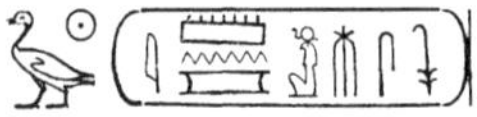

10. 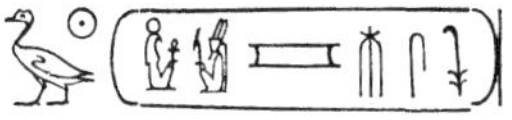

11. 

12. 

13. 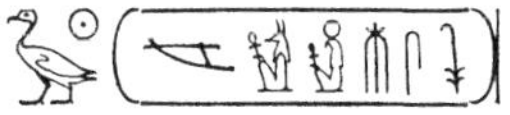

14. 

Sesetsu, or *Sesetsu-meri-Åmen.*

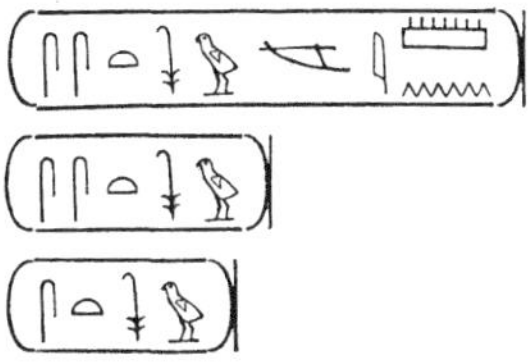

Lepsius, *Königsbuch*, No. 420; Chabas, *Voyage*, pp. 99, 285.

Nefert-åri Meri-Mut, a wife of *Rameses II.*

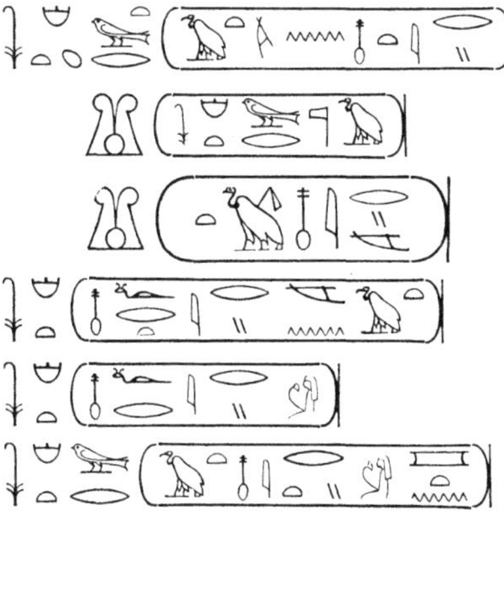

L. D., III, 175, 189, 192, 193, 195, etc.

Ȧst-Nefert, a wife of *Rameses II.*

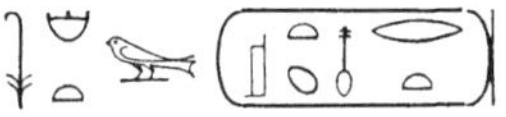

L. D., III, 174, 175.

Rā-maat-neferu, daughter of the Prince of Kheta, and a wife of *Rameses II.*

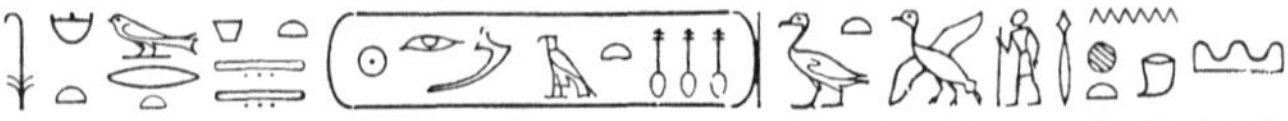

Petrie, *Tanis*, I, V, 36 *b*.

Sons and daughters of Rameses II.

A. From the Temple of Abydos (Mariette, *Abydos*, I, plate 4).

... SA-TEM  Mariette, *Abydos*, I, 4 *e*, 19.

... ER-PA-RĀ 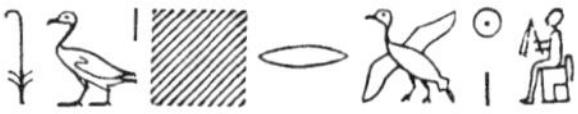 *Ibid.*, 20.

....ERT-MȦ-RĀ  *Ibid.*, 21.

...USR-KHEPESH 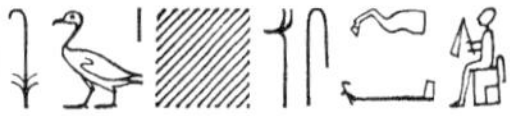 *Ibid.*, 22.

RĀ-MESSU-MER-...  *Ibid.*, 23.

RĀ-MESSU-SA-KHEPERȦ  *Ibid.*, 24.

... MERI-MAĀT 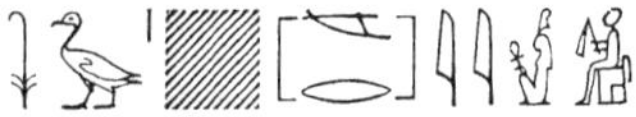 *Ibid.*, 25.

MERĀTHERE-THET 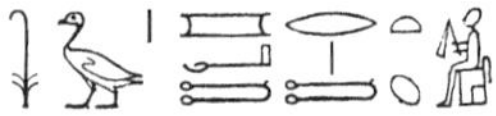 *Ibid.*, 26.

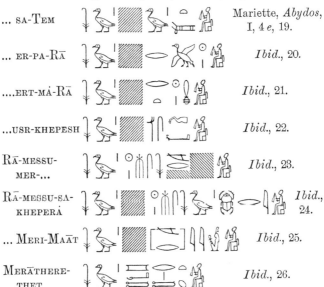

...-...-NEB  Mariette, *Abydos*, I. 4 *b*, 23.

...Ā-ȦMEN  *Ibid.*, 24.

RĀ-MESES-SA-TEM 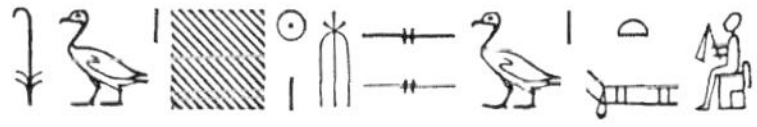 *Ibid.*, 25.

... MENTH-ḤEQU 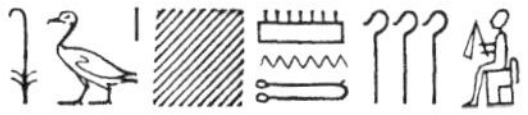 *Ibid.*, 26.

... MENTH  *Ibid.*, 27.

ḤERU-ḤER-UNEMI-F 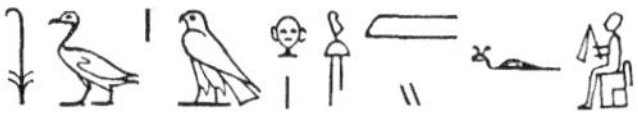 *Ibid.*, 29.

ȦMEN-EM-ȦPT 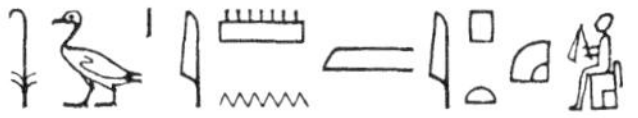 *Ibid.*, 30.

MENTH-EM-UAST 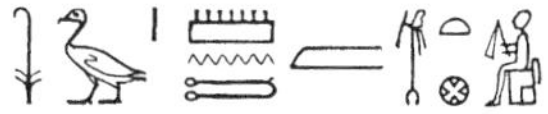 *Ibid.*, 31.

SA-ȦMEN  *Ibid.*, 32.

SA-PTAḤ  *Ibid.*, 33.

...-MERT  Mariette, *Abydos*, I, 4, 4.

...-ȦNT  *Ibid.*, 5.

...-RU  *Ibid.*, 6.

NEFERT-ȦRI  *Ibid.*, 7.

ȦST-NEFERT 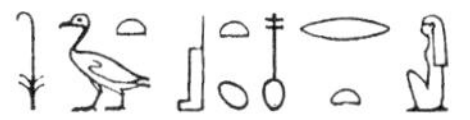 *Ibid.*, 8.

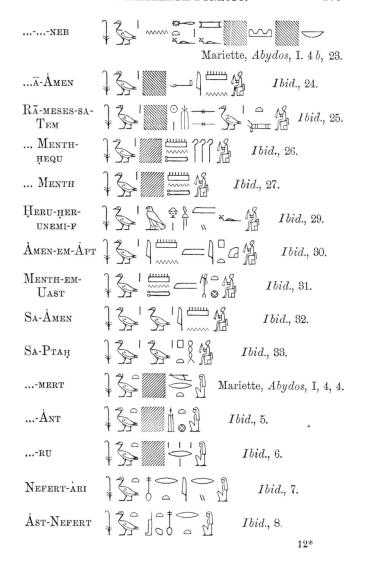

...-TAUI	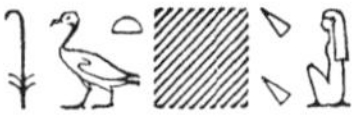	*Ibid.*, 9.
...-ȦN-ȦNEHET		*Ibid.*, 10.
...-I		*Ibid.*, 11.
...-ḤET-Ā		*Ibid.*, 12.
MERIT-SEKHET		*Ibid.*, 13.
...-ȦNT		*Ibid.*, 14.
...-KHESBEṬ	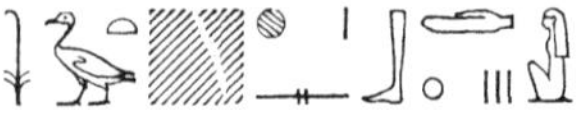	*Ibid.*, 16.
MERIT-ȦTEFS		*Ibid.*, 17.
...-MERTU	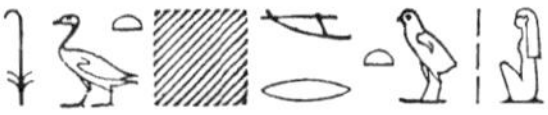	*Ibid.*, 18.
...-ḤĀP	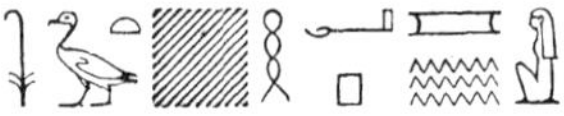	*Ibid.*, 19.
NUB-EM-N...	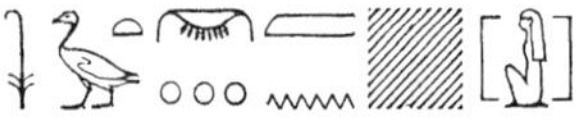	*Ibid.*, 24.
ḤENT-PA-...		*Ibid.*, 25.
ḤENT-...	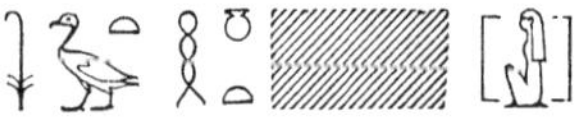	*Ibid.*, 26.
ȦSIPU...		*Ibid.*, 27.
...-NUB-ḤER-...	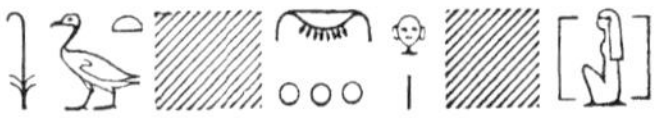	*Ibid.*, 18 *a*.

Shepsi-ḥer-ȧtef-s  *Ibid.*, 19.

Ḥent-...  *Ibid.*, 20.

Mert-mȧ-Ḥāp 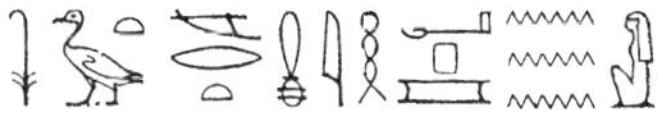 *Ibid.*, 22.

Mert-ȧtef-s  *Ibid.*, 23.

Nub-em-Ȧnt 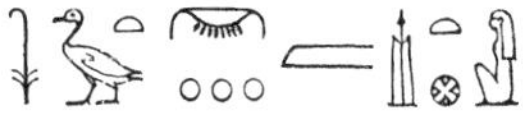 *Ibid.*, 24.

Ḥent-sekhemu  *Ibid.*, 25.

Ḥent-pa-ḥuir 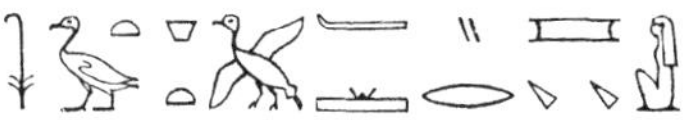 *Ibid.*, 26.

Pipui  *Ibid.*, 28.

Bak-Mut  *Ibid.*, 29.

Renpit-nefer 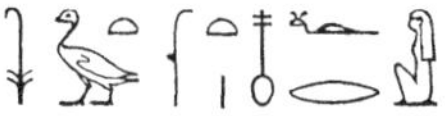 *Ibid.*, 30.

Neferu-Rā 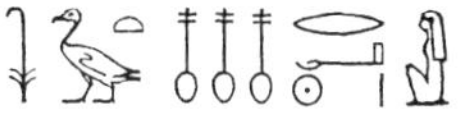 *Ibid.*, 31.

Meri-neter  *Ibid.*, 32.

B. From the Lists at Wâdî Sabû'a, Abû Simbel, the Rȧmesseum, and the Temple at Derr (L. D., III, 168, 179, 183, 184, 186).

Ȧmen-ḥer-unemi-f 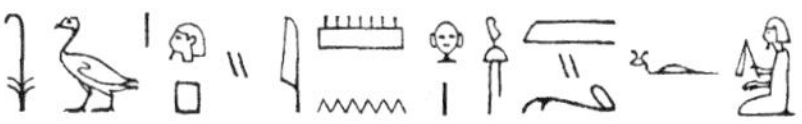

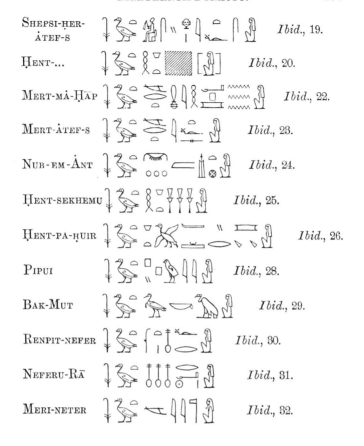

Khā-em-Uast 

Ȧmen-ḥer-khepesh-f 

Set-ḥer-khepesh-f 

Rā-messu 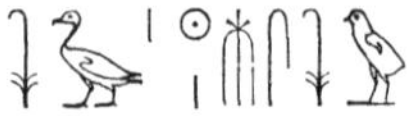

Rā-meses 

Rā-mes 

Pa-Rā-ḥer-unemi-f 

Khā-em-Uast 

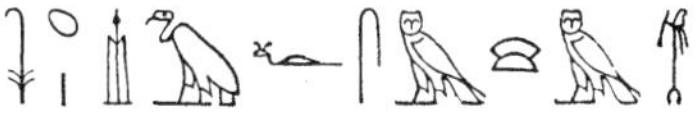

Menthu-ḥer-khepesh-f 

Neb-en-kharu 

Ȧmen-meri 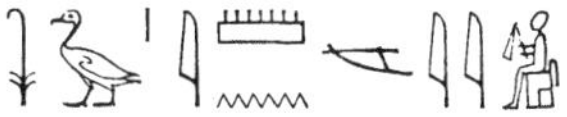

Ȧmen-em-uȧa 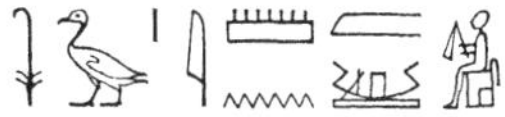

Set-em-Uȧa 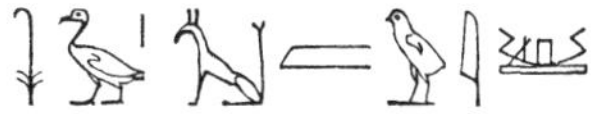

Seti 

Setep-en-Rā 

Rā-meri 

Ḥeru-ḥer-unemi-f 

Mer-en-Ptaḥ 

Ȧmen-ḥetep 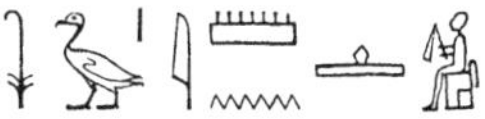

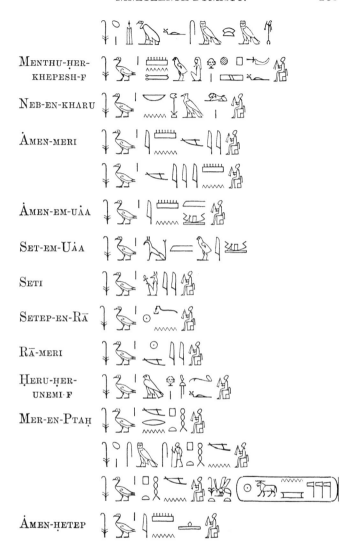

Ȧtef-Ȧmen 

Meri-tem 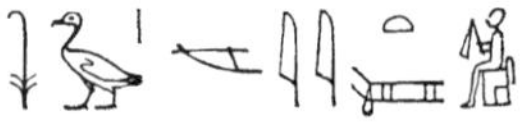

Tem-meri 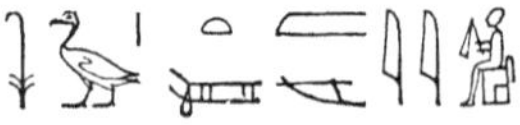

Neb-en-ta-neb 

Rā-meri 

Ȧmen-em-ȧpt 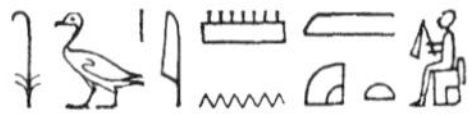

Senekht-en-Ȧmen 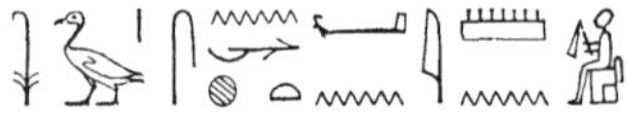

Rā-meses-mer-en-Rā 

Teḥuti-mes 

Ṣa-Menth 

Rā-meses-mert-mȧ-Ra 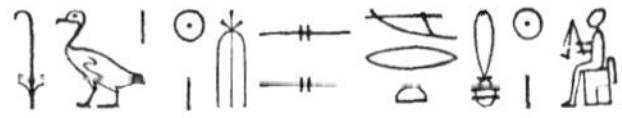

Khā-em-Uast 

...-Ȧmen 

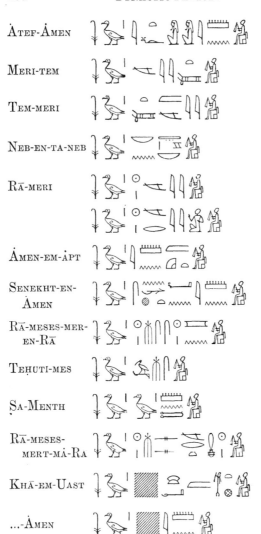

BATHȦĀNTHȦ, or BATAUĀNTHȦ, or BANTAUĀNTU

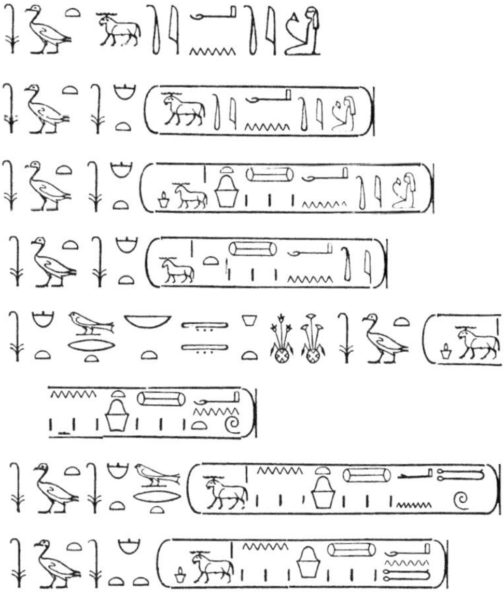

ȦMEN-MERIT

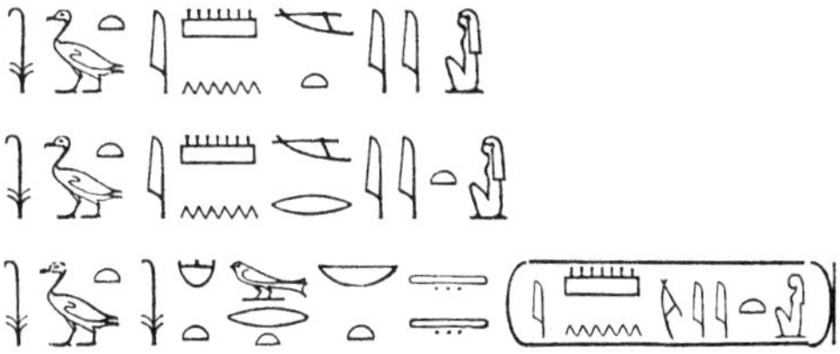

BAK-MUT

NEFERT-ȦRI

NEBT-TAUI

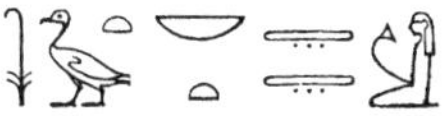

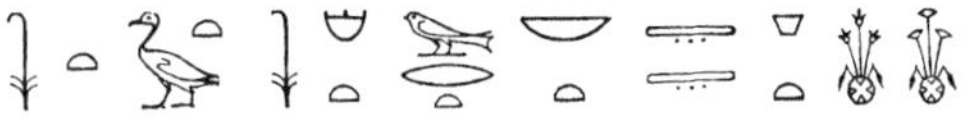

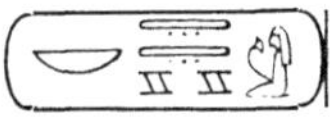

ÀST-NEFER 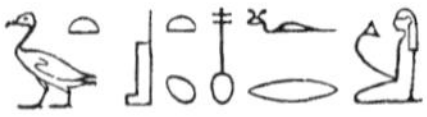

ḤENT-TAUI 

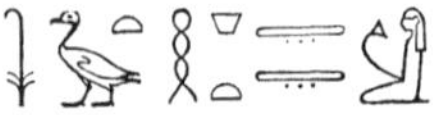

URN-RE 

NETCHEM-MUT 

MER-... 

ḤENT-PA-...-RU 

TUMMERSET 

Àni, a prince, governor of Nubia.

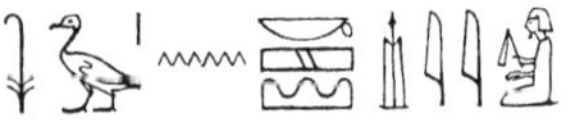

Champollion, *Monuments*, plate 4, No. 2.

Àmen-em-àpt, a prince, governor of Nubia.

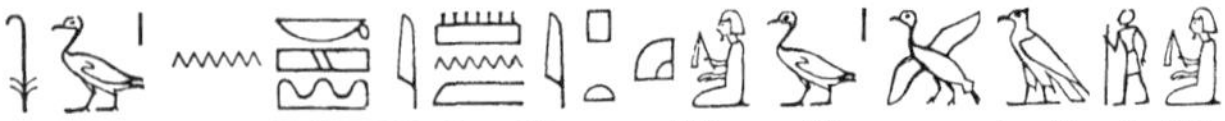

L. D., III, 176 f. ; Champollion, *Monuments*, I, pl. 68, 69.

Setau, a prince, governor of Nubia.

L. D., III, 195 *b*, *c*.

Messui, a prince, governor of Nubia.

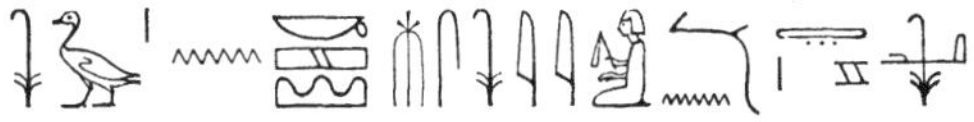

Champollion, *Notices*, p. 614.

Pa-ser, a prince, governor of Nubia.

L. D., III, 176 f.

Nekhttu, a prince, governor of Nubia.

L. D., III, 195 *d*.

Mer-en-Ptaḥ Ḥetep-ḥer-Maāt.

I. Horus names	1. KA-NEKHT-ḤĀĀ-EM-MAĀT.
	2. KA-NEKHT-ḤĀĀ-EM-MAĀT-ḤENK-SU-EN-RĀ-EM-KHERT.
II. N-U names	1. KHĀ-MȦ-PTAḤ-EM-KHENNU-ḤEFENNU.
	2. KHĀ-MȦ-PTAḤ-EM-KHENNU-ḤEFENNU-ER-SMEN-HEPU-NEFERU-EM-KHET-TAUI.
III. Golden Horus name	ĀA-KHEPESH-ḤU-SATI.
IV. Suten Bȧt names	1—3. BA-EN-RĀ-MERI-ȦMEN.
	4. BA-EN-PTAḤ-MERI-ȦMEN.
	5—6. BA-EN-RĀ-MERI-NETERU.
V. Son of Rā name	MER-EN-PTAḤ ḤETEP-ḤER-MAĀT.

1. 2.

I. 

Temple of Karnak (ed. Mariette), Ramesseum, rocks at Silsilah, etc.; Petrie, *Tanis*, II, plate 7.

II. 1. 

2. 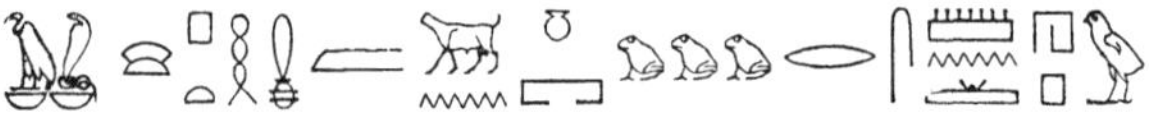

Temple at Karnak. And see *Aeg. Zeit.*, XXXIV, 1; *Recueil*, XVIII, 159; L. D., III, 199 ff.

III. 

Stele at Cairo, *Aeg. Zeit.*, XXXIV, 1.

IV. 1. 

2. 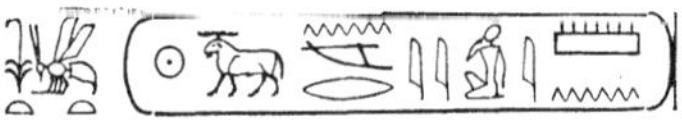

3. 

4. 

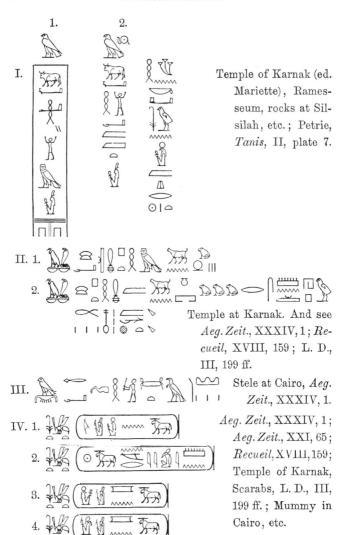

Aeg. Zeit., XXXIV, 1; *Aeg. Zeit.*, XXI, 65; *Recueil*, XVIII, 159; Temple of Karnak, Scarabs, L. D., III, 199 ff.; Mummy in Cairo, etc.

5. 6.

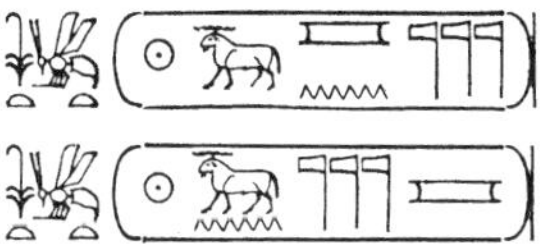

V.

Inscriptions at Silsilah (L. D., III, 200*a*), ʿAmâda and Wâdî Ḥalfah (*Recueil*, XVII, 162; XVIII, 159), etc.

Ȧst-Nefert, wife of *Mer-en-Ptaḥ*.

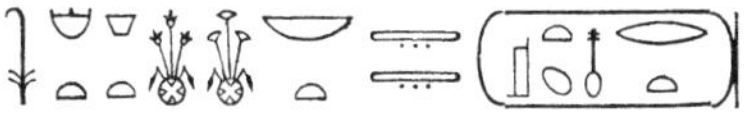

Champollion, *Monuments*, p. 114.

Seti-Mer-en-Ptaḥ, a prince.

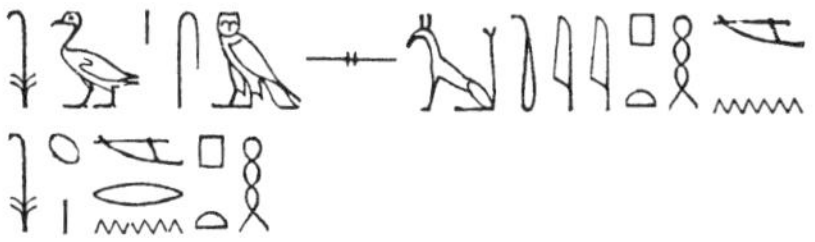

Mes, a royal scribe and governor of Nubia.

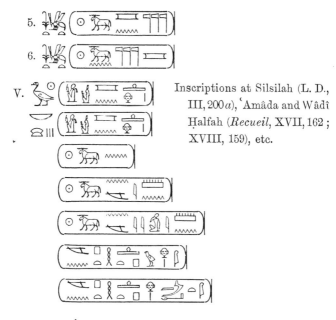

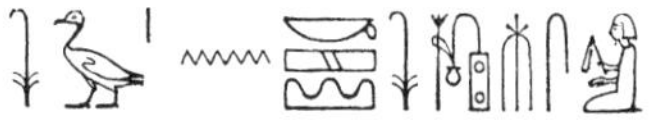

L. D., III, 200 f.

Ȧmen-meses Ḥeq Uast.

I. Horus names 1. Neb-seṭu-mȧ-Ptaḥ-tunen.
2. Ka-nekht-ur-peḥti-mȧ-Ȧmen.
3. Ka-nekht-meri-Maāt-smen-taui.

II. N-U name Ur-bait-em-Ȧpt.

III. Golden Horus name ...

IV. Suten Bȧt names 1. Rā-men-mȧ-setep-en-Rā.
2. Rā-men-mȧ-setep-en-Rā-meri-Ȧmen.

V. Son of Rā name Ȧmen-meses. With additions: Ḥeq-Uast, Meri Rā.

1. 2. 3.

I. 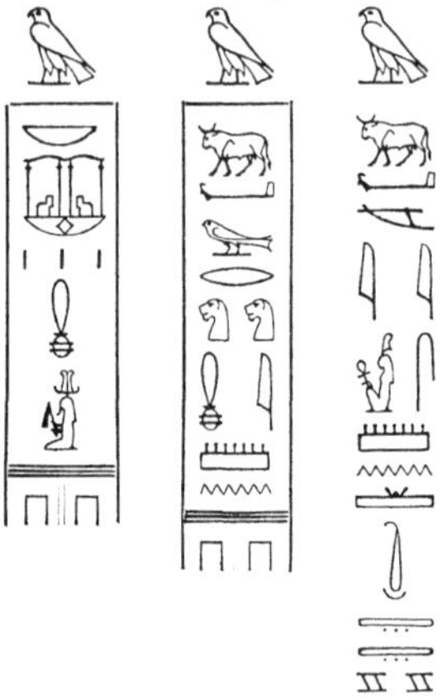

Temple at Karnak, L. D., III, 201.

II. 

Temple at Karnak.

IV. 1. 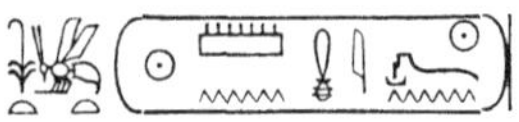

2. 

L. D., III, 201, 202; Daressy, *Recueil*, X, p. 143.

V. 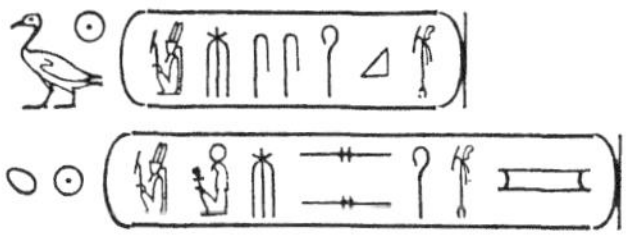

L. D., III, 201, 202; Daressy, *Recueil*, X, p. 143.

Baketurnre, a queen.

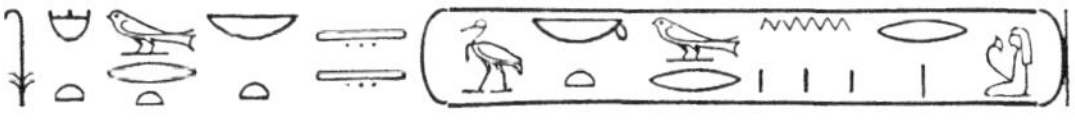

L. D., III, 202 *g*.

Ta-khāt, a royal mother.

L. D., III, 202 *f*.

Seti-Mer-en-Ptaḥ.

I. Horus names 1. KA-NEKHT-MERI-RĀ.
2. KA-NEKHT-MERI-RĀ-SMEN-TAUI.
3. KA-NEKHT-MERI-RĀ-ÅMEN-SA.

II. N-U name MĀK-QEMT-UĀF-SEMTI.

III. Golden Horus name ĀA-NEKHTU-EM-TAIU-NEBU.

IV. Suten Bât names 1—4. RĀ-USER-KHEPERU-MERI-ÅMEN.
5, 6. RĀ-USER-KHEPERU-SETEP-EN-RĀ.

V. Son of Rā name SETI-MER-EN-PTAḤ, and MERI-ÅMEN.

1. 2. 3.

I. 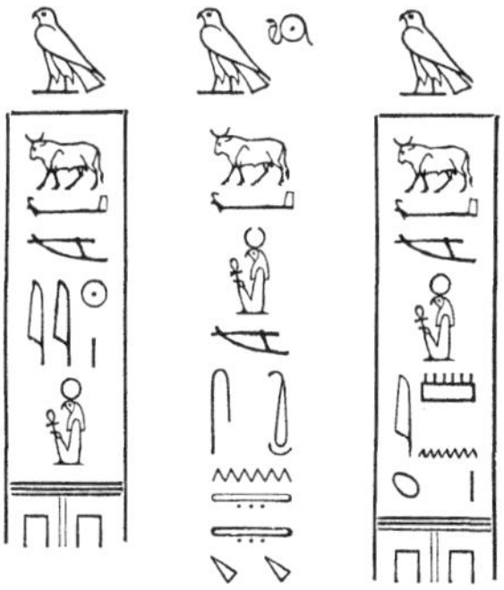

Temple at Karnak.

II. 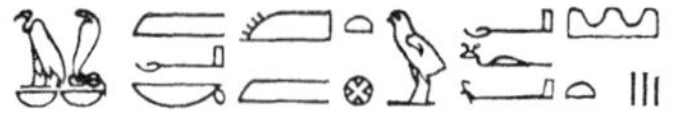

Temple at Karnak.

III. 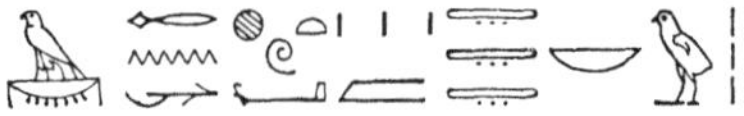

Temple at Karnak.

IV. 1.–6. 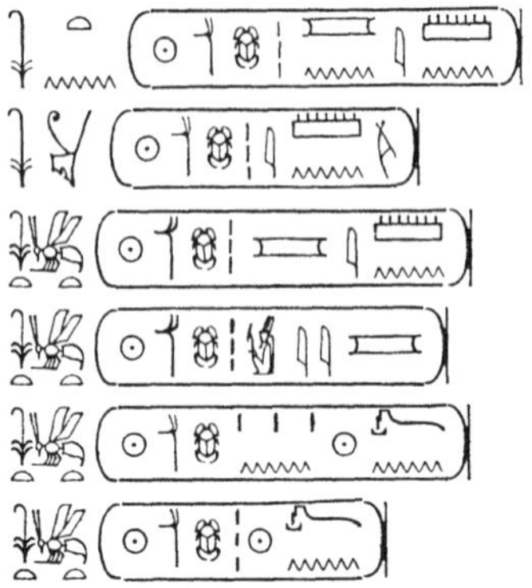

Temple at Karnak, L. D., III, 237 *c*; Stele at Abû Simbel, L. D., III, 204 *e*; Champollion, *Notices*, II, pp. 131, 194, 263 ff.

V. 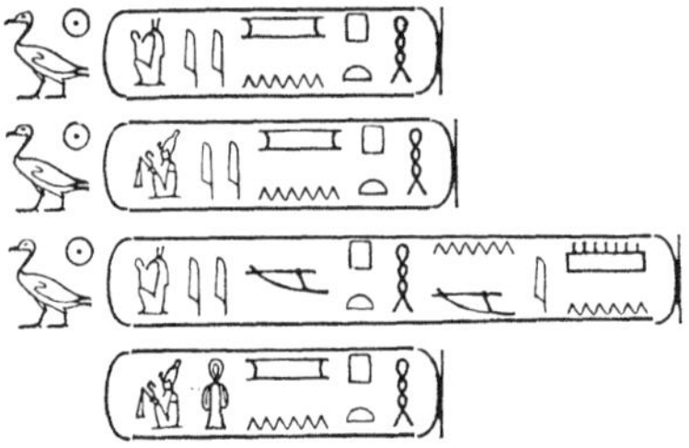

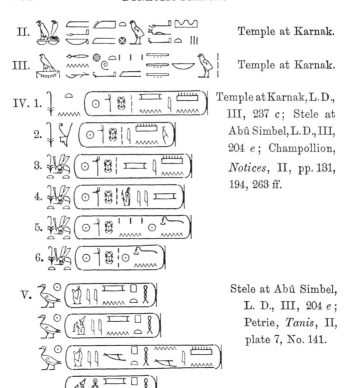

Stele at Abû Simbel, L. D., III, 204 *e*; Petrie, *Tanis*, II, plate 7, No. 141.

Mer-en-Ptaḥ Sa-Ptaḥ.

I. Horus name — Khā-em-Bàt (?).
II. N-U name — ...
III. Golden Horus name — ...
IV. Suten Bȧt name — Khu-en-Rā-setep-en-Rā. With addition : Ȧri-Maāt.
V. Son of Rā name — Mer-en-Ptaḥ Sa-Ptaḥ.

I.

IV.

L. D., III, 201 *a*, *b*, *c*, *d*, 202 *a*, *c*, 204 *d* ; Petrie, *Season*, No. 278.

V.

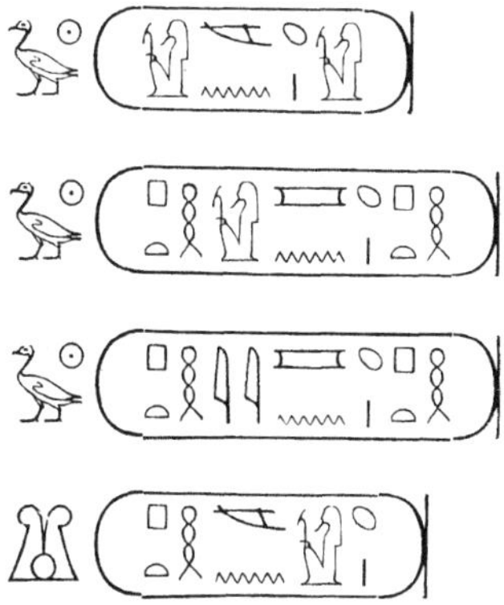

L. D., III, 201 *a*, *b*, *c*, *d* ; 202 *a*, *c* ; 204 *d*, etc.

Ta-usert, a queen.

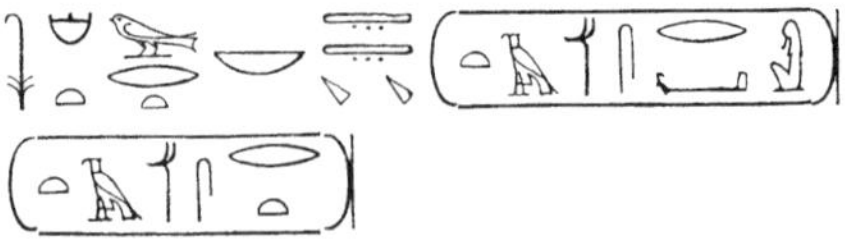

L. D., III, 201 *a*.

Seti, a prince, governor of Nubia.

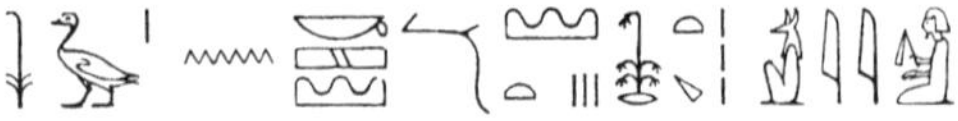

L. D., III, 202 *b* and *c*.

Ȧrsu, a Syrian.

Great Harris Papyrus, Plate 75, line 4.

Set-nekht.

I. Horus name KA-NEKHT-UR-PEḤTI.
II. N-U name ...
III. Golden Horus name ...
IV. Suten Bȧt names 1. RĀ-USER-KHĀU-SETEP-EN-RĀ.
2, 3. RĀ - USER - KHĀU - SETEP - EN - RĀ-MERI-ȦMEN.
4. RĀ-USER-KHĀU-MERI-ȦMEN.
V. Son of Rā name SET-NEKHT-MERI-RĀ-MERI-ȦMEN.

I. 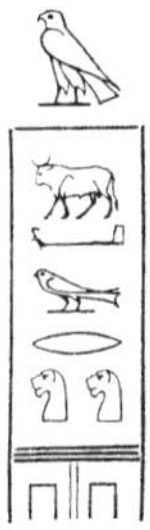

Temple of Karnak.

IV. 1. 2. 3. 4.

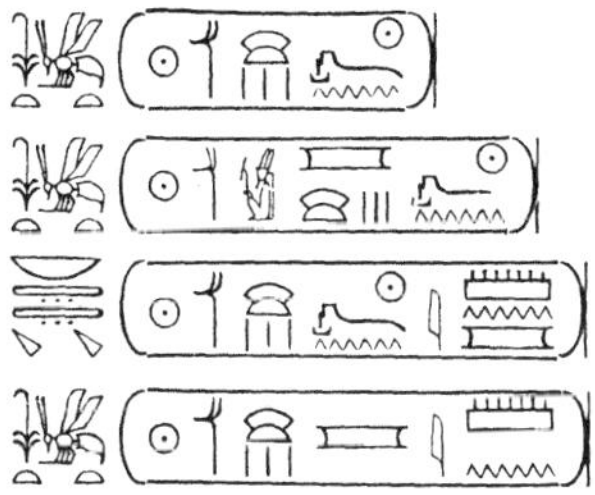

L. D., III, 204, 206 *d*; Weill, *Recueil*, p. 215, No. 118; Mariette, *Abydos*, II, plate 52; Harris Papyrus, No. 9900; Column in the British Museum, No. 64.

V.

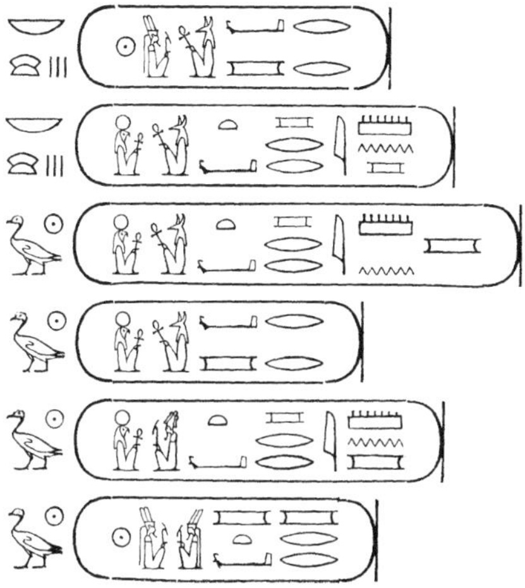

L. D., III, 204, 206 *d*; Temple of Karnak; Harris Papyrus, No. 9900, etc.; Column in the British Museum, No. 64.

Thi-mer-en-Ȧst,* wife of *Set-nekht.

Mariette, *Abydos*, II, plate 52.

Printed in the USA/Agawam, MA
May 30, 2014
590308.003